Struck Down

but

Not Destroyed

A Novel Based on a True Life Story

Jane E. Morin

Copyright © 2018
ISBN: 978-0-578-41599-4
First Edition
Cover design by Christina Bond
Editors: Sharon Bartles, Gaetan Morin

Publisher: Ingram Publishing. Contact: ingramsparksupport@ingramcontent.com

FlyAway Media is a division of Jane Morin Evangelical Association and the Flyaway logo are trademarks of FlyAway Media.

Table of Contents

From the Author

I hope this story of tragedy and triumph will change your life and allow you to realize this great truth; that that no matter how hard things get, you have a GREAT BIG GOD that is crazy about you!

I want to thank some very important people in my life who have helped make this story available to you. But before doing so, I want to express how very grateful I am to the Lord Jesus Christ who brought me out of a life of great trouble, remorse and shame and set my feet on a firm foundation of faith that keeps carrying me through this present darkness. May all the glory and honor go to Him who is FAITHFUL and TRUE!

"But you, O LORD, are a shield about me, my glory, and the lifter of my head." (Psalm 3:3)

I want to thank my precious husband Gaetan for his encouragement that kept me writing and reliving some very difficult days of my past so that others would benefit from them. You have always been my *Boaz,* and I am so very grateful for the love we share with one another and for our wonderful Lord Jesus. We surely make a GREAT TEAM!

I am so grateful to my sister Sharon who spent many days editing the manuscript and keeping me focused on the project at hand. It is so wonderful that God saw fit to allow us to be a part of each other's lives.

For the rest of my family members and friends who have been waiting a long time for this book to be written, I want to say one thing. May it encourage you and remind you just how faithful our God is and what a joy it is to serve Him! No one is perfect, but we do serve a *perfect* God who loves to take our broken messes and create beauty from ashes. After all, according to Ecclesiastes 3:11, *"He makes all things beautiful in His time."*

After His Heart,
Jane Morin

Dedicated to my mother, *Edith.*

Foreword

Life changing books are written by changed lives. We are moved because they have been moved. These types of books are so powerful because the authors have been shaken to their core, and their experiences shake us. I believe this book will be one that will shake lives because of the life of Jane Morin.

Jane Morin was leading praise and worship in a church in Odessa, TX, where I was preaching a revival meeting several years ago. My wife and I instantly fell in love with her and her husband from the first moment we met them. As we learned of her testimony, we saw how God had brought her from a life of rejection and despair to a life of much joy and victory. In 2 Corinthians 1:3-4, it says, *"Blessed be the God and Father of our Lord Jesus Christ, the Father of mercies and God of all comfort, who comforts us in all our affliction so that we may be able to comfort those who are in any affliction with the comfort with which we ourselves are comforted by God."*

Jane has let God use her past struggles to help others through their struggles in life. Her tests have become testimonies of God's goodness, mercy, and grace. What Satan meant for evil, God turned around for good. It is obvious how much Jane loves the Lord and desires to bring others to Him. I believe this book will be one that will so inspire, encourage, and bless your heart in such a deep way that you will want to encourage others with it.

Rev. Larry B. Jordan - Evangelist

We are hard pressed on every side, but not crushed;
perplexed, but not in despair; persecuted, but not
abandoned; *struck down, but not destroyed.*
(2 Corinthians 4:8) NIV

You, dear children, are from God and have overcome them, because the one who is in you is *greater* than the one who is in the world.

(1 John 4:4) NIV

Introduction

As she removed the loaded gun from her black leather handbag, she peered intently into the golden-framed mirror hanging directly ahead. Her chest was rising and falling, and her breathing became more erratic as Maggie gazed into the mirror. To her dismay, the reflection before her was that of an unrecognizable image unknown to her former self. Her thoughts focused on the sudden turn of events that took place earlier that week.

A drunken Harold had arrived home early from work three days ago. This occurred in a matter of weeks after she had allowed him to move back in with the promise that he would leave the bottle once and for all. Simultaneously, on that same day, Harold left her for another woman. However, because she knew the other woman, this consistently succeeded in causing Maggie grief and anger, all at the same time. In just a few moments, Harold grabbed his work clothes from the closet, and without another word, he left. As if that was not enough torment for one night, a few short hours later, the nightmare was compounded by yet more tragic news that had reached her.

Maggie was informed that her eldest son had succumbed to a tragic and untimely death. Now, here she was three days later at the funeral home waiting for her beloved son's body to arrive. She excused herself briefly to use the facilities.

"*Maggie, it's time,*" she whispered. This was not exactly how Maggie had planned it, but it would have to do for now, because time was not on her side. After all, in a matter of minutes, everyone in town would know all about the horrific act that Maggie had just committed.

A dark presence seemed to encapsulate the bathroom. It muttered, "*That's it….go ahead! It's the only solution to your grief woman,*" the ominous voice slithered softly in her ear.

Lifting the gun to make sure it was loaded and ready, she looked at her desperate reflection in the mirror once again and then carefully placed the muzzle on her abdomen and uttered, "Forgive me Go…"

Maggie, now lying in a pool of blood, was disturbed by the commotion gathering outside of the locked bathroom door. As Maggie's breathing shallowed, her distant past began to torment her as she lie helplessly recalling the beginning of all her broken memories.

1

Paris and Freedom 1949

Just living is not enough…one must have
sunshine, freedom, and a little flower. -Hans Christian Andersen

Maggie was only eighteen when she decided to run off to Paris and take a modeling job that had been offered to her. Frank, the movie producer in Hollywood, had connections, and though he could not have her picture-perfect face filling the big screen for his own movies, he was sure that Maggie had that special something. That something that would eventually bring her back to California to stay, once and for all. He called his photographer friend in Europe and told him of the beauty that had auditioned in a screen test a few years ago, and to see if he had received the package.

In Hollywood, Frank had pulled out a duplicate of the yellow folder that he had airmailed Antoine and dialed his good friend's phone number.

Antoine had just walked into his modeling office when the phone rang. "Hello. Antoine Lartigue speaking."

Frank anxiously answered. "Antoine, how are you, my friend?"

"All is well. I suppose you are calling about the package you sent me?"

"Yes. I received your call requesting any referrals for your next lead model. Listen, I have all the confidence in the world in this young lady named Maggie. I sent you her headshots and a short bio for

14

consideration. I believe she is going to do really well there. No doubt, her father is a force to be reckoned with, but now that she is out of school, he won't be able to keep her from her ambitions forever." Frank maintained.

His friend had indeed received the package the day before and was now fumbling through his desk as Frank was telling him all about Maggie. "Here it is..." he replied as he opened up the secured packaging.

Antoine fumbled through a few pictures and then began to hold one particular portrait up to his eyes and focused. "I see what you mean. She has a sophisticated, yet innocent appearance that will make the public eat her up. Look at that beautiful red, curly hair and a warm, inviting smile. While Frank, she is irresistible!"

"I am so glad that you agree. Maggie is a born natural too, you'll see. You do right by Maggie, you hear me?" Frank insisted.

"No worries there my friend. Don't worry about a thing. Thanks again for introducing her to me. She will get along fine with the other girls, and they can watch out for her. She does appear naïve, but she has the stuff I'm looking for. We will be in touch soon!"

Antoine then hung up, reached for some office stationery and decided to not waste another minute before he began writing Maggie Adler directly with an offer of a modeling job on the spot. She should have graduated from high school by now, and since that was the only stipulation demanded by her father before she followed her dreams, he was confident that the offer would be more than enough to get her to come out and work for him. He would enclose a pass for the journey by ship and some travel money before mailing it that afternoon. He knew if he took care of the monetary obligations needed for her trip that she would be less concerned.

One Month Later…..

It was June 10, 1949. The date had finally arrived, and Maggie said her final goodbye's to her family on the pier just before embarking for Brussels, then on to Paris. She had a sense that things would now be turning around for good in her life. The air was thick with humidity, but the sky was clear, and a slight breeze helped it not seem as unbearable. The misty gray waters were relatively calm ensuring a smooth journey for the day. She loved the ocean and the idea of sailing to another country on the ship, but it was almost more excitement than she could bear. Oh, she had been away from home before, but this was different. She actually had a job, and now no one could prevent her from becoming what she always wanted to be, famous.

As she boarded the ship, she made her way to the top deck and looked down to where her parents said they would be standing to wave her off. There they were too, her Mama was apparently crying but still trying to smile. She waved to Maggie and then pressed her hand to her lips to deposit a kiss and then waved again and again. Maggie returned her kiss and several waves. Her father merely put his hand up once and waved in a somewhat salutatory manner. Then, as the ship left the port and started its journey, her parents stood there on the deck until they no longer could see the vessel within view.

During that entire farewell, as she stood there, her thoughts were all over the place. She would have what she always dreamed; and that was to become the star Maggie knew she could be, as well as, be free of her overbearing and controlling father. He meant well, or at least she thought that he did, but why did he make her life so miserable? He told her how proud of her he was, but warned her if it did not work out in Paris, not to come back home.

She thought to herself, "What kind of support is that?" On the other hand, she had gotten used to his lack of support in her life, so she really wasn't that taken aback by his disdainful remarks. She never understood why her mother agreed to suffer all these years with his contentious manner, yet never said a word. At least Maggie would not be under his thumb anymore. Whatever came her way, she was going to make it because there was no way now that she could afford to fail.

Her papa, William Adler, had always worked so hard, and he was very successful. He was only five feet, five inches tall, but his height did not stop him from becoming one of the most popular in his field. He and her mama had stowed away on a ship from Russia to come to the country where freedom reigned. It was an arduous affair as they both were quite young. Her mama was only fourteen years old, and her papa was all of sixteen.

They were best friends, and when they arrived in the states, William and Opal married as soon as it was legal to do so. Opal was forced to lie about her age so that they could be married. Afterward, William was assuring her that he was always going to be there to take care of her. Shortly following, William served the country in wartime, then came back and received an education in interior design. Now, as Maggie sailed onto a new life, her father was working as an interior decorator for the White House. People from all over the world appreciated his work, and William took his job seriously. He ensured that the White House maintained a certain standard of excellence for not only the people of the country but for all who would enter its doors, as well as the residents. He had a keen eye for design and could quickly create the perfect setting for any room. William had mentioned that his father had taught him a thing or two about interior design as well. It was something about his Russian Jewish heritage of which he was very proud. He was an assuming man, but there were those moments that came and went throughout the years, when his big brown eyes would turn to mush. He would be overcome with love and pride over his family and all of their accomplishments. It was rare, but it did happen. That is how Maggie knew that deep down inside, under that brass exterior that she and her Mama and siblings often encountered, was a man who was capable of love, though he rarely displayed it.

As Maggie pondered about him, she realized he was one person at work and an entirely different person at home. Once he got home, his kind and genuine demeanor, in which everyone else respected him for, turned into a demanding and bickering man that seemed discontent with anyone and everyone.

She never understood what she had precisely done to deserve his scorn through the years. He had stood between her and fame on more than one occasion. This time, it was out of his hands. He could not stop her if she had a means of survival, and a job, far away from home. It was somewhat concerning to think of traveling all alone, but frankly, she preferred the conversation of a total stranger over talking to her father any day. Their last conversation the night before she embarked on her journey left her feeling insecure, and questioning her decision. Her father had that kind of control over her. He made her feel that no matter how good something looked and no matter how much she wanted something good to come from it, he would make it seem impossible for her to attain it. She tried to wipe him out her mind as she went to the concierge to pick up the key to her cabin. Afterward, the steward picked up her bags that she had placed in front of the check-in counter and directed her to follow him.

"Ma'am, your room is right around this first corner, up one flight of stairs and the third door down to the left." The man was very tall and wearing a white jacket with gold buttons and donning a navy blue collar with blue slacks to match. It resembled a navy uniform but was custom made for the stewards on board.

Settling into her living quarters for the next ten days, she found the accommodation's not too elaborate but suffice. She asked the kind steward that had helped her carry her bags to the cabin if she may have a cup of hot tea. He gladly replied and shortly returned to her cabin within minutes offering her a teapot and a delicately, violet-flowered china cup on a tray. Then the steward kindly placed it down on the simple wooden table that folded out from the wall and offered, "Should I pour you a cup?"

"Oh, I can get it, thank you!" Maggie insisted.

"Anytime you need more, just let me know ma'am. There will be a luncheon upstairs soon, and you should find your seating accommodations inside your travel itinerary." He then stepped back and closed the cabin door.

Once he left, the steward remembered what he was told about Maggie and how he needed to take extra care to help her feel comfortable and at ease. Her ticket to Brussels included all the other perks and tips expected for such service, as the concierge had received the orders earlier on from Antoine. After all, Antoine knew she might feel a bit uncomfortable traveling all alone. After that, Antoine would meet her at the Brussels port of entry and then she would take a train with him to Paris. It was all so exciting and more than she could absorb at the moment when she started to think seriously about it. It also would have been otherwise a very risky ordeal for one to take on, not knowing Antoine, but Maggie felt confident that Frank had not steered her wrong. She actually called Frank right away to confirm his business relationship with Antoine, and he was delighted to hear that she had taken Antoine up on the offer. He insisted, *"Maggie, I told you that you would find a way to make it big one day. I wish you all the best, and feel free to call me and let me know how you are getting along."*

She remembered his kind words before she sat down to enjoy her tea. Now seated on the comfy chair across from her bunk, she poured herself a cup of hot tea as she felt herself begin to relax. Leaning back into the comfort of the plush, green covered seat, and placing her feet up on the ottoman in front of her, she sensed a particular snug of peace embrace her. As she looked across the room at the single bed, it was tidy and covered with a spread that donned English lavender, one of her favorite flowers. Additionally, there was a tall sculptured glass vase on the side table filled with yellow Forsythia. It certainly added more color and interest to the cabin. Above the pillow on the wall was a small sconce and next to the other side of the bunk was the ship porthole. She could see the gray bluish waves rolling back and forth across the deep waters of the Atlantic Ocean in which she was all too familiar. Living in New York, she had many opportunities to stroll the beachfront and swim in the refreshing summertime currents when the heat had become unbearable. She spent days swimming in the salty waters, and now she was headed to a place she had never seen, but always dreamed of going to, Europe.

She looked downward, glaring into the cup of hot tea, and slid her finger lightly on top and around the gold rim before taking a sip of it. The warm English tea had a touch of mint added to it, and it comforted her as she inhaled its essence and took a moment to calm her anxieties. It appeared that her dreams were coming true and she couldn't help but feel a sense of accomplishment. She had to admit that her beauty had absolutely nothing to do with her, as she was born this way. Her mother ensured her that she was indeed unique, but not to let it make her prideful. She was not very tall at five feet and four inches, but her slim figure, big brown eyes and dynamic smile coupled with long, curly red hair that silhouetted her entire body made her appear bigger than life. Her nineteen-inch waistline showed that she was willing to deny whatever food she needed to keep her curvaceous figure. Though she was grateful for possessing a natural beauty, she never understood what the big fuss was when young men were introduced to her or when they resided in her presence. She was a bit shy and oh so naïve, especially when it came to the opposite sex. She had only dated a few times so she would be the first to admit that she knew nothing when it came to having a relationship. Unlike her sister Fran, who was lovely and outgoing, and never knew a stranger, Maggie was initially much more reserved.

Perhaps she was more like Roma, her oldest sister, who kept everything bottled up inside and knew how to avoid conflict by just doing everything she was told to do. Her mind wandered off about her two twin-brothers that Mama had given birth to many years before. They had both died a horrible death from yellow fever that struck and was prevalent in those days. Though Maggie had never met them, Mama spoke about them every year when their birthday came around. Moses and Michael were only two-years-old when they succumbed to the illness. Oh, how it must have crushed her Mama's heart that terrible day. Now, as she sat in the cabin on the cruise liner, she realized it was the anniversary of their death. She paused, set the tea aside, put her shawl over her head and bowed respectfully, as

Mama had always taught her to do. She was thinking once again about her Mama after she finished the *El Maleh Rachamim*, the Jewish prayer for the dead. As she embarked on her journey to Paris, Maggie's Mama was most tearful, and whispered in her ear, *"I will be praying for your success, my sweet daughter."* As Jews, Maggie's family were very devout and Orthodox in their faith, and her mother had taught her to keep faith when times were most difficult. It would be something that Maggie would sporadically turn to all the years of her life. Opal, Maggie's Mama, was also shy, and a gentle soul. Maggie could still feel her Mama's loving arms around her before boarding the ship. Mama had long, salt and pepper hair with tender, brown eyes that comforted Maggie so many times throughout the years. Mama was much shorter than Maggie, and she also was unfortunately what one might call a fleshy woman due to some health issues. Her weight had been something that she always had to contend with as long as Maggie could remember. Maybe that is why her father always talked down to her mother. Maggie admitted to herself the fact that there are some things in life you will never understand and shrugged off her curiosity about her parent's relationship as she picked up her teacup and sipped in her resolve. It was time to stop thinking of her past. She needed, for now, to put aside the thoughts of her family and all these melancholy memories and start focusing on her bright future.

As Maggie shook her head and tried to clear her mind once again, she wondered how she would ever be able to model successfully with such an introverted spirit, but immediately decided to place her fear aside. After all, Mr. Antoine Lartigue had contacted her, mainly sight unseen because of Frank. She liked Frank. He was always so kind to her, and though he was terribly disappointed at her father for making her come back home after Frank had offered her the movie contract, he did not hold it against her. He assured her that she had the talent and the look that Hollywood needed and that he would not forget her, and he hadn't. She made a mental note to write a thank you letter to him that evening from aboard the ship.

After slowly sipping the warm and fragrant tea down, she heard people rustling outside her cabin door and thought it might be time for the luncheon. She decided to freshen up her makeup, apply some red lipstick, brush down her blue sleeveless cotton-laced dress with the palm of her hands to make sure it was not wrinkled, and then she grabbed her ivory lace shawl before stepping out to join the other hungry travelers. It was going to be a long ten days on the ocean liner, but she was up for the challenge. She was not going to permit her shyness to allow her any excuse to stay holed up in her quarters. She wanted to see the world, and since the opportunity came knocking on her door, she was going to open it up wide.

"Ms. Adler?" the young stewardette called out as she entered the dining hall.

"Yes, that's me," Maggie answered quietly.

"Oh, come right this way ma'am, as we have the perfect place right here by the porthole for you to enjoy your meal and the lovely scenery. There should be a few other guests joining you soon," she smiled.

The stewardette was wearing a pastel, long- sleeved, airy pink dress with a built-in tie that had been bowed at the front collar. Additionally, she had on a white cap and matching apron, and was wearing white shoes.

After assisting her to her table, the woman left in a scurry to greet the other guests and to take them promptly to their assigned seats. Almost immediately, there was a middle-aged couple, Nan and Robert Charles joining her, as well as a businessman named Tom Emmett. Nan had lightly salt and peppered hair and was dressed in a green silk dress with a shawl that complemented her eyes and beautiful fair complexion. Robert, with white hair, was dressed in a gray pin-striped suit, with a white shirt, green silk tie, and cufflinks that looked like emeralds that matched his wife's dress color. Tom was quiet but seemed relaxed. His chocolate-brown suit and red and brown striped tie looked nice with his blonde hair, brown beard, and hazel eyes. One seat was left open, but that didn't last for long. After the stewardette took their drink orders, and those seated got acquainted, a gentleman appeared and apologized for being late.

"Hello, my name is Jonathan Bentham." After realizing where and whom he was seated next to, he spurted out, "How lucky can a guy get? I am seated next to this lovely lady," he smiled as he took his seat promptly.

"And what might your name be?" Jonathan looked at Maggie as if no one else was seated at the table.

She put him off as she looked down at her lap, then up and across at the couple and replied, "This is

Mr. and Mrs. Charles and to your left is Mr. Emmett, and you can call me Maggie." She nervously grinned.

Mr. Charles reached over and offered a hand of introduction, "You can call me Robert, and this is my wife, Nan."

After a proper introduction, he turned to shake hands with Mr. Emmett and then settled back into his seat. The stewardette appeared again with drinks and promptly took Johnathan's drink order. "I will return in a few minutes. You can all look over the menu and when I return, simply let me know."

Maggie took a quick inspection of the man seated next to her and decided that his black, three-piece suit, white shirt and burgundy tie looked nice. He had dark hair, large black eyes, and a dark complexion as if he had spent the summer in the sun. The scent of the pomade that he used to make his hair shiny could not go unnoticed, as well as his dimples and bigger-than-life smile. She was sure that he attracted many women, but she was not interested. She drew her attention to the menu, and though it had a variety of delicious looking dishes available, she quickly found one of her favorite lunch items, Bagel and Lox with Tomato Basil Soup, and settled on it at once.

The stewardette came back to take everyone's orders and, after leaving, the host for the banquet appeared at their table and approached her. He handed her a single rose tied up inside lace ivory paper donning a beautiful peach ribbon. I almost forgot about this Ms. Adler. This is from Misseur Lartigue, at Le Modele Exclusif. He then gently placed it in front of Maggie, smiled and stepped away.

26

"So, you're a model?" Johnathan stated somewhat animated. "Well, I must say that I have never met a model before Ms. Adler. In fact, I guess none of us should take that as a complete surprise, now should we?" Johnathan queried as he looked across the table at the other guests with his huge dimpled smile.

"Don't let him intimidate you, dear," Nan said.

"Thank you, Nan," Maggie replied as her eyes became set on the rose and small note card attached. She then picked up the softly colored, peach and ivory rose out of curiosity and lightly placed it under her nose enjoying the subtle, pure fragrance before putting it beside her flatware.

She then carefully opened the small envelope that contained a notecard that read, "*Bon Voyage! See you in Brussels. – Antoine*"

"I guess this is Mr. Lartigue's way of letting me know that he is making sure all things are going well for the journey. How thoughtful," she admitted.

"Oh, so Mr. Lartigue ….as you call him…..is he your boyfriend?" Johnathan asked.

"No, he is my new agent," Maggie spouted back embarrassingly and explained.

"Mr. Lartigue owns the photography company that hired me as a model last week. I have to say, he sure has made every effort to ensure that my journey is comfortable and for that, I am most grateful."

"Well, congratulations on your new opportunity. I know that you will do well!" Tom piped up.

"I couldn't agree more," Johnathan interjected.

Nan and Robert looked at each other acknowledging the single men at the table who couldn't take their eyes off of Maggie, as well as, her discomfort in their actions.

"Perhaps after we finish dear, if you want to go up on the deck with us Maggie, you are more than welcome," Nan invited.

Maggie almost let out a sigh of relief as she responded, "Thank you so much Nan, but I don't want to get in between you and your time with Robert."

"Are you kidding?" She giggled. "We have to take this journey every six months. I would welcome someone breaking up the monotony a bit," Nan laughed.

"We would enjoy showing you around the ship and spending time with you," Robert pitched in.

"Well, if it's not any trouble, I would enjoy that too," Maggie smiled as she looked at Nan. She noticed that Nan and Charles were much older and she felt a bit more comfortable knowing that. She had no intentions whatsoever of giving in to the whims of the single man sitting next to her who's staring had become annoyingly persistent.

The stewardette appeared with Johnathan's drink, and checked on everyone else to ensure that their glasses were filled, and then scurried off again in a matter of minutes. When the food came, Maggie could not believe how much food was on her plate. It was enough for both lunch and dinner. She ate slowly enjoying the food and casual conversation that turned into a rather pleasant affair.

2

Modeling, Marriage, and Two

The past is the beginning of the beginning and all that is
and has been is but the twilight of the dawn – H.G. Wells

Antoine was standing on the dock, waiting for the passengers to disembark when suddenly he spotted Maggie walking down the ramp. Her long red hair was blowing in the wind behind the green flocked jacket that she wore over her long, silk green dress. Maggie had brushed back the front of her hair on the top of her head and secured it with an intricately designed, gold, tri-colored stoned barrette given to her by Nan as a good-luck charm. He could tell that she would look stunning in anything that she put on, and Antoine was taken aback by her rare beauty. She was even more beautiful than the picture that Antoine had seen of her. He raced passed others waiting for family members and friends and he walked briskly up the deck and smiled.

"Hello Ms. Adler, my name is Antoine Lartigue. I am so glad that you made it. How was your journey?" He spoke gently as he reached out to shake her hand.

"It is nice to meet you Mr. Lartigue, and please call me Maggie." She shook his hand, then gently let go and kept talking, "My journey was delightful, and I want to thank you for taking care of every detail. I am most grateful."

"It was my pleasure, and you may call me Antoine." The towering, handsome man added. Maggie noticed his tall, lanky build, long brown hair, and goatee. He wore a twill newsboy cap and a leather vest over his plaid shirt with nicely creased brown slacks. Antoine took a glance at his gold watch and then looked up towards the street and bent over to retrieve her bags. When he looked up, she saw his piercing blue eyes sparkling like the blue skyline.

With bags in hand, Antoine asked her to follow him through the crowd to the waiting black taxi directly ahead at the curb. After they got in, the cab headed straight to their next destination.

Maggie thought she was a good reader of people and that it would help her in France, as she did not know the language very well. She could not stop herself from looking out the window and seeing the beautiful, old-world scenery. She read up on the area in France where she was going, and a little bit about Brussels, but the pictures and the information gathered could not compare to actually being there. Antoine spoke with a thick European accent, but that did not phase Maggie. Perhaps her New York accent was somewhat strange to him, as well.

Antoine watched Maggie as her eyes perused every corner of the city of Brussels along with every building and every person walking along the city streets.

Antoine broke the silence by stating "I have made accommodations for one of the other models to show you around Paris this coming weekend if you don't mind? I think it is essential for you to understand the culture there."

Smiling and now more relaxed she replied, "I would love that very much, Mr. Lartigue…, I mean Antoine."

She began to be more at ease in knowing that Antoine was all business, yet a straightforward individual, and one in which she could communicate. He looked nothing like she anticipated. He must have been in his early thirties, which made her relax all the more. She was excited about such a fantastic opportunity, and she was going to work hard to make sure her modeling career was successful.

As the taxi pulled over, she noticed that she was in front of a train station. Antoine had told her that they would need to take a train from Brussels to get to Paris which was about five hours away. As they unloaded, Antoine spoke in French to the taxi driver, then Antoine quickly took her bags to the ticket counter as she followed.

"I will pick up our tickets at the will-call window, and we should be ready to leave in about forty minutes. The restrooms are to your left as you enter the depot area." Antoine informed.

Antoine thought of everything, and she was glad because a restroom was needed. As she walked in, she saw an older woman washing her hands. Maggie smiled and went on into the stall. When she came out, the older woman was still there washing her hands. The woman saw Maggie in need of the sink, so she shut it off and moved to the side. The sink area was minimal, and Maggie pushed her shoulder strapped purse behind her as she bent slightly to wash her hands.

The older women kept an eye on Maggie's purse as Maggie reached to turn on the water. Maggie caught a glimpse of her looking intently at the bag via the mirror in front of her and quickly turned to dry her hands and leave. The older woman just smiled, but Maggie held her purse tightly underarm and began to have that all too familiar feeling of mistrust that often guided her life. As Maggie left the bathroom, she quickly found Antoine and took her place in line with him. She did not mention anything to him, but then a lady in line behind them yelled out, "My purse is missing! I just had it at the window!!"

The lady could not find it, and she went to the ticket window to inquire. When she returned without a purse, somehow Maggie knew that the older lady had taken it. "Antoine, excuse me, I will be right back....."

Maggie went to the ticket counter to let them know of her suspicions, as the older lady she had seen in the bathroom passed her again and just smiled. Maggie walked quickly to the window and asked for the manager. The attendant operating the window clarified, "I am the manager. How can I help you, Mademoiselle?"

Maggie softly spoke, "Sir, I think that the older lady over there may be responsible for the missing purse as she was eyeing my purse in the restroom moments ago."

"Thank you, Mademoiselle. I need to make a call." Then he turned around to call security immediately.

Maggie went back to the line but was careful not to make eye contact with the woman again.

The manager picked up his phone, spoke a few words in French and immediately two policeman from the back of the station approached. They saw the older lady, spoke briefly with her and took her with them to the end of the long hall off the side of the depot to interrogation. After about fifteen minutes, one of them came out with the younger woman's missing purse and brought it to her. Before handing the purse over to her, they asked the victim if she could identify a few items inside. She told them that there should be a small silver compact mirror with the engraved initial J.E.M. on it.

After confirming the silver compact mirror, the policeman asked her to look inside and make sure that everything was still in place, and it was.

Antoine leaned forward and whispered, "You knew?"

Maggie just halfway smiled and nodded.

"That kind of instinct is relevantly important for modeling. You will see what I mean once we start working together." Antoine whispered.

The train whistled as it came into the depot and the passengers all started picking up their bags and getting ready to board. Once inside, Antoine had gotten a luxury parlor room that included posh seats, a private bar, and fresh fruits, with coffee and juice as well as a domed window at the end of the railcar. Maggie had never ridden on a train like this before, and Antoine suspected that she had never seen such accommodations either.

Maggie never let on how impoverished her family was, regardless of Papa's excellent job. The truth is, right before she left, her sister Roma was institutionalized by her husband who said that she was mentally incompetent. Roma did suffer from depression that would lead to other ill behavior. Maggie's parents gained custody from her brother-in-law, but that meant fighting in court, and steep lawyer fees. It was pretty stressful, and there were no extra monies to be spoken of available for her or her other sister. Maggie worked part-time at an art studio to make some money to support herself. She was glad that she did, as it took care of clothing and other needs so that she would not lean on her parents for much. In all of her years, she would have never imagined traveling in such a manner as the elite, and it was somewhat difficult for Maggie to adjust.

As they entered the more private area, Antoine smiled and asked, "Can I get you something to drink?"

Maggie smiled, "I would like some water, thank you."

"As she discovered the extended red leather seat, she sat and carefully crossed her legs and just relaxed with her head tilted back. Maggie's fatigue set in from the traveling, but she was almost to Paris.

As Antoine brought her some water, he noticed her admiring the view. She had been on a train before, but she had never ridden in such luxury. Maggie looked outside and saw that Brussels was quickly falling behind them, and the picturesque countryside was taking over. She could see the wildflowers and an abundance of hawkweed, which many people thought were flowers, take over the meadows and valleys that they were passing along the way. Hawkweed lit up the countryside with bright yellow blooms that imitated sunflowers. She then noticed a lavender farm straight ahead, and she leaned back and breathed in hoping to catch the fragrance to no avail.

"It's lovely, yes?" he asked.

"Oh my goodness, yes! It looks like a Monet out there." She was referring to the famous artist Claude Monet, known for capturing nature's beauty in his work.

"Monet, you say? You have an appreciation for the arts, I see." Antoine continued.

"Oh, yes. Papa would take my sisters and me to the art museums back home, and then he would drill us on names and art forms. Papa is an interior decorator, so he has such a keen eye for color and design. I suppose I got that from him. Plus, I worked in an art studio before coming here. I have always had an eclectic love for the arts.

"Well, speaking of family, my grandfather was a photographer, and so was my father. Now, I am keeping the family trade alive. You may have heard of him, Édouard A. Lartigue?"

Maggie burst out, "Your father is Édouard A. Lartigue?"

Antoine replied, "I can say the one and only. You are familiar with his work?"

"I have some Paris magazines back home with some of his work in it. He has a good eye for fashion and well, beautiful women." She shyly answered.

Antoine smiled. "He taught me everything that I know about the business, and now I am living out my dreams making other people's dreams come true."

Maggie was pleasantly surprised and asked, "May I see some of your work...., that is if you brought any with you?"

Antoine got up and retrieved his briefcase, then opened it up to take out some articles and returned to the seat next to her. "Here is Maudelina. You will meet her tomorrow. She is now modeling for one of the most exclusive haute couture stores in Paris."

"She is so beautiful...my goodness!"

"Well, I only work with the best, Maggie. I already have a meeting lined up with you at another high-end department store seeking a model to fashion their new line. I know that you are the perfect fit. You'll see."

That was the one thing Maggie had difficulty doing. She never was good at feeling like she measured up to anything well. Her father constantly belittled Maggie, and always told her how useless she was. In doing so, Maggie still believed that she was far less desirable and far less gifted at anything. Looking at Antoine's work, she was astonished that he thought she was every bit as capable as Maudelina.

She pressed, "Antoine, I hope that I don't let you down. I mean, I will work hard for sure, and I am a good listener. Thank you so much for believing in me."

Smiling he offered, "Listen Maggie. I know that you have little experience, but I also know that when Frank refers someone, he has every confidence in them. I understand that you might encounter a learning curve, and that is perfectly normal. I am surrounding you with professionals who can help you.

All of the women who work for me are the best of the best! Nothing like learning from the best, oui?"

Maggie laughed, "Well, if you put it that way. I pray your confidence in me rubs off." she lightly giggled.

Antoine got up and went to the other side of the railcar and set his briefcase down. "I am going to let you rest now while I finish up some advertisements that I need to have ready by Monday." As he looked at the advertisements, he would occasionally glance over at Maggie and started realizing how special she was and how his customers were going to enjoy a fresh face.

He heard Maggie move, and she had actually put her legs up on the seat and snuggled in with the blanket, all while sleeping. Her head rested now on the curved back of the chair, and he could see how uniform and perfectly shaped her face was. He also could think of one client who would pay extra for a look like that, and so Antoine got to work getting ready to pitch a new face for the new clothing line.

About thirty minutes before arriving at their destination, Antoine called out "Maggie....? Maggie?"

Maggie stirred from her place and realized that she had been sleeping for the remainder of the train ride. "Oh, I am so sorry for falling asleep like that! I think the time change is starting to affect me."

Don't think anything of it Maggie. That is why I got the extra room on the train because I could foresee that you would need some rest. I am so glad that the accommodations worked for you to be able to sleep and get caught up. It is time to get ready for our arrival now," he prompted.

Maggie walked to the back of the train car to experience the view. Antoine looked at her and knew that her naive charm was going to win the public over, as well.

Shortly, the cabin staff went around announcing that the arrival time would be approaching soon. Antoine put away the items he had taken out of his small briefcase to read. Maggie's bags were still packed, so there was no other preparation.

Once they got off the train, Antoine secured a taxi once again. As they rode through the city, Maggie's eyes studied every building, every architectural design, and every fashion boutique window. She was like a sponge. She honestly had a sincere appreciation for fashion and design.

As the taxi driver arrived, Antoine announced, "This is the Gallo Hotel of Paris, and your accommodations have been handled. I will get your bags for you."

Antoine got out, and as the taxi driver placed the luggage on the curb, Antoine dug in his pocket for a gratuity. After settling, he motioned to Maggie to follow him inside.

Maggie looked up following the architectural design of the hotel as it climbed several stories and remarked, "This is incredible!"

"It's the best hotel in town. You will stay here for a few weeks, and if everything works out, I will secure you a permanent apartment near the other girls so that you can get to know them much better."

"Thank you so much, and I assure you that it is my every intention for this opportunity to work out well. I will make sure of it Mr. Lartigue!"

"Antoine....please." he smiled.

"Antoine, of course," Maggie corrected.

"The chauffeur is coming here in the morning at 7:30 a.m. to pick you up and bring you to the studio. We always start early in the morning. There is always food at the studio, so do not be concerned with breakfast. See you tomorrow?"

"Yes Sir," Maggie grinned.

"Now let me get you inside and checked in," Antoine insisted.

Antoine opened the door for Maggie as they entered the hotel lobby. A smiling concierge greeted them as they entered and a bag boy had already retrieved her luggage from the taxi driver instantly.

"How can I help you Monsieur?"

"Mademoiselle has a reservation under Maggie… I mean, Margaret Adler," Antoine spoke up.

"Ah… here she is. May we assist you to your room Mademoiselle?" the concierge requested.

"Thank you, sir," Maggie replied.

Antoine turned to look at Maggie, "Now get settled in and feel free to eat in the hotel dining area. The food here is authentic French cuisine." Then Antoine reached in his pocket and pulled out a gratuity and gave it to the man carrying her luggage up to her room.

"Thanks again Antoine for everything. You won't regret this," Maggie said most confidently.

Antoine laughed lightly, "I have a feeling that you are very right!"

As Maggie arrived upstairs, she thanked the doorman and then closed the hotel suite after he deposited the bags in her room. The room was covered in gold, plush material and designed with beautiful artistic inlays of flowers and gold on wooden paneled doors and windows. The restroom was all done in pure ivory marble. She had never seen such a beautiful suite. *"Oh, my Antoine, you have spared nothing to get me here,"* she whispered. As she looked out her large glass window, she recognized the *Jules Abbe de Arts* that she had read all about in a magazine.

"This view is spectacular," she thought to herself and smiled once again as she stood there momentarily soaking it all in.

Opening her luggage, she unpacked, and then decided to check out the hotel food, since she was famished. She never liked dining alone, and so she thought perhaps she could order food and have it delivered to her room. As she picked up a small thin leathered book sitting on the entry table, Maggie realized that she could order from their menu, but she did not recognize any of the meals, as it was all written in French. *"Oh my! I guess I better learn some French or I will never survive."*

She quickly changed clothes, freshened her makeup and ran a quick brush through her hair before pinning it up out of the way. She then left to go down to the restaurant to eat so that she could inquire of what foods were on the menu. Once she arrived and was seated, a tall, handsome waiter came to her aide. "What may I get you to drink mademoiselle?"

"Some hot tea please," Maggie nervously replied.

When the waiter returned, he also brought with him an English menu so that Maggie could order more efficiently. "Thank you so much for thinking about that," she offered as she took the menu from his hand.

The waiter placed the hot teapot and teacup with saucer down as he said, "My pleasure. I will return in a moment mademoiselle to take your order?"

"Yes, thank you, Monsieur."

When he walked away, she practiced saying Monsieur without a thick Northeastern accent.

After ordering and eating a most delightful meal, she retired to her room, took a long bath and readied herself for bed, knowing that she needed to arise at 5:30 a.m. so that she was not late for the chauffeur arriving the following day.

A Year Later..............

"Give me a left profile Maggie, and look at that vase as if you wish to pick up the daffodils displayed in it." Antoine directed.

"That's it, Maggie, stay there, don't move," Antoine continued to lead as he walked around her 360 degrees taking a load of pictures. "Beautiful work Maggie. Our client is going to love this one!" Antoine exclaimed. "Now, unbutton the top button of your blouse and lean a bit forward towards the vase again."

Maggie recalled the first time that Antoine had her change clothes and model some loose coverings used for modesty. He never asked her to reveal her body openly, but he liked to take playful, provocative photos of her in his clients' showroom clothing. The client, *France L' Fashion*, created a new clothing line and requested Maggie's pictures for display. They placed her work on their front windows and inside the store. They also asked if Maggie would be willing to come to the department store and do a meet-and-greet with potential customers when the clothing line debuted. Antoine answered affirmatively for her.

A few weeks later, as Antoine and Maggie got in the limousine to leave for the clothing debut, Maggie stated, "I am not sure what they expect of me at this event Antoine. I am a model, and I am terribly shy when it comes to meeting new people, as you know."

"Just be yourself, smile a lot and make people feel comfortable around you. You can do that naturally, without any lessons from me," he winked.

She took in a breath when they arrived at the department store. Placed upon the display window was a bigger than life poster of Maggie modeling their latest clothing line and an invitation for all to come inside and meet her. Her heart was racing, but Antoine took her hand and placed it on his arm, and smiled as he leaned over to her ear, "Relax Maggie. These people already love you!"

As they entered the store, the owner and associates all begin to clap, and she could hear customers excitedly respond, "Maggie Adler just walked in!"

Antoine introduced her again to the owner of the store and the creator of the new clothing line called, *Pearl of Light* because all of the designs were created to be worn during the summer month. They were light and flowing, and Maggie looked gorgeous in every picture taken of her as she wore the *Pearl of Light Collection*. That day, she chose a flowing pastel green chiffon coverlet to wear over a flowered A-line sleeveless dress that revealed the beauty of her legs and accented her long, auburn hair. The v-neckline was an added feature that accentuated her olive complexion as well. The owner stepped up next to Maggie, and they posed as she gracefully enhanced their clothing line once again, and Antoine did what he did best…took more pictures.

The debut of the clothing line was a great success. The store was full of people, and the clothing was flying off the store racks as women of all ages came in to choose from the variety of designs offered by the *Pearl of Light* line of clothing.

Maggie was only expected to stay about forty-five minutes, so people rushed to meet her and get her autograph. Maggie was somewhat overwhelmed by the response of the public to her, but she began to relax and take it all in. Antoine saw that her face had naturally relaxed and he took some random shots of her greeting customers. Those were some of the best pictures because Maggie's smile was so genuine and those who met her knew that she had a heart of gold for people of all ages. All of a sudden, it appeared that Maggie was in her realm, soaking up the opportunity and making the *Pearl of Light* clothing design irresistible. Antoine was very pleased that Maggie adapted quickly to the assignment, and he knew that if she kept learning how to deal with the public as well as she did today, that her modeling career would take off to new heights very quickly. She had matured a lot since her arrival in Paris.

The owner of the store had a grin on his face that could not be wiped off. He was delighted and told Antoine that he had found just the right model for their clothing line. When the time came, he escorted them both out of the store and to the waiting limo that had never left the curb.

"Thank you so much, Mr. Lartigue and Ms. Adler for a wonderful clothing debut. I am very well pleased, and I will be in touch again soon!" Mr. Beltane insisted.

"You were fabulous Maggie!" Antoine exclaimed as the limo pulled away from the curb. "I don't think I have ever witnessed you like I did today. You are definitely a shining star!"

Maggie slightly blushed and smiled. "Thanks, Antoine, I really did enjoy myself today," she admitted.

Antoine dropped Maggie off at her apartment and left, but not before letting her know that there was a new project awaiting her talent the following week. Maggie was pleased to be chosen among the models to do some of the grunt work. It mattered not to her as she was making a name for herself and the other girls were just as excited for her too.

As Maggie climbed the burgundy-carpeted stairwell to her apartment, she heard Claire call out to her. "Maggie, hold up!"

Maggie had become best of friends with Claire since the second day of her arrival in Paris. Claire had been very cordial, and she had shown Maggie around Paris, and much about professional modeling techniques. They would practice modeling at the apartment and holding poses so their stances would look natural. They also did their daily exercises together. They understood that a model out of shape was a model out of a job.

Maggie looked down the spiraled staircase as Claire advanced.

"Maggie, tonight there is someone I want you to meet. His name is Sam Milner, and we have a double date if you are game?"

"I don't know...I have had a big day already Claire."

"The day is young Maggie. Take a nap and wear that red and black gown that looks like a million bucks on you, huh?"

Maggie smiled and decided that she would not mind a little company, and so she nodded yes and continued up the flight of stairs to her apartment. She did not have any work for a few days so a nice break away might be just what was needed.

"Sam Milner.......hmmm...seems familiar but I can't place who that is," she pondered.

As she entered the apartment, she took off the flowing coverlet and plopped on the bed sideways and fell asleep. When she awakened, it was 4:00 p.m. and so she took a bath and got dressed and ready for her blind date.

"Hmmm...a date with someone I have never met. I am glad Claire will be there!" she said out loud as she looked in the mirror.

A gentle recognizable knock came to the door, and Maggie smiled as she let Claire in. "You look beautiful Maggie. Here, let me help you with the back of your hair." Maggie sat down, and Claire took the back of Maggie's hair and placed it in a quickly twisted updo in just a few minutes. "There….do you like it?" Claire exhaled.

"It's so different, and so grown up looking…and glamorous. Yes, I think I do----thank you!"

Maggie reached for some English Lavender perfume and lightly dabbed some on her wrist and behind each ear. Then she picked up her black rhinestone clutch purse and black silk wrap, and they both left and went downstairs in time to see the gentlemen waiting for their arrival. Claire waived to Hugo her date, as she scurried down the stairwell.

Maggie took a bit more time, and as she seemed to glide down the staircase so gracefully, Sam's eyes looked at her in a very pleasing, recognizable manner.

As she stepped off the staircase, Sam smiled, "And so we meet again Maggie…..my name is Sam Milner," he said as he stretched forth his hand to greet her.

When her hand met him, he lifted it to his lips and placed a soft kiss upon it. Maggie tried not to blush, but she was taken aback by his looks and demeanor, and one more thing, she recognized him! It was Sam from the voyage to Brussels. He had eaten one evening with her aboard the ship as she journeyed to France. She remembered him as being a bit shy and reserved, and very gentlemen like, so she enjoyed being around him. Afterward, he had asked her if she wanted to take a walk on the upper deck and she was delighted to accommodate him. After that, they ate the remaining meals together, which was only for a few more days, and took walks nightly on the promenade deck.

When she arrived in Paris, she had all but forgotten about him. She had no time for a long-term relationship as she had to learn the ropes of modeling. She had to become successful no matter what and dating was not a priority whatsoever.

Maggie smiled, "Nice to see you again Sam."

"You two know each other?" Claire inquired.

"Yes, Ma'am. I met Maggie on the trip from the states to Brussels a year ago. Frankly, I am surprised she remembers me! However, when you said that my date would be Maggie, I was not sure it was her, because I couldn't remember her last name while journeying here. However, I am completely delighted to see her again!"

Maggie smiled as Sam continued, "Shall we go now ladies?" as he offered his arm to Maggie. Hugo followed suit and extended his arm to Claire as they walked out to Hugo's vehicle. Maggie and Sam sat in the back.

"You two comfy?" Hugo asked before pulling away from the curb. Maggie blushed again and off they went.

Dinner was delightful, and Maggie and Sam had no problems being together and talking and laughing. When they got back to the apartment building, Hugo and Sam walked the girls inside and said goodnight. Sam planted a soft kiss on Maggie's cheek and whispered, "Can I call on you tomorrow night?"

Maggie smiled, "I would like that very much."

Two Years Later…

"How are you feeling Maggie?" Sam asked.

"I am doing as well as expected, I suppose."

Maggie had just laid down out of extreme fatigue. She was very saddened as she missed her modeling days, but Antoine said there was no room in the modeling business for a pregnant woman. Maggie was able to hide her pregnancy for a few months, but since she was carrying twins, her figure appeared to change overnight. Her husband Sam was delighted that she was expecting but concerned now that her health was at risks as Maggie had some early on complications that could not be ignored. The doctor said if she wanted a safe delivery, she would have to try and rest as much as she could. At that time, Sam was stationed outside of France so that they would steal as much time together as possible. One night, they decided to elope, and when Antoine heard, he was delighted, that is until she became pregnant. He released her from her contract and told her that modeling would be a most challenging career for a mother with children. That is when Sam requested to a transfer back to Virginia, and so they moved to the states.

Maggie loved modeling, but she loved Sam more. He understood the sacrifice she made to be with him, and though her job had kept her very independent, once they married she became much more co-dependent and controlling of his time. It was near impossible for him to have a perfect day at work because when he came home, she would complain about how long that he had been gone.

"Honey, I have to work so that we can eat, and when I say *we*, I mean you, the babies and me," Sam explained as he put his hands on the front of her now visible baby bump.

"I know, but my family is so far away and not willing to help in any way. Papa won't speak to me and won't allow anyone else to either. I suppose it is because we never married in the synagogue. I'll try and be more understanding, okay love?"

"That's all that I am asking sweetheart."

The next morning Sam kissed her as he left for work, but she was so exhausted that he refused to wake her up. She was doing well, but the doctor thought she might not make it full term. That worried Sam, as he knew how Maggie had prepared the nursery as much as possible. She wanted a very normal life for the babies, but she had no idea what to expect or how to care for babies. She never even babysat, so caring for two babies at one time was for sure going to be a challenge.

She was now a little over seven months pregnant. It was about 3:00 p.m. when she noticed a sharp pain run across her abdomen and her worst fears took over. She called her neighbor Joslyn and asked her to please take her to the hospital and to call Sam. Joslyn, who had become a dear friend in just a short amount of time, came right over, called the command office where Sam's ship was docked and left a message for him to get to the hospital.

Joslyn was more than a neighbor to Maggie; she was her only friend. When Sam and Maggie moved in, Joslyn and Ricky came over with an apple pie to welcome them as neighbors and instantly

Maggie and Joslyn hit it off. Joslyn's sweet demeanor matched her tender green eyes, long ash-blond hair and slender build. She was very unassuming, a bit older than Maggie and more confident about everything in life. Secretly, Maggie wished she could be as optimistic about life as Joslyn always appeared to be.

Joslyn carefully helped Maggie gather her things and assisted her to the vehicle as they had planned ahead of time. Joslyn could never have babies, so she was very excited to be a part of Maggie's life and to be with her for the big event, although Maggie was apparently having the twins too early.

"Oh no!" My water just broke all over your car!"

"It's Okay Maggie. That's why you are sitting on that thick blue blanket. It washes so don't worry, okay?"

Maggie nodded and held her stomach as her face grimaced in pain. I think something is wrong. It's too early to have these babies. Oh, Joslyn, what am I going to do?"

"We're doing it, Maggie! I'm getting you to the naval hospital as fast as I can. Just hold on now, we're almost there!"

As they pulled up in front of the hospital, she saw Sam running towards the vehicle. He opened the door and without hesitation, bent down and slid one arm around her waist and his other arm under her thighs and then picked Maggie up and carried her inside the hospital corridor.

"Thank you Joslyn. I don't know what we would do without you," he spouted.

"Hang in there darling," he assured her as he rushed inside. The nurse could immediately tell that Maggie was in horrific pain. The charge nurse quickly arrived and when she realized what was happening she called back for a gurney. Two more nurses came and helped get Maggie on the gurney and then swept her off with them towards the end of the hall.

The charge nurse then patted Sam on the arm and said, "You stay here, and I will keep you informed as to what is going on, okay?"

Sam nodded disappointedly but understood.

Joslyn came walking in shortly afterward and joined Sam in the waiting area. She could see his temple muscles flex, revealing the tension in his body. She reached out and laid her hand on his arm, "Relax Sam, I have heard that they are outstanding here about keeping expected fathers updated. They'll come out shortly and tell you something. You'll see." she gently assured him.

When she looked up, she saw another sailor coming in the doorway, and he looked around until he saw Sam and rushed over to him. "You okay buddy?"

"Yes Harold, I am okay. She is in the back, and I am waiting here for some news." Pointing to Joslyn, he said, "You remember Joslyn, Ricky's wife from the Christmas party last year, don't you?

Harold smiled, "Of course I do."

"She helped get Maggie here. Are you already off for the day?" Sam inquired.

"Yeah, I went in early, and so they let me off. I thought you could use some company, so here I am. Can I get you anything?"

Harold had befriended both Sam and Maggie right after they moved to Virginia. He wasn't married, but he would tease Sam about how beautiful his wife was and that he better watch out. It was just a joke, and Sam played along. Sam and Harold both worked in the photo lab onboard, so they had a lot in common and had shared many days and long night shifts working together. Harold enjoyed Sam's sense of humor and Sam liked that Harold could take things as they were happening and not get all stressed out much like some other crew members did.

The three of them sat there in the waiting area for a few hours before they heard anything, and then as if on cue, all heads turned as there was a rushing sound of someone scurrying down the hall. Sam looked up, and it was the charge nurse that had promised to give him updates.

As she approached she started talking, "She is delivering now, and it should be soon, as the babies are tiny. I will be back out as soon as possible. Don't worry, as Dr. Hodges is one of the best, even with premature babies." She then dashed back down the hallway.

"Let me get you some coffee or something Sam." Harold insisted.

Sam shook his head in agreement. "Can I get you anything Joslyn?"

Joslyn smiled at the handsome man with a dark tan, "Sure. I suppose I could use an orange soda if you can find one."

"I'll be back." Harold smiled.

It was just a matter of minutes when the nurse appeared again. She came rushing out of the room just long enough to tell Sam that he had twin girls, but that they were being cared for and placed inside incubators because they were so small at three and a half pounds each.

"Though they are healthy, there is still a risk, but the doctor thinks they will survive. I will come to get you as soon as they are somewhat settled." Then she disappeared again behind the double metal doors near the end of the hall.

"Girls? I'm a Papa of two baby girls!" he laughed and then his brow furled in concern.

"Everything is all right, did you hear what she said? They are small but healthy, so they should be fine. Try and relax Sam, as you will see them shortly. Oh, here comes your friend," Joslyn announced.

Harold walked in, and Sam was standing looking down the hall. "Any news?"

Sam was startled by his voice, and quickly turned, "We have girls, twin girls! Isn't that wonderful?"

"Congratulations Papa!" Harold rang out. Here's coffee for you too!" He then handed Joslyn her soda after opening it, and then the three of them toasted in celebration to the new arrivals.

After about an hour or so later, the nurse stepped into the hall smiling and called out, "You can come and see your babies now Mr. Milner. They are in the nursery. We have wheeled them up to the window for you to get a better look. They are both in incubators, and doing well."

3

Maggie is Lost

*Not until we are lost do we begin
to understand ourselves –Henry David Thoreau*

It had been almost twelve months since the twins were born and Maggie had battles of her own. She appeared to be overcome with anxiety and symptoms of depression, though during this time it was frowned upon for new mothers to complain about depression or baby-blues, as it was called, so she remained quiet about it. Maggie loved her precious girls with all of her heart, but she just could not muster up the strength for the day in and day out responsibilities of caring for them. Sam had seen her slipping away into a form of malaise, and he was not sure what to do about it. He spoke to his best friend Harold about it, but Harold could not offer any advice, being that he was a single man without any idea as to why women would act or behave strangely after childbirth. He loved his friends, but he had no idea on how to help them through this transition of life.

Maggie found herself pining away each day, and trying to live up to other people's expectations. The months moved on slowly, and the baby girls were becoming more demanding to care for as they went from crawling to walking in what appeared to be overnight. Maggie and Sam had moved from their tiny apartment into a house, and now Maggie found herself unable to become acquainted with neighbors or anyone else.

It was almost a year now since she had the girls and they were a handful. She could not understand why she always felt inadequate and aggravated at everything and everyone around her. As hard as she tried to just smile in the presence of Sam and the girls she understood now that she was merely going through the motions. Regardless, if she had a big birthday party to get ready for or not. The twins would be a year old in just four days. Leanne and Laney Milner were the center of her world, and that world was spinning out of control. The emotions inside of her would never settle. She had no other extreme stresses other than motherhood, so she could not even reason as to why she was experiencing these feelings of deep despair. At times she truly was happy, though it seemed that her emotional highs were the highest and her lows the very lowest. There was no middle ground or stability of her emotions. She could never just take things as they were. She always wanted change, something new or exciting, and she had lost all of her self-esteem and worth after giving birth. Her body no longer looked like her famous modeling magazines. She fought to take off the last five pounds of her pregnancy weight, and she stayed mentally and physically drained.

Suddenly a sound disturbed her from her deep thoughts. "Mama…mama..," she heard Laney crying out.

Maggie ran to the nursery as she knew both girls would be awakened now and ready for lunch. She rushed in, "Hey angel, Mama is here." Then she swooped down in the crib and picked up Laney. Immediately she heard Leanne stir from her nap and so she put Laney down on the throw rug and picked up Leanne from her crib as well. She had gotten used to taking care of two babies with very little help. Sam helped a lot when he was home, but he worked twelve-hour shifts, and that left her with the girls all day. They were usually eating dinner when he came in the door. Soon, it would be bedtime, and then Sam would assist with that. He loved his girls so much. He could see how they were growing and how beautiful they were becoming. The twins looked a lot like their mother, but they had his dark straight hair and cheeky smile. The girls were his whole world, and when he had days off, he would take the girls outside for a stroll in the park and play with them unending. His parents lived a distance away in Florida as well as Maggie's parents. Neither of the grandparents on either side was readily accessible which made the raising of two very active twins a bit more challenging.

Sam helped Maggie get things ready for the birthday celebration the next day. He borrowed some extra tables and glassware from some friends on the base and invited his best friend Harold and another couple over for the celebration. His parents were going to come to the party, but Maggie's parents could not make it. It was a disappointment for Maggie indeed; however, her parents sent gifts and promised to come for a week-long visit very soon. Maggie's parents had warmed up to their grandchildren, especially since Maggie had twins. Her mama was so pleased and loved holding the girls, as it reminded her of Moses and Michael. On their last visit up to see Maggie and the family, she told Maggie, "*God has redeemed our family by giving us these precious twins.*"

The day of the party arrived. The girls looked lovely in their pink dresses, and the room was full of people who had watched them grow up over the past year. Maggie was wearing a matching dress that coordinated well with the girls' dresses. She loved dressing up and making all of them match. She even made Sam wear a pink tie. He wasn't too thrilled about that, but he did it to keep the peace. Even their good friends Joslyn and Ricky came to celebrate the day.

While Maggie was in the kitchen preparing the punch, Joslynn entered, "Hey Maggie, How are you doing? Can I help you with anything?"

"I'm fine Joslyn… I am so glad you and Ricky could make it to the party. Isn't it wonderful??" she added.

"It sure is… I cannot believe it has been a year! Those girls have grown so much, and they are just beautiful." Joslynn beamed.

"Well, they are a handful, but I would not have it any other way. Could you please get me some ice out of the freezer?"

"I sure can," Joslyn replied as she walked toward the refrigerator.

The women chatted with small talk as Maggie continued getting things ready. When they entered the dining room, Harold said, "Well…look at you, Maggie. All of you girls look amazing today. I need to get a picture of this."

Harold reached in his carry bag and retrieved a camera. "Hey Sam…get over here by your ladies, and I will get a picture of all of you. Just stand by the girls high chairs. Everyone else just gather around."

Everyone complied as Harold took control of the room. "Here we go… on three," he said holding his camera up and ready for the shot as he counted off. After he took a handful of pictures, he dismissed everyone. Immediately the party went back to life as the guests mingled and began dotting on the birthday girls. The party was a great success. When everyone finally left, the cleanup began. Harold had stayed behind to help Sam and Maggie finish putting things away. He then shook Sam's hand vigorously and kissed Maggie on the cheek as he was leaving saying "See ya'll soon." His distinct country accent was unmistakable, and Maggie found it to be charming.

After the party, Sam finished cleaning up everything allowing Maggie to tend to the girls and get them ready for bed. Harold had put the extra tables in the back of his truck and said that he would drop them off at the McCane's house on his way into the base. That was so helpful, and Sam really appreciated having a friend like Harold in times like this.

Maggie thoroughly enjoyed the day. She loved being around her friends and family at certain times, and as she got the girls ready for bed, she was singing their favorite lullaby. Leanne started rubbing her eyes and wining.

"It's okay baby girl. You've had a long day and you will rest well now." She continued. She put them both to bed and before she shut the light off, both of them had already closed their eyes. That usually wasn't the case. The girls would chat with each other, in their baby talk, as they did most nights before going to sleep. One night Sam recorded them after he had put them to bed. They would giggle, and sit up in their cribs and chat like sisters do, even when they were eight months old. Leanne was the oldest of the twins by five minutes, but she always took charge. She seemed to know that Laney had an unusual eye problem that stopped her from seeing everything as clearly as Leanne could, so Leanne protected her by holding on to her wherever they went. The girls were inseparable, and both Sam and Maggie considered themselves doubly blessed to have such precious angels as daughters.

It had been a few months since the party and Sam happened to come home a few hours early. The base sent him home because he had a little bit of overtime. He wanted to surprise Maggie and the girls, but the surprise was on him. As he walked into the house, Maggie was lying on the couch reading modeling magazines, and the girls were sitting on the floor with soiled diapers. There were dishes in the sink, and the girls looked as if they had not been taken care of all day. Their hair was tangled, and food was on their faces.

"What's going on here? Maggie are you okay?" he asked as he picked up Laney who had stood and reached up for him.

"Oh, you're home! I am fine..." she replied.

"Why aren't the girls dressed and cleaned up honey? You are just lying there rereading those magazines. I don't understand it. Can't you see that those days are gone? This is your life now. These girls need you!" Sam blurted.

"Sam, I was going to take care of them. I have the girls all day, every day to myself. So what if they are dirty! I was going to give them a bath before dinner," she grumbled back at him.

"Can you see what this looks like Maggie? We have been dealing with this for months. I can't take it anymore, and I can't fake it anymore. You need help. I do not know what happened to my wife, but you are not the same woman that I married. I see glimpses of her from time to time, and that's is all. I am not saying that I do not love you. I just cannot keep on living like this. It's not fair to the girls or me."

"It's not fair? What's not fair? I'll tell you what's not fair! Me giving up my career in modeling just because I got pregnant! Me, here all by myself every day trying to keep up with everyone else's expectations! What about my needs and wants! You don't even look at me with love anymore Sam. I agree that at night I am totally exhausted, but you try taking care of these girls from 6:00 a.m. until 8:00 p.m. every day for over a year and see how much energy you have left at the end of the day!!" she angrily responded.

"I'm not going to talk to you about this anymore Maggie. All we *do* is talk about this, and nothing happens!" Sam retorted.

"Fine! Cook your own dinner and take care of the girls tonight. I am going out!" So, Maggie got up, went to the bedroom, and got dressed and ready for an evening at the club. She had not been out dancing in over a year. Sam was too aggravated and weary to fight with her anymore. He gave in.

"Go ahead…see if I care!" he said under his breath.

Maggie put on her dancing dress, makeup, and high heels and was out the door in about forty-five minutes without a single word. She got in the vehicle and drove off speedily down the neighborhood road. As Maggie turned the first corner, a driver was flashing his lights at her. She looked up and noticed it was Harold. She pulled over on to the side of the road, and he turned around and pulled up right behind her.

Harold got out of his car and ran up to Maggie's window. "What are you doing out here looking like that this hour of the night?"

"I'm going dancing. I am sick and tired of not getting out to do anything anymore."

"Where is Sam?"

"Home with the girls!" she snapped.

"Hold it there sweetheart. You don't have to bite *my* head off. Want some company?" he smiled.

"Why not…sure."

"Are you going to Larry's?"

"Yes… see you there."

Maggie took off and kept driving furiously as if she was taking her anger out on the vehicle. She could see Harold trying to keep up with her, so she decided to go the speed limit and start acting a bit responsible. She was glad that he had spotted her car. She really did not want to walk into a club and not know anyone. She liked Harold a lot, and he had always been a special friend to Sam and to her. It put her mind at ease to know that Harold would be with her that night.

As Harold followed his thoughts were all over the road. "*Why would Maggie go out dancing without Sam?*" He knew they were experiencing some arguments as Sam had told him most of what was going on. That is why Harold would come over a few nights every week just to help around the house or keep them company. He loved both of them dearly, and he really loved the girls. He hoped one day that he would marry and be as lucky as they were to have children just like them. Being the oldest of sixteen children in his own home, he often was left to babysit and take care of the younger children. His father was an alcoholic, and it forced his mother to work outside the home to try and make ends meet. His mother could not do much but be a waitress or housekeeper as she had no other real work skills. That is how his parents met. His mother, Betty, was waitressing when James came into the diner one day. From that day on they were together everywhere they went and married in just six months after meeting. James wasn't a heavy drinker then, but when times started getting difficult and the depression years hit, he lost his job, and he could not support his family anymore. He handled that pain by drinking alcohol as it numbed him from the distress of being a failure.

Now, Harold liked drinking. Honestly, he always liked drinking and started drinking when he was about sixteen. His Dad would sit outside and offer Harold a beer every night. Soon one turned into two and Harold got hooked. Though he graduated from high school, he never had any ambitions to go to college. Harold wanted to be a mechanic someday and own his own shop. But before that, he always aspired to be in the Navy. So, upon graduation, Harold walked down to the offices of the Navy and registered for service as soon as possible. Harold was not real tall, but he was muscly and fun to be with. He had a good sense of humor, but he did not talk very much. He did his best to mind his own business and tried to help others when he could. There wasn't anyone who didn't like him. After being in the Navy for a year, he decided he wanted to learn more about filming and photography. That is when he was assigned to the film lab, and that is where he met Sam. They hit it off immediately and became best buddies in just a few months. They had a lot of the same interests, and everyone started calling them "the clones," because they even had the same mannerisms after a while.

As they arrived at the club, Harold thought that it was good that he was there to keep an eye on Maggie. He knew a woman that beautiful could get in trouble fast around all these Navy men and he would be there to ensure her safety and take care of his best friend's wife.

He walked up to Maggie's car parked just in front of him and opened her door. "Come on beautiful… let's get this show on the road."

"Oh Harold ……you're so silly!" she laughed.

They walked into the club, found a seat and Harold ordered them some drinks. Maggie always enjoyed her red wine, so he knew exactly what to get for her. As usual, he just ordered a beer on tap. As soon as the drinks came, the band started playing an upbeat song, and Maggie asked Harold if he wanted to dance.

'Uh…Maggie… I am not very good at those fast songs, but when a slow one comes around, I will take you out there."

Almost on cue a tall blond man walked up to the table and asked, "Are you going to take her dancing or do I have to?"

"It's up to her," Sam nervously replied.

"Well, it is my favorite song... let's go!" she answered the stranger.

He reached down and helped her up from the table, and they walked out on to the dance floor. They started dancing the swing dance, and Harold was surprised at what a good dancer Maggie was. He had not been out with Sam and Maggie dancing for a long time, so he had forgotten how she quickly became the life of the party. Things were no different that night. She was smiling ear to ear, and every man in the club was watching her. There were only a few couples on the floor at that time but the way Maggie moved with such ease over the dance floor, it appeared she was gliding. When she came back to the table two men approached and asked if they could dance with her too.

"Oh, no fellas. Thanks anyway. Can't you see I am here with a date?" she smiled as she looked at Harold.

Harold knew Maggie enough to know that her words were a cue that she was a bit uncomfortable with all the attention. So he spoke up, "Yup fella's, you're on your own the rest of the night, this beauty is mine," He winked.

Actually, Maggie thought what Harold said was very kind and sweet, and she told him so. "Thanks for stepping up. I really don't want to dance with strangers. The fast song was okay because we really did not get too close to each other. I had fun, but I am so glad you are here Harold."

She sipped the rest of her wine, and when the waitress came by, she ordered another. Now, Maggie wasn't very good at holding any kind of alcohol, and that meant even one glass of wine as it loosed her inhibitions. Harold knew that he better keep a close eye on her. Momentarily a slow song began, and she looked up at him.

"Are you going to take me out there now?" she prodded.

Harold smiled, "Sure....let's go."

They walked out on to the dance floor, and he put his arm around her small waist. Instantly he realized they had never danced together before. She put her arm upon his shoulder, laid her head against his breast and followed his lead as if they had danced liked that a million times. He could smell her perfume and feel the softness of her hair against his cheek and then it happened. His mind went somewhere else. Somewhere to a place where he and Maggie could be together forever. He loved her, and he never realized it until they danced together that night. Oh, it terrified him to think that he could care for his best friend's wife this way but he couldn't help himself. One dance led to another and another. At the end of the third dance, before the music stopped, Maggie looked up into his eyes with seriousness. It was apparent she was feeling the same way, and before they both knew it, their dance turned into an embrace followed by a gentle kiss that neither one of them ever forgot.

By the end of the evening, Maggie was a bit lightheaded from the wine and Harold agreed to follow her to make sure she got home alright. It was after midnight before Maggie drove up into the driveway. Harold parked behind her, got out and helped her out and walked her to the door. Sam had gone to bed. Every light in the house was out as if he did not expect her to come back home.

"I had a wonderful time with you tonight,' Maggie stated.

"Me too…can I call you tomorrow during the day?" he asked.

"Yes, I'll look forward to it." She smiled before she reached up to kiss him goodnight. His heart was beating so hard he couldn't think straight. He then pulled her away, "Maggie, not here. Not with Sam....you know.........?"

"Sure....goodnight." she said as she opened the door and disappeared.

Sam was in bed, but he never fell asleep. He heard her come in and shut his eyes relieved when he realized that she was home. Sam had called his parents that night and talked for a few hours with them about what he had planned to do. He wanted no harm to come to Maggie, but he cared about the welfare of his children. He, through the counsel of his parents, decided to get a divorce and fight for custody of the children. His parents had decided to temporarily move closer to assist him in the children's care. It wound up after a very long six months, that both of them were granted custody. The girls would stay at his parent's home during the week with him, and Maggie could see them anytime that she wanted, and have them every other weekend. It was unusual for a woman not to get sole custody of the children in those days, but Sam had gotten a good lawyer who contested her battle for sole custody due to her instability and unsound mind.

Meanwhile, a year later Sam's ship had been ordered overseas, and he was going out of the country. He made arrangements with the court for the girls to remain with his parents who were moving back to Eau Gallie, Florida in less than a month. While he was gone, Maggie could visit them there and take them home to her new place in Miami, Florida every other weekend. He had no idea that Harold had put in for a transfer to the Florida base and that he and Maggie were now an item. They kept that a secret. He knew Maggie went out on the weekends when he had the girls, but he did not know that Harold was with her. However, some of the guys on the base knew all about it and when he confessed to someone else about his divorce one of them piped up.

"Well, I'm not surprised being that your best friend takes her out dancing every other weekend," one of his shipmates sarcastically snorted.

Sam turned around stunned and spouted, "What on earth are you talking about...Harold?" he inquired.

"You didn't know? We thought everyone knew by now. They certainly do not hide it from anyone at Larry's. Sorry, bud...I did not mean to antagonize you. I'm just stating facts."

Sam walked away profoundly disturbed and in deep thought. All those months Harold had been consoling him and telling him that he was making the best decision on behalf of the girls to get a divorce. He had gone drinking with him on a few Friday nights at the officers club, but they never drank as much as they talked. Harold was never much of a talker anyway. He was sure a good listener though, and Sam needed someone to listen. Sam never thought that in a million years his best friend would do such a hurtful thing to him. Now he understood when news came for Harold's transfer why all of that had happened. Maggie's folks were in Florida too. She had recently told Sam that she had procured a two bedroom apartment when she heard about his leave. She knew his parents were moving to Florida too, so it made sense. Before then, on the weekends when she did not have the girls, she would drive over to Harold's and spend the night after they went dancing at the club. Now, in another month both Sam and Harold would be gone from Virginia. Harold would be in Florida and Sam in North Korea. It was more than Sam could bear. He wanted to tear into Harold and rip him apart limb for limb, but he did not want to sacrifice his Navy career over it...so he let it slide for now.

"Hey, buddy.... How's it going?" Harold asked as he entered the ships photography lab.

Sam was just starring off into space. He had no reply, and he did not care if Harold needed a response or not. He was steaming inside. Sam decided to get up and walk out of the area, and in doing so, he pushed Harold's shoulder to the wall deliberately as he exited the room. Harold was confused merely because he had no idea that Sam knew anything about him and Maggie.

"Commander Ryan, report to the captain's office immediately." The announcement rang over the entire ship. Harold had never been summoned to appear on the captain's deck before, and he hurried as soon as he heard his name.

He saluted his superior, and when Captain Miles saw him, he replied, "At ease." I need to talk to you about your transfer."

Harold carefully entered the quarters and replied, "Yes sir?

"I want you to know that your transfer has been postponed for six months. The Admiral says he needs both you and Sam to be on this initial journey over to North Korea as he needs all the eyes that he can get on board. After six months, you can be stationed in Florida or wherever you want to go. Do you understand?"

"Alright, Sir…," Harold responded, saluted and quickly left.

This was going to mess up their plans, but he and Maggie would work around it. He knew that Maggie had procured an apartment a few blocks away from her parent's house. He had given her the money to do so. Harold agreed that he would make sure that Maggie was set up comfortably and send her money to help keep things stable while he was gone. He would call her later that day to explain things.

"What??!! You're going to Korea too?" Maggie cried. "You can't Harold. I need you here."

"What do you want me to do sweetheart? I can't go against a direct order. It will work out. You'll see." Harold answered softly.

"I'm pregnant Harold!" she blurted out.

A long silence fell over the phone as Harold tried to allow those words to soak in.

"Are you there.....?" she cried.

"I'm here sweetheart...and well...that does complicate things. We can only do the best we can do. If you are more comfortable living with your folks for the next six months, that will be fine. I will forfeit my deposit on the apartment, and we can work this out, Maggie. We'll talk tonight. I have to go now." Then he hung up.

Maggie hung up and suddenly felt like her world was spinning out of control again. Her folks had never met Harold, but when they heard that she was dating him, they were concerned. Maggie was not sure how they would react to her being pregnant and unmarried but what choice did she have? She had to come clean. She picked up the phone and called her parents. Things had been rough between them since she married Sam, but they seemed to overlook the issue once the girls were born and they became much more supportive after the divorce. They were delighted grandparents, and her mother loved having the twins around. It reminded her of her of Michael and Moses before the fever took their lives. How she missed her precious sons, but when she held the girls in her arms, she would hold them as if it was the last time she would ever get to do so, knowing how fragile life really could be. Opal was a woman who had experienced so many significant losses.

When Opal and William came to the states, they had stowed away on a ship that was headed for America. As they were running for the boat, Opal's parents were gunned down by the Czar. It was terrifying. The last words she ever heard her mother

Rebecca say was, *"William, take care of her..."* and so William had. Opal knew nothing about paying bills, or how to do any business transactions. She leaned on William for everything. He kept her that way because it was easier to control the family if he was in charge of everything.

The phone rang... "Hello," Opal answered.

"Hi, Mama... how are you?" Maggie tried to smile.

"Oh Maggie, I am well... How are you darling?"

Maggie continued on talking, and she told her Mama everything. Her Mama was upset, but she did not reject Maggie. She asked Maggie to let her tell William everything, and they would get back to her as soon as they could. They were empty nesters so allowing Maggie to move in with the children for six months would not be that difficult. After all, she could get to know her granddaughters better. She just hoped after William expressed his anger that he too would see things her way.

A few days passed, and Maggie and Harold had spent the night together trying to figure out what to do about the upcoming months when he would be gone.

"Maybe we should come back here when you get back. After all, I still have base privileges as Sam has not taken me off of them yet. I can have our baby here and make sure that is paid for at least," Maggie negotiated.

"Well, since your parents called yesterday and said that you and the girls could stay there, I think that might be a better solution. It would be easier to pick them up in Eau Gallie than for you to drive there every other weekend in your condition. So, a temporary move to Florida might be a good solution...," Harold agreed.

The following months were very trying on Maggie though her parents were gracious enough to not ridicule her for getting pregnant out of wedlock. However, her father's disdain over the matter could not be overlooked. He was very unhappy with the choices his daughter Maggie had been making, and he made it clear, maybe not in word, but his actions often spoke louder. He had a few words to say to her and when she asked him questions. He just replied with a "yes" or "no" or nodded. He never conversed with her on anything of importance. Her Mama was different. In fact, her Mama seemed cheerful every day as long as the girls were allowed to be in their home. Because Sam's parents liked to travel, they allowed Maggie to keep the girls for weeks at a time. That was a good thing for Maggie, and it kept her mind off of Harold and the morning sickness and aches and pains of pregnancy. She would go up for visits to the doctor once every six weeks. It was a long drive, and she rented a hotel when she did so.

On the drive up the girls asked, "Hey, Mama, isn't this where you and daddy used to live…here in this town?" Leanne asked.

"Yes, honey," she smiled.

"I miss daddy …don't you Mama?" Laney asked.

"Um…girls …now you know that your daddy and I do not live together anymore. There is a reason for that. I do miss him but not in the way you think I should."

"Oh, I know Mama… but wouldn't it be nice if you could be friends again and we could all live in our home together?" Laney reasoned.

The girls did not know that she was pregnant with Harold's baby. She had kept it all a secret from anyone but her parents and her oldest sister who lived in town. It was hard. She felt ostracized enough. Soon she would not be able to hide her pregnancy from Sam's parents either. She had not figured out how she would explain it, but when the moment arose, she prayed she would have the right words. However, when she went to the Jewish Synagogue with Mama and Papa, it was different. The congregation thought her husband was overseas and that she was pregnant again by him. Opal and William never said another word about it. They just let people believe what seemed natural. She had not been to the synagogue in years, but Papa said that was his only stipulation if she was going to live with them. She had to attend the synagogue with them faithfully. Maggie really did not mind it. She actually had missed going to synagogue and since Sam had no desire to go, they always just stayed home with the girls.

The six months was almost over, and she was due to deliver in just a month. Maggie made plans to move back to Virginia. She let Sam's folks know in a letter that she was moving and that she would not be able to see the girls for six weeks. Maggie told them that she was pregnant and close to delivering. She also let them know that the baby was not Sam's. She did not have a place to keep the girls in Virginia as of yet, but if the plans changed she would let them know. Maggie thanked them for caring for the twins and assured them if they needed anything that they could reach out to her. They had her parent's phone number, and she would make sure that her parents had all the current information on her location.

Sam's parents agreed to come and pick up the girls on that last weekend. Maggie was very emotional knowing she would not see them for a long time.

"You girls be good now. Mama will see you again as soon as possible. I love you very much." She gave them each a long embrace and tender kiss before standing up and walking back to the porch. She stood there blowing kisses and waving to them until the vehicle was out of sight.

Her Papa had brought her luggage out and put it in her vehicle. "Are you alright Maggie?" he asked.

"Oh Papa, it's so hard. I know I have made poor choices in life. Please find room in your heart to forgive me" she paused. "I never meant to hurt you Papa."

William stepped in closer and took his daughter into his loving embrace. "Well, I was hurt, but I forgive you, Maggie. I am not going to waste any more time thinking about it. Now you be safe and please call us when you arrive in Virginia. Here is some extra cash for a hotel along the way. You do not need to drive thirteen hours while you are pregnant. Understand?"

Maggie hugged him back, and they stood there for a brief moment. She remembered his loving arms around her only a few times in her lifetime. She was cherishing the moment when suddenly she heard, "Can I have one too?" her Mama interrupted.

Maggie smiled and reached over for her Mama. How she had grown to admire her Mama. She was much stronger than Maggie had given her credit for. Yes, she was controlled by Papa, but she had a way of getting around his tactics and moments of control when she had to do it. Maggie hoped she never had to live with a man like her father.

Maggie kissed both of her parents again and then got in her car and drove off. Opal stood on the porch watching her drive down the road until she could not see the car in the distance any longer.

Maggie drove for almost eight hours with only one gas break and two restroom breaks. She was getting tired, and so she decided to look for a hotel. There in the distance was a sign for the Roadway Suites in Charlotte, North Carolina. She had stayed there once with Sam, so she knew that it was a beautiful place. Once she got inside, she rented a room. The clerk saw that she was very pregnant and so he offered to carry her luggage to her room. She was thankful. Maggie slept well that night, except for the time when the baby would kick and wake her up.

It seemed this baby was a night owl just like his sisters. The twins kept her up so much at night that she slept a lot during the daytime when she was pregnant with them. And now this baby felt like he or she was doing jumping jacks in her tummy. *"Goodness sakes child, please calm down. Mama has to drive a long way tomorrow, and I need rest."*

Suddenly it was as if the baby heard and instantly calmed. *"Hmmm... I like obedient children,"* she giggled and then fell off to sleep. Morning came quickly but she was rested. She went down to the front desk to check out and the morning clerk asked if she needed help with luggage again. She smiled, "That would be very nice of you, please."

Once everything was in the car, she drove to a local diner to grab a quick bite to eat. She was hungry for a good bagel and locks. Something she often craved with the girls as well. As she ordered the waitress was surprised that Maggie was traveling alone and in her condition.

"How in the world are you managing a road trip in that condition?" she asked.

"Well...one mile at a time...," Maggie laughed. "It's not the most comfortable drive, but I am actually enjoying the time alone."

Maggie put in her order and asked for a crème soda to go with it. After eating until she was full, she left the ticket and money on the table with a tip and walked away. Once she was on the road again, she turned on the radio and started singing to some oldies and lost all track of time as she drove on toward Virginia.

It was around three o'clock in the afternoon when she pulled into town. Harold would be getting in that evening, and they agreed to stay at a local boarding house for the birth and recovery. Then, as Maggie and the baby could travel, they would move to Florida. Maggie had an afternoon doctor appointment on base, so that would take up some of the waiting time for Harold to arrive.

When Harold got in that evening, he was surprised at how big Maggie had gotten, but he was delighted to know that his baby would be arriving in a matter of weeks. The doctor told Maggie that she was already starting to dilate a little but to not worry. That some women tend to do that a few weeks before delivery. Since they were staying a few miles from the base hospital, it would not be a problem at all to get her there once she went into labor.

"I missed you so much Maggie," Harold said as he wrapped his arms around her from the backside. He placed his hands on her stomach and said, "You too little fella...," he smiled as he tapped her gently on her baby bump.

"And how do you know it's a boy?" she laughed as she leaned back into his embrace.

"Well, it better be since I bought him boy clothes...," Harold answered. Then he held up a small Navy sailor suit. "Do you like it?" he asked.

"If we have a son... great...but a girl... not so much." she laughed as she turned around and tapped him on the nose at the same moment. She loved how he teased her. They sat down and Harold asked her if she wanted a soda to drink as he popped open a beer. "I got you a crème soda...your favorite," he insisted.

"That sounds great...and how about some....," and before she could finish the sentence he pulled out a bag of sour cream potato chips. "You remembered!" she gleefully replied.

"Oh, you will find out that I never forget anything. The guys tease me about that on the ship all the time," he said.

Speaking of the ship caused him to pause as his mind went to the photography lab. Sam and Harold had kept things amicable between them merely because a time of war was not a time to turn on a shipmate. They had to work together for their department to be successful. They needed each other, and so they were forced to work out their differences so that the rest of the shipmates would not be affected by the recent events in their lives. They were no longer buddies though, and in that first month their shifts were split up so that they rarely had to work together. The captain had received word of what had happened, and that is the only way he could intervene. Schedule changes did make it easier for the two men to live on the same ship for six more months. The vessel would port for a month and then go back out to sea. Sam had a week of leave coming to him and so as soon as they docked, he caught a taxi to the airport and flew out to see his girls.

The next day, after they got some rest, Harold approached Maggie about an opportunity that he was given. "How about after the baby is born we move to California. I have been offered a big promotion and lots of extra money which will come in handy with the kids. What do you say?"

"How can I do that? The girls live in Florida honey. I can't travel every other weekend to Florida and with a baby….," she stated in a concerned manner.

"Well, I have a plan," Harold said.

He went on to tell her of his plan, and she felt like she was between a rock and a hard place. She agreed to it no matter how risky it sounded. Once she started thinking about it, she suddenly felt a sharp pain across her abdomen. The stress of such a decision had caused her to go into labor.

Harold called the naval base and told them he was taking his wife to the hospital. Everyone on board thought they were married, but they were not married. Harold had put Maggie down as the beneficiary of all his policies and placed her under his medical

75

coverage at the base too. He did not want anything to happen to her or the baby.

Maggie could barely walk to the car. Harold did his best to get her there and get her comfortable, and then he took off quickly toward the hospital. When they arrived, a nurse came quickly out the door.

As Harold got out to help Maggie, the nurse informed, "They called us from the base and told us that you were on your way, Mr. Ryan. How is Mrs. Ryan doing?"

Maggie looked back at Harold, and he replied, "She needs to get inside," he smiled.

It had dawned on Maggie what he had done. He had told them they had gotten married the previous night, and so the paperwork was in place with her new name …that is, her new name to be, as soon as the real marriage took place. She did not seem to mind, but she would have liked being in the know about it. It felt like there was an undercurrent in his behavior that she was not familiar with. He was very assuming of things. Now wasn't the time to argue though, because the labor pains were taking over her reasoning abilities at the moment. She did not fear the labor, she feared what the next step in their relationship was going to bring, and Maggie wasn't sure she could follow through with it.

Harold waited all alone in the waiting area. He had friends, but not close friends like he and Sam used to be. Just shipmates. Maggie's labor lasted about two hours before they took her to delivery. He thought that was really fast, but when she got to the hospital, she was already dilated to a seven. It would be a matter of minutes now before he knew anything else. The nurse in the reception area kept him apprised of the situation. He was anxious. Anxious for his child to be born, eager to know if Maggie would be alright and worried if Maggie could follow through on his plan to go to California. His mind kept thinking on how to make it all work out when suddenly his thoughts were interrupted.

"Mr. Ryan, your wife has delivered and the baby is doing well. Your wife is in recovery, and the baby is in the nursery now getting checked out. Congratulations on having a baby boy. I will come to get you as soon as they get him ready," the nurse informed him before she took off down the hall again.

Harold was elated. "A boy.... I had a boy!" he almost shouted.

The receptionist laughed, "You....had a boy?" she laughed again.

He laughed along with her. Well, I am glad I did not do the hard part....," he answered.

He could not sit any longer. He paced back and forth once again and waited for the nurse from the baby nursery to come out and take him back. After about thirty minutes she called to Harold down the hall. "You can come now. I have him up at the window," she smiled.

As Harold walked up to the window, he had butterflies in his stomach. Nothing had made him feel so inadequate, or as helpless as a newborn baby. He could take a storm at sea with fewer nerves than he was experiencing at that moment. Suddenly when he laid eyes on his son, something happened. An instant calm to the storm inside of him became apparent. He looked into his son's eyes and realized that he had his Mama's curly red hair and olive skin, as well as dark eyes. He was beautiful and Harold stood there silently as tears filled his eyes. No one had ever seen Harold cry. He was such a tough guy, but something about this baby broke through that rough exterior of his. He was all mush. He put his hands on the window trying to get the baby's attention. The nurse inside picked up the baby and held him up closer so that his Daddy could inspect him through the protective glass. Harold just stared and smiled and stared some more. His son was the most beautiful thing he had ever seen on this earth, next to Maggie.

The nurse placed the baby back down in the bassinet and whisked him off to see his mother. By then Maggie was anxiously waiting to see her son. She was still woozy from the drugs they had given her in labor, but she was alert enough to know that she had a boy. As the nurse approached, she could see red hair peek through the top of the blue nursery blanket.

Maggie smiled as they placed her son in her arms. "Here's your sweet boy honey. He is precious….," the nurse added.

"He definitely is….," Maggie agreed. She checked all his fingers and toes, just like she had done with the girls. Then she kissed his sweet face and held him ever so close. "Oh, Maxwell. You are the most handsome boy I have ever met. I love you so much, my sweet baby," she whispered.

The nurse was standing there and said, "Oh, I love that name...Maxwell. Is that what you said?" she inquired.

"Yes, his name is Henry Maxwell Ryan," Maggie stated.

The nurse wrote it down and asked Maggie if she had spelled it right before entering it into the record. Maggie agreed that it was written correctly.

"I'll be back in about thirty minutes to take the baby to the nursery. You can feed him though. Here, I have a bottle all ready for you," the nurse stated.

Maggie thanked the nurse without ever taking her eyes off of her son. There was something so extraordinary about this baby, but she did not know precisely what it was. Maybe it was because he was conceived in so much love, or perhaps it was because he was her baby. It did not matter. She worked with Maxwell until he took the bottle with ease and he drank every drop. Apparently he was famished. Come to think about it, she had not had breakfast that morning, and it was now one o' clock in the afternoon. *"The poor fella probably was starved,"* she thought to herself.

Harold got word of the baby's name, and he was pleased. Maggie had not shared that with him. After the baby was fed, they took him to the nursery and allowed Harold to come in and see Maggie. There he stood at the doorway. He looked different to her. More resolved and bathed in peace. She was pleased that he was so happy about the baby and the name she had selected.

"How is the love of my life," Harold chimed in.

Maggie smiled, "I am tired but doing well....or were you talking about the baby??"

Harold giggled, "Both of you. He sure is a handsome little fella, huh? He looks a lot like you sweetheart."

"I thought he looked like you...," she laughed.

Baby and mother were doing very well. Harold spent the next days on board the ship working and a big part of the evening at the hospital with Maggie and Max. Maggie was in the hospital for a week before she was released to go home. Harold came by and picked up his family and took them to the boarding room. He had paid for a six-week stay, while they decided whether they would be going on to California or not.

When Harold would look at Maggie taking care of Max, he began to see her in a different light. He had watched her interact with the twins, but something was different here. She was more calm and deliberate. He was glad that Maggie had this time with Max to be alone and adjust to the new baby. If everything worked out like Harold thought it would....Maggie, Max and the twins would all be living together in California very soon.

4

Seven Years Later

*A lie that is half-truth is the darkest
of all lies –Alfred Tennyson*

At the age of five, Lizzy Ryan was ready for kindergarten. Her peaches and cream complexion made her look like a china doll in a glass window. Lizzy was excited about the possibility of going to school, just like her two older brothers Max and Bruce. Everyone knew she was happy because Lizzy was singing. Her family lived in downtown Muskingum, Oklahoma, inside a one-story bungalow, with white painted trim and terracotta colored shingles. A towering oak tree stood over the entire front yard providing shade and respite during the hot summer season.

Maggie Ryan, her Mama, was a petite, olive-skinned, full-blood Jew married to a self-proclaimed atheist. Lizzie had no idea that Mama had been married before to someone else, or that she had children from a previous marriage. She had seen the girl's pictures on the mantle in the living room, but she never inquired as to who they were until years later. Now, her Mama did not honestly believe that Harold was an atheist. She just thought he had a bad church experience that had turned him away from God. Harold, who was of average height, dark curly hair, steel blue eyes, and with a muscly build, was the type of man who liked to say things to get a stir out of people. Most of the time, he used that tactic inappropriately. In the past, Maggie would have never been attracted to a man like that, but now, after seven years, something had caused him to change and perhaps, not in a good way. Lizzy never felt like he had time for her, so she stayed by her Mama's side at all times, but today was different.

All morning long Lizzy sang and sang over and over again the song she had made up about getting to go school. Singing was her favorite form of enjoyment. Her Mama was such a marvelous singer too. Lizzy remembered the stories about how her Mama Maggie and how her Mama used to sing on the radio in Washington, D.C. when she was only fourteen years old. Her Mama's long red hair, dark cocoa eyes, and bright smile helped her on later in life. Having the former occupation of a Paris model, her Mama was continually reminding Lizzy to stand up straight and to walk properly. She could also dance beautifully. When Maggie was only sixteen, she went to Hollywood and was in a screenplay with Rita Hayworth. Initially, they selected Maggie, as the director said the two girls looked alike; however, Maggie was just a little bit prettier. Lizzy would never argue about that. Looking at her Mama, she admired her slender figure and her fashion sense. She agreed that her Mama was someone she wanted to emulate. Unfortunately, Papa Adler, would not allow Maggie to drop out of school and become a movie star. He permitted her to go to California to follow her dreams, thinking she would inevitably fail. Nevertheless, when it appeared that things turned out just the opposite, he could not let his daughter go through with it. This was the beginning of many years of disappointment to come for Maggie.

When Lizzy and her Mama were home alone, Lizzy would witness this light-hearted, talented and fun-loving side of her Mama. However, when her Dad came home, everything usually got serious. She never remembered being particularly close to her Dad. He was gone a lot with his Navy job, until the family moved to Oklahoma, his home state. Lizzy was born in Brooklyn, New York at Bethel Hospital; the same hospital Maggie was born in twenty-six years earlier. She always thought that was special. She hoped one day to go back and see the city where she came into the world. Her dream was to visit the Statue of Liberty.

The afternoon arrived, and her Mama began to fuss over her, preparing Lizzy for her first day in kindergarten. It would only be for half a day but Lizzy was so excited.

"Now, Lizzy, when you get there, you do everything the teacher says, and you will be just fine. Understand *Mama-la*?"

Mama-la was a name that Lizzy's Mama used to call her when she was a young child. "Yes Mama, I am not afraid. This is going to be so much fun!"

Her Mama finished putting Lizzy's long red curly hair back into a ponytail. She topped it off with a few green butterfly barrettes. Then, she bent down and inspected her daughter from head to toe.

"Lizzy, you look lovely. My little girl is ready for her first day of school!"

Lizzy clapped her hands and started singing the little nursery rhyme she had been singing all day. Her Mama walked with her out onto the front porch and directed Lizzy to walk down the sidewalk just one block away.

"Now, when you get there Lizzy, Mrs. Flowers will meet you at the sidewalk. See all those kids down there?"

"Yes, Mama....can I go now?"

Bending down one last time, she gave Lizzy an enormous hug and a kiss, and whispered, *"My little girl is going to school today,"* as if she could not believe it herself. "Have fun sweetheart."

"I will Mama… bye," she answered as she scurried to meet the other kids. She noticed the scent of her Mama's perfume as she had given her one last hug before leaving and it had comforted her of any insecurity.

Max, Bruce, and Lizzy played outside a lot, and she knew that she was more than capable of walking to school. Something inside made Lizzy turn her head around and look back at the house. When she did, there was her Mama watching her walk every step of the way. Raising her hand to her mouth and then outward, she blew a kiss in Lizzy's direction. Lizzy pretended to catch it and throw one back. Inside the house, Allen, her little brother, was napping, so her Mama watched Lizzy until she was sure of her daughter's safe arrival to the school.

Lizzy thought to herself as she met her teacher on the sidewalk, "*I certainly am all grown up now,*" even though she was still found herself sucking her thumb during the school day. She was wearing a blue and green plaid dress and black and white saddle oxfords, which she grew to detest throughout the years.

"Hi, Lizzy….," Mrs. Flowers called out as she greeted her. She was uncommonly tall, with shiny, dark brunette hair, and a slender build. She was wearing a red plaid skirt with a white ruffled, shell blouse. She donned a whistle around her neck and held a stack of papers under her left arm.

Mrs. Flowers took Lizzy's hand and placed her in line with the other children. She looked down the street, smiled and waved towards Mrs. Ryan to let her know all was well. Acknowledging the signal, her Mama turned and went back inside the house.

Lizzy was a shy child and kept quiet until she had a chance to get to know you, which usually took only a few minutes. The children followed Mrs. Flowers inside. They sat at their new tables that had eight chairs each, all made of wood and blue-green seats. There were two sets of tables in the classroom. Mrs. Flowers took roll call and started the day by explaining to the students what they could expect.

Lizzy thought that school was a lot of fun. She did some coloring and singing the alphabet song. Max had taught her that song, so Lizzy was a little bit bored waiting for the other kids to learn it. She liked Mrs. Flowers though and thought she was funny. She reminded Lizzy of her Mama.

When school let out for the day, she practically ran all the way home with her older brothers. Lizzy gabbed all the way home telling them how big she was now that she was getting to go to school.

"Look what I made today....look!" She proclaimed to her brothers as she held up her art piece. Then she pointed to a rainbow she had decorated. "I know what color this is too! Oh! Max, we sang the alphabet song!"

Her brothers laughed at her, and while giggling Bruce added, "Lizzy, you've got a long way to go!"

"What's so funny?" She could not understand their actions, because she was so serious.

Nevertheless, her Mama was waiting to greet Lizzy at the door, and she covered her in hugs and kisses. Then her Mama saw the artwork Lizzy had in her hand and a huge smile came across her face. Her Mama had a smile that could fill up the entire universe. Lizzy loved seeing her smile and being so happy.

"Oh Lizzy, you did beautiful work today and I love the colors you chose for your rainbow picture. Let's hang it up right here in the kitchen!" Maggie proudly boasted.

She knew her Mama was proud of her little girl that day. Lizzy was proud of herself too, except for one thing.....

Watching Mama prepare supper, Lizzy interrupted, "Mama, how can I stop sucking my thumb? No one at school does that."

"Well, honey, that will have to be your decision to stop. I am sure you will figure it out. You are such a smart little girl." Maggie smiled again.

Her Mama was gifted that way. Lizzy did figure it out that night as she slept with her favorite thumb-sucking hand under the pillow, and did the same thing all week. Presto….! She had accomplished what had seemed to be the un-accomplishable! Yeah, she sure *was* growing up!

Lizzy's younger brother Allen was only sixteen months younger than she was. He was sweet, and he always thought she was so smart. That was until they were all much older and her older brothers convinced him differently. Brothers! She wanted a sister, but Mama said that would be impossible.

Around the second week of school, Lizzy saw her brothers outside riding a big bicycle, and she wanted so badly to join them.

Lizzy ran out the door, "Max, will you teach me how to ride on that big bike?"

"Lizzy, you're too little for this big bike," Max scolded.

"Come on Max, if you give me a push I think I can do it! I know I can….really! Please…?" she begged.

Lizzy always thought Max was older than he was. He seemed taller than most kids his age, and he was very strong for an eight-year-old. His olive complexion helped him tan easily, and he had freckles lightly sprinkled across his nose. He was a bit lanky, with curly red hair, but still a handsome boy.

Well, Max usually gave in to her begging so he propped her up on the high seat of his bike as he balanced it from behind.

He asked, "Are you ready? I'm going to give you a push now."

"Alright, let's do it!" she gleefully responded.

Max gave Lizzy a big push. Well…as big of a push that an eight-year-old can provide, and she went sailing down the side road. The air was blowing on her face, and she looked around at how fast things were going by. This was nothing like her little red tricycle. Because there was a downward grade to the road, Lizzy was going excessively fast. She could barely reach the pedals correctly, and frankly, after convincing Max to push her, she realized that she had no idea how to control the thing. Then it happened. Lizzy looked up and closer, and closer the back end of a parked car had started coming towards her.

She could hear Max yelling, "Lizzy------turn the handlebars!"

It was too late. Her glorious moment of freedom came to an abrupt end as the front wheel hit the shiny silver bumper of the blue '57 Chevy parked near the curb. The bike came to an immediate halt as her body kept flying up, over, and onto the top of the car. After her head hit the top of the car where she finally landed, Lizzy cried out, part in fear and part in pain.

Bruce ran ahead to get the bike while Max ran on and climbed onto the car to help Lizzy get up and walk her back to the house. There was no apparent damage to the car.

"Are you okay?" Max asked as he walked her to the front door.

"I'm okay Max, I'm not hurt anywhere," she tried to convince herself of it. Nothing was really hurt except her ego.

"Maxwell, what were you thinking?!!" Mama scolded.

"Mama, I asked him to push me. It ain't his fault," Lizzy insisted.

Of course, her Mama scolded her and told Lizzy that she was too little for Max's bike. Lizzy half smiled and shrugged her shoulders at Max, knowing it was not his fault.

"You sure you're okay kid?" he asked.

"Yeah, I'm okay."

This would be the first of Lizzy's cuts scrapes, bumps, and bruises acquired from play days with her brothers. The older that they got, the boys became more annoyed with her. They often ditched her by running off to hide when they wanted to play. Lizzy would pretend that it did not hurt her feelings. After all, she was perfectly capable of entertaining herself, and she loved to read.

By the time first grade came, her family had moved to Cherry, Oklahoma. They moved out on to a small farm just east of town. The farm had about five acres, but no one lived directly around them, so it seemed so much bigger. Life there was initially quiet, and the family enjoyed planting a big garden and caring for all kinds of animals. Their house was an old, small, white farmhouse that only had two bedrooms. Lizzy's Mama said they would build a room just for her very soon.

Initially, the house set up on foundation blocks and was not fully sealed enough to keep animals and whatever else wanted to get underneath from doing so. The bright white siding on their new home made the dark black trim look even darker. There was a small barn in the back part of the property. Her Dad expanded the barn a few years later. There was no well house, yet, but that too was resolved within the first year, as her parents worked together to build a small shed around it.

There was barbed wire that sectioned off the acreage and behind the house there was a huge blackberry patch that one either loved or hated, depending on the time of year and the work involved.

There were big oak trees all around the main lot where the house stood, and through the years, Lizzy took it upon herself to plant flowers and make flowerbeds with red brick borders. She loved being outdoors, and she especially enjoyed gardening. Frankly, Mama did not seem as happy as she used to be in the city. She started thinking that Mama missed her friends in Muskingum. Also, Lizzie would hear people talk about being poor and never realizing it, but that wasn't the case for her. She knew just how poor her family was when it came to material things anyway. It was more noticeable now since they had moved out to the farm. For instance, Mama would get very stressed out if someone got sick, and she appeared to take it out on them. Lizzy supposed it was because there was no money for a doctor. Thus, when she got a sore throat or felt ill, she kept it to herself.

She never understood Mama's melancholy moments. Sometimes Mama would just sit on the couch and daydream. One time Lizzy walked through the living room, and Mama said, "You know what Lizzy? One day I am going to paint that ceiling cranberry and the walls a beautiful eggshell cream. What do you think about that?"

As Lizzy tried to imagine the room painted as her mother had seen it, she noticed once again the pictures of the two girls that looked so much alike on the mantle, sitting at their usual place of prominence.

"Mama, can I ask you something?" Lizzy inquired.

"What is it Mama-la?"

Mama always answered a question with a question. Lizzy did not know anyone else who did that. "Mama, who are those girls on that shelf up there? They sure are pretty."

Maggie suddenly got very quiet. Lizzy looked at her and waited. She could tell that her Mama was thinking about what she was going to say.

"Well Lizzy, come over here and sit next to me," her Mama insisted as she patted the empty space on the seat next to her.

Lizzy went over to the davenport and sat down with her Mama as she drew her in close and began to tell her a story. "A long time ago, I gave birth to those two girls. They are your sisters. They have a different father than you do."

"Mama, how come they do not live with us?"

"That is a very long story dear, but mainly because their daddy kidnapped them and I have no idea where they are living to this day. Someday though, I will find them, and they will know how very much their Mama truly loves them," she hopefully responded.

"Oh Mama, that is so sad," Lizzy said as she hugged her Mama tightly. "I am here for you Mama…I will never leave you...I promise."

Changing the subject, Maggie asked again, "So, do you think this room would look pretty in those colors?"

"It sounds beautiful Mama…..but I have never seen a ceiling painted that dark before. Have you…?"

"Not cranberry per say…..but yes…..I have seen ceilings with murals or darker colors on them."

Lizzy always wondered why her mother sat and daydreamed like that. She saw it as a harmless activity, although she did worry that Mama might be very sad because they never seemed to be able to fix up the house the way her Mama had dreamed it could be.

As time went on, one summer Allen and Lizzy decided to build a natural border to the front yard by transplanting cedar saplings from the rest of the acreage. Years later those trees grew so large that you could not see the house that was hiding behind them.

The Ryan family soon accumulated chickens, geese, rabbits, sheep, goats, and a big old bull that their Dad called Ferdinand. Lizzy knew then that they did not have a lot of money, because she only had a few outfits of clothes, and they never really did a lot of things outside of home life. Lizzy went to school and noticed that most everyone else had new clothes periodically, as well as new shoes. She was given only one pair of shoes a year, and they were fitted larger than needed so she would have growing room. When summer came, Lizzy went barefoot. That did not bother Lizzy too much as she always had an aversion to shoes.

By the time Lizzy was in first grade, she could read the newspaper fluently. Her teacher, Mrs. Moore, impressed by her capability, used to buy Lizzy books to take home so she would have something to read. After being in first grade for only two months, Lizzy had already read every book up to the third grade level in the library. She loved reading. It seemed like the one thing Lizzy could do right. Actually, she liked everything about school back then. She had become somewhat of an awkward, introverted child. Her Mama did not know what had happened to her, but she indeed suspected something. A few years later, Lizzy thought the cat was out of the bag, but luckily, she was able to keep her dark secret hidden.

Lizzy began to remember…when they lived in Muskingam, she never recalled ever feeling afraid or threatened by anything. Life was normal, or she thought it was. Then, after starting school, at the age of five, her entire world was altered one dark night. Her parents had gone out with Uncle Tommy and Aunt Lynn. Lizzy had never met them before. Aunt Lynn was her Dad's sister. Something about Uncle Tommy made her feel strangely uncomfortable, but she was a shy child when it came to adults. All the kids were at the house with older cousins who were babysitting them. Lizzy got tired, and her cousin told her to go into her parents' room and lay down because the kids were all playing in her bedroom, and her brothers' bedroom.

She crawled up into the big bed and fell fast asleep in just a few minutes. She awoke in a way that no young child should ever have to awaken. The room was dark, and she felt someone put their arm around her waist and put their hand in her panties.

"Lay still Lizzy, and I won't hurt you," he whispered. It was a man and he smelled like beer.

"Don't be afraid.....it's okay. Do not tell anyone, or I will hurt you. Understand?" her uncle threatened.

Then his lips closed tightly over her mouth as he continued touching her underneath her panties. It hurt, and she could not understand why Uncle Tommy would do such a thing to her. Lizzy wondered what she had done to make him think she wanted this.

"Tommy....? Tommy, where are you?" Lynn called out.

"I'm coming out," he yelled, and then he swiftly left.

Mama came in as Uncle Tommy left, and Lizzy pretended that she was still asleep, but she was so scared. She was also embarrassed because she had wet all over herself.

When her Mama realized it, she inquired, "Lizzy, are you okay?"

"Yeah, I'm just tired," Lizzy insisted, not wanting to get into trouble.

Her Mama picked her up and refused to put Lizzy down until everyone left. Afterward, Lizzy got her pajamas on and went to bed, never saying a word. She did not know Mama suspected something terrible had happened. It was then that she had started wetting her bed regularly. Lizzy kept having nightmares about her uncle, and because the tragic event happened in the darkness of her parents' bedroom, she suddenly had become afraid of the dark. Her Mama never mentioned anything to her about it. Each night her Mama would come into her room, console her, and ask her why she was so upset, but Lizzy would make up stories. Lizzy started to suspect that her Mama knew something, but she continued to hide the truth from her. After all, she was too young to understand that she would not get in trouble or that it was not her fault that something like that had happened to her.

After the family moved to the new house, Lizzy felt safer. She still had nightmares, but at that time, she had to share a double bed with her little brother. In the same room, her other two brothers had to share another bed as well. They were building a room for Lizzy, but it was not finished yet.

"Good night Maxy-Laxy," Lizzy giggled.

"Go to sleep Lizzy," Max responded.

"Good night Bruce-Lucy," she continued.

Allen laughed at her, but Bruce said, "That's enough Lizzy."

Allen and Lizzy whispered silently, "Hey Allen, you want me to tell you a story?"

He whispered with a smile, "Sure Lizzy."

Clearing her throat, she thought about it for a second and started, "Once, in a very dark forest, there was a tiny….itty….bitty….smitty…..weeny…."

Allen started laughing out loud, and Lizzy chimed in just as the door opened. It was their Dad. "You kids better get to sleep and stop talking!" He had his belt in his hand, and that was enough to make them obey.

Silence fell over the room and soon everyone was asleep. She felt safer being in the same bedroom with all her brothers. However, when her room was ready, and it was time for Lizzy to have her own space, she started having nightmares and wetting her bed again, as well. Her Mama would come in, change the bed, and would clean her up. Never once did she complain.

"Lizzy, are you sure you are okay?"

"Yes, Mama. I just have bad dreams all the time."

"You want to talk to me about them?"

"Not tonight. Maybe sometime but not now." she carefully answered.

Looking back, Lizzy realized her Mama knew what happened. She never saw Uncle Tommy or Aunt Lynn ever again. In fact, Mama said that no one could ever go visit the Ryan family in Muskingham, Oklahoma ever again. Some other uncles would come to their home, and Lizzy really liked them. Uncle Will used to come over to their house and play dominoes with her parents. He was her favorite uncle, and he seemed to always dote on Lizzy.

Whenever someone would come for a visit, Lizzy's mother would embarrass her by asking her to sing for everyone. By then, Lizzy knew she had a unique voice. Kids at school would talk about how pretty her voice was. Lizzy's favorite class was choir. It was during that time that Lizzy also began to notice how much drinking was going on in their home. Her Dad seemed to drink a lot. The more he drank, the louder he talked and the more he laughed, unless her Dad got mad about something. Then watch out. At that time, she did not remember her Mama ever drinking. All of dad's family drank as far as she knew, so the kids just tried to stay out of the way and just be good.

Later in life Lizzy would realize that Harold Ryan, her Dad, was the epitome of a soul raised under alcoholism and abuse. He kept the curse alive that had passed from generation to generation. In doing so, he eventually became the very thing he hated, an abusive alcoholic.

Sometimes, on a Saturday, after her Dad had been at the bar all day, he would come home drunk. He then would load all the kids up in the back of the pickup truck and take them to the corner store, about a mile away. He would give each of them a quarter to spend, and they were thrilled.

"What are you getting Allen? " Lizzy inquired.

Allen smiled, "I don't know yet."

"I do…," Lizzy proclaimed, as she reached for a drink called a *Chocolate Soldier* and a candy bar.

After everyone got their goodies, their Dad would drop them off at home and go back to the bar. The kids did not care. They spent most weekends at home alone, without any adult supervision. This was the norm. However, during the summer, they did go fishing a lot. Her Dad would drink like crazy, but as long as everyone behaved, her Dad stayed in a good mood and things would be fine. Her Mama seemed to tolerate it.

After everyone got a bit older, the fishing trips stopped, and both parents began to drink heavily and all weekend long.

One Sunday morning, after Lizzy awakened, she had to walk through her parents' room to enter the rest of the house. As she walked through, her dad was lying across the bed with his head hanging off the side. Her mom was lying on the floor where she apparently vomited, as she lay there in it. She was passed out. Lizzy had to step over her mom to get out, as well as the mess, and so she was extremely quiet, hoping not to disturb either one of them. The sight of her parents in this state mortified her. Usually when she got up, her parents were already up and out of their bedroom. When her parents came out of their room much later that day, they both complained of bad liquor and headaches. Lizzy and her brothers stayed outside all day to avoid any run-ins with their parents.

Lizzy was about nine-years-old when she realized how much her parents were fighting after they got drunk. They really had some humdingers too. Lizzy just knew one day that they would kill each other. Lizzy and her brothers were terrified to be in the same room with them when they had been drinking. They witnessed all kinds of things that children should never observe between adults, nevertheless their own parents. The fights would get bloody, and many times the local police would come out to put an end to it.

"Maggie, what are you doing?" Harold yelled.

"Take him away!" Maggie demanded as she looked at the police officer. Then looking back at Harold she screamed, "You son of a b-----!"

"You better be gone when I get back you no good bit-----!" he retorted.

The police hauled Lizzy's Dad out more than once, but her Mama would go right down and bail him out, and never press charges. Her Dad would shoot off the gun inside the house when he got outraged, which was often. Her Mama was not innocent either. When she was irritated at his drinking, she would pick at him, which would only make things worse. It never made sense to Lizzy, because Mama had started to drink too. Mostly, what irritated her Mama was that her Dad would stop and get a few beers to drink right after work and on his way home. She also suspected, and often accused him of having an affair.

Supper would always be ready at 5:30 p.m. The kids knew that no matter what they were doing, they had better be in the house at that time to eat. Suppertime was usually a silent time at home. No one was allowed to talk at the table, just eat. Oh, Lizzy's Mama and Dad would say a few words, but the kids were raised to just be quiet and eat everything on their plates and to never complain.

One day, Lizzy's Dad came home all irritated. As everyone sat down to eat, the conversation began with Mama, and an outburst soon followed.

"What the h----- you talking about woman?!" her Daddy burst out.

"You were ten minutes late, so…. where did you go?" her Mama glared back.

Standing up, he reached for the underside of the table and flipped it onto all of the kids and Maggie declaring, "D---------you! You go to h----!"

The fight was on and the kids scattered like roaches to their rooms. They all went to bed hungry that night. Lizzy knew that none of her friends at school knew what her family really was like. The more they fought, the more withdrawn she became. It was safer that way.

One Saturday evening, Lizzy and her brothers were home alone. It got very late, and Lizzy went on to bed around 12:30 a.m. Right before she fell asleep, she had an awful vision. It was her parents, and they were in a terrible car accident. She even knew the location on Elm Lane where it had taken place. It terrified her, and she got up and ran to Max and told him what she had seen.

He said, "Lizzy, you were probably dreaming. Don't worry…just go back to sleep. I am sure they will be home soon."

Before she got back to her room, the telephone rang. It was her Dad. He had told Max that they had been in a car accident and that their mother had been taken to the hospital. Max was in shock. He looked at Lizzy standing there and then he asked, "Are you guys okay Dad?"

"We will be ….. But I will be here for the rest of the night Max. Can you hold the fort down?" he asked.

"I got it dad….," he answered trying to get the words out after being so shocked.

"I will call you tomorrow morning. All you kids need to go to bed," Harold pressed.

"Alright, Dad," Max said. Then he heard Harold hang up.

As soon as Max put the receiver down he looked at Lizzy who was crying and saying over and over again, "I knew it…,I knew it….I saw the accident happen….I don't know how….but I knew it!"

Max held her close for a few minutes. Allen was already asleep, but Bruce was still up. "Lizzy that is so weird … I have never heard of anyone envisioning an accident like that. We need to tell Mom and Dad about that when they get home."

Max interjected, "Now you two need to get to bed. I am on my way to bed too. Dad is going to call in the morning and we will have more news. Okay?"

"Yes…," they both agreed as they walked to their rooms.

Lizzy laid in bed and worried herself to sleep. It was strange how she had actually seen the accident and the location. The following morning her Dad did call and say that he was coming home, but that her mom would be in the hospital for about a week with a broken collarbone and injured knee.

After Harold got home, the boys told him about Lizzy's vision, and he was amazed. "Lizzy, where did you say the accident happened?" her Dad asked.

"I think a few blocks off of Eleventh Street and Elm Lane. I could probably take you to the location. I have seen it many times riding on the school bus," she answered nervously.

"I do not know how you could possibly know that, but that is exactly where we got in an accident. Your mother thought she saw something in the road and she reached over and jerked the steering wheel. It sent the car off the road and….."

97

"Directly into a telephone pole….," Lizzy finished his sentence.

"Come here baby girl." He held her for a moment and then said, "We are going to have to be very strong when Mama comes home. She is going to need a lot of time to heal. That means extra chores for all of us …understand?"

"Yes sir," they all responded at the same time.

Meanwhile, Lizzy had noticed that her Dad had his arm in a sling and she asked, "What happened to you, Daddy?"

"Well after we crashed, your Mama was silent. She would not answer me no matter how many times that I called out her name, and I could not get out of the car. I started ramming this arm against the driver's door until I caused it to break open. The doctor said that I dislocated my shoulder, but he was able to put it back in place. I will need to wear this support for about ten days and take some meds for the pain, but I am going to be fine. I was just so worried about your Mama that I guess I was out of my mind trying to get out of that vehicle to get us some help."

"Oh, Daddy….that sounds terrible! You thought Mama had died, huh?" she cried.

"Well…yes….the thought did go through my mind. But Mama is going to be fine. Do not worry." He looked up at all of the kids, "I am sorry this accident happened, but we will all get through this. Everything will be okay….you will see."

Each of the children one at a time hugged their Dad and then went on about their day. None of them had ever seen this side of him. This kind and thoughtful and caring side.

Lizzy thought to herself, "This must have been why Mama married him. Daddy really did have a good heart, but when he was drunk, he was a monster."

Once Mama came home, all of the kids realized how much pain she was in. It was summer, so there were no school obligations to take care of. They spent time doing all the chores, and with Max's help, Lizzy was able to provide dinner on some of those nights. On the other nights, their Dad would go out and bring home what they called TV dinners, or go get some fried chicken at a fast food restaurant in town and bring that home for supper. Actually, for the next few months, things were pretty calm around the house. Lizzy's parents did not go out to the bar to drink at that time. Her Daddy still drank, but he kept it down to only two or three beers a night. Things were rather nice.

However, by the time school started, everything had gone back to its usual routine. School all week, and on weekend's they were home alone again while their parents went out to drink. Lizzy was only in fifth grade, but she got to where she did not like school anymore, and her Mama never understood why, as Lizzy wasn't one to complain.

5

School Days Continue

*We don't stop going to school
when we graduate –Carol Burnett*

Lizzy actually had very few friends. Most kids mistook her introverted manner as Lizzy thinking that she was too good for them. Therefore, Lizzy became the object of their bullying, and she learned to walk on eggshells at home and at school.

Fifth grade was difficult. First, it appeared that no one liked Lizzy at all, and then Lizzy had an incident at school that caused her great embarrassment. She also noticed that she was different too. Girls at school were talking about getting their periods, and she had not even started showing any signs of puberty as of yet. Of course, if she had, Lizzy probably would have ignored them.

Lizzy learned how to navigate her own way through adolescence with little knowledge or really not caring anything about it. That was until she started menstruating. All of the girls in her class began their cycles many years earlier… but Lizzy was what one would call a late bloomer. Many years later, when she was almost fifteen… it happened to her, and it sent her into panic mode.

However, in fifth grade, her Mama had signed a piece of paper giving Lizzy permission to see the film *All About A Woman's Body* at school, but the trauma of her younger years impaled her. Lizzy did not want to know about any of that.   She remembered being in that stuffy classroom that day.

"Okay, young ladies, we are going to start the film now. If you have any questions, you can save them for the end of class," her fifth-grade teacher, Ms. Stine, instructed.

Then, Ms. Stine flipped on the film projector, and up on the screen flashed the diagram of a naked woman. That is all that Lizzy could remember. She came to in the hall with her teacher applying a cold washcloth to Lizzy's head and asked, "Lizzy, are you okay? You fainted in class."

Lizzy was so embarrassed. She had actually fainted at the sight of just a diagram of the reproductive system glaring up on the wall. Lizzy could not tell Ms. Stine why she had done so, and Lizzy wasn't even sure why she had anguished over the moment herself. Sexual abuse enforces strange things upon the mind of a victim, and Lizzy's reactions to life were becoming more and more like her mother's…..most inappropriate, and like that of an over-reactor.

"I'm okay," Lizzy insisted.

Ms. Stine offered, "I can call your mother, and she can come to get you if you would like dear."

"Uh…no, that won't be necessary."

"Would you like to go back inside for the remaining of the film?"

"Not really," Lizzy answered nervously.

"Okay honey, you can go to the library and find something to read and at 2:30 p.m. you can come back to the classroom, alright?" Ms. Stine asked while she reached in her pocket to write Lizzy a hall pass.

That sounded great….Lizzy could read and forget all about this most embarrassing moment. Ms. Stine handed her the note and Lizzy took off down the hall towards her favorite place in the entire school. She'd rather be reading than anything else at that moment in life.

A few days later, on the bus ride home from school, she got off the bus as two girls followed her.

"Slow down you!" Jody called out. She was a tall girl with blonde frizzy hair and not really liked by too many people.

"Yeah, you stupid idiot, we'll show you!" her sister chimed in.

They both jumped on her and hit her repeatedly with their fist, feet, and anything else that they could throw at her. When she gathered enough strength to finally push them off, they ran home. They were friends of the girl at school named Nita. That girl was a constant fear for her, as she had beaten Lizzy up at school many times. Lizzy never told anyone, because she thought she would be worse off for doing so. Lizzy would lay in her room at night and say out loud, *"That Nita Green is mean to the spleen!"*

Kids at school knew they had a patsy for all their jokes, and they took advantage of it. This treatment had been going on the entire fifth grade. By the time Lizzy was halfway through fifth grade year, her grades began to fall. She hated school because she knew the kids would make fun of her or attack her, and she wanted to quit.

She told her Mama, "I hate that teacher Mom. She is always so mean to me."

Lizzy knew that was a lie, but she wanted out of the class where Nita was so people would stop picking on her.

"Sweetheart, I am so sorry. I will go up to that school in the morning, and I will take care of this, I promise."

Her Mama went up to school the next day, and Lizzy was placed in a different class of people with all new faces. They were kinder to Lizzy, for a while anyway. Several months later, one girl got jealous that Lizzy knew how to find every word in the dictionary faster than anyone else in the class, so she beat her up during recess. All Lizzy could do was take it and keep her mouth shut.

One time, a bunch of kids decided to play soccer. They counted off everyone they wanted on their team. Lizzy was not selected, so when she was the only one left, the girl team captain sarcastically said, "I guess we're stuck with you!"

Now Lizzy was good at soccer so she could not understand why they felt that way. After all, she had grown up with brothers playing soccer, softball, football and climbing trees. It happened, during the game that the opposite team kicked the ball out near the street, and it rolled under a car parked near the curb.

Lizzy, trying to please everyone yelled out, "I'll get it!"

After she crawled under the car to get it, Lizzy came out and Dwayne, on the opposing team kicked her in the stomach.

She let out a cry, as the other kids, said, "Crybaby! We don't want to play with you anymore!"

Lizzy did not even know what she had done, but she left them all to play on their own after that. Lizzy figured out, before the end of fifth grade, that this kind of treatment was her destiny. She concluded that she was meant to be ridiculed, and hurt by others. By then her brothers had started playing tricks on her and being hateful as well. And, because she never spoke up about this, they never got in trouble for it.

After arriving home that day, she went into her room and found her pet parakeet dead. It was traumatic as Polly's head was missing, and her body was lying on the top of Lizzy's chest of drawers. She also noticed that the cage door was opened. She suspected their cat had gotten to her. It upset her, but she knew she had to do something.

Lizzy started thinking that her Polly needed a proper burial. It was years ago when she was four years old, but she remembered seeing Robert F. Kennedy's funeral on television. So, Lizzy decided that she was going to bury her favorite bird in the same manner. She asked the boys to help, and surprisingly they went along with her plans. She got a shoe box and put Polly's body in it and then sealed it tight with masking tape. Bruce told Lizzy that he had dug a hole over by the tree in the front yard and Allen gave Lizzy a cloth to wear on her head like a laced funeral hat. They walked out the front door with the box in hand.

As soon as they stepped away from the house, Lizzy began to choreograph the event. She said that she and Allen would follow Bruce as he walked in front of them with his arms extended carrying the box of the deceased in his hands. She told Allen that when they got to the burial site, that he needed to salute the coffin along with Bruce. Allen agreed. So as they walked slowly and somberly through the front yard approaching the tree, Lizzy started to really cry. As soon as Bruce laid Polly's box in the ground, he and Allen saluted the dead bird and then Lizzy bent down and picked up some earth and covered the casket. The boys then reached down and finished covering the home made casket. Afterward, Lizzy said, "Now we have to bow our heads and say some kind words."

Lizzy led them. "Sweet Polly …we give you back to the earth that brought you forth. We are grateful for our time together. I will never forget your sweet bird tweets and songs waking me up in the morning. I am sorry that George the cat got to you. I did not know that he knew how to open your cage door….you poor bird. Now you just rest in peace…okay, Polly? Amen."

Lizzy had taken a block of wood out that she was carrying in the pocket of her dress. She had carved out Polly's name on it, and the date she died. She put it at the head of the grave. Afterward, Lizzy insisted that they had to leave the grave in the same manner that they had arrived, sauntering with their heads held high.

Allen inquired, "What is sauntering Lizzy?" He and Bruce always wondered where she got these highfalutin words that she used.

Because Lizzy was such a good reader, her teacher held a special test for her and discovered that Lizzy's placement was at the top-ten percent of the nation when it came to vocabulary and writing. Lizzy never thought that her vocabulary or writing was exceptional and she played it down when she was talking with her friends. She feared they would make fun of her and hit her again.

Lizzy explained, "Just walk the way that you did when we first came down here Allen."

So the boys followed her directions until they got to the front porch and then relaxed. "I'm glad that's over!" Bruce exclaimed.

It was another afternoon later that summer when the boys had built a tree house. They also made what they called an elevator. Unknowingly to Lizzy, they had planned to get her on that thing, so they called out, "Hey Lizzy, Come up here with us!"

Like a dumb lamb, she thought they really wanted to play with her. Lizzy was so excited, as she climbed up high into the tree and finally reached the tree house. She could climb a tree every bit as good as a boy. When she arrived, they showed her their elevator. It was a board tied to two ends of a rope and tossed over a higher branch.

"Hey, get in it Lizzy! It will be fun!" added Bruce.

"I'm not getting on that thing!! You're crazy!"

Allen persuaded, "Oh, it's safe, we've already been playing on it!'

"No... I'm not stupid!" Lizzy replied.

As Lizzy turned away, her little brother pushed her out onto the so-called elevator, and the rope instantly broke and....well, one can only imagine. Luckily, Lizzy landed flat on her back. Max, the oldest brother, was the first to arrive on the ground looking down at her thin, still frame as it lay under the broad oak tree.

"Lizzy....Lizzy are you okay?!"

All she could do was look at them. The impact of hitting the ground had knocked every bit of the air out of her lungs.

Bruce interrupted, "Say something!!"

She tried hard to get a breath of air, but when Lizzy finally felt her lungs fill up, she breathed in and then let out a huge bellowing cry.

Her Mama came running out the back door, and towards all of them. She saw Lizzy on the ground.

Wiping her hands on her apron, she asked nervously, "What is wrong *Yenta*?" That was because she did not know what had taken place. Now the name *Yenta* meant busybody, and when her Mama got mad at her, that was the term she always used to refer to Lizzy.

"They pushed me out of the tree house," Lizzy cried.

"They what!!!! Get in that house......all of you!" her Mama furiously spoke. Then she looked under Lizzy's shirt and noticed a big bruise forming on her upper spine between her shoulder blades. She held Lizzy's hand all the way to the house as she spoke in Yiddish, and in terms, no one understood. That was except to know that her Mama was very angry. All Lizzy could understand was "fifteen feet!" She knew

106

Mama was talking about how far down Lizzy had fallen out of the tree house.

Well, the boys got a beating with a belt and Lizzy had a big black bruise on her back when that day was over.

Lizzy looked at her Mama, "I'm tired, I am going to lay down."

Her mother gently said, "Mama-la, let me look at your head before you lay down." No outward bump was ever found, but Mama worried about Lizzy for a while that day and kept coming into her room to check on her. Lizzy slept for three hours. After she awakened, she was very sore but appeared okay. Her Mama catered to her needs all day long after that, and by the next day, Lizzy went outside to play like she always did. Looking back at that event now, she realizes she could have broken her neck or something. The boys never again tried to hurt her.

As Lizzy continued to grow older, she became more and more aware of the dysfunctional family she had. She could not label what was wrong with her family back then, but she was able to articulate it in later years. The arguing and fighting escalated annually, and at the age of eleven, she wondered if there would ever be an end to it.

That next summer she had been going barefoot as usual around the property. Lizzy never thought anything of it. Her feet were tough, and she could do anything barefoot, even outside. She managed somehow to get her big toenail infected, and it really hurt. The nail was extricating itself to a degree, and her Mama said it was going to have to come off. She was terrified and in pain.

When her Dad got home that night, and after supper, he said, "Lizzy, I have to cut that nail off, or you are going to really have a bad infection in there."

"No Dad, it's gonna hurt!"

He gently put his arm around Lizzy in a manner she had vaguely remembered, and said, "Listen. You sit right behind me and give me your foot. Put your arms around me, and every time it hurts you can squeeze me as tight as you need to. We need to get medicine under that nail, or you will get sick, understand?"

Lizzy did understand, because the previous year she had gotten a bad rash on her bottom and the back of her legs from poison ivy. Her Mama assumed that she had been sitting in it. She was afraid to tell her parents that she was constantly itching. She had scratched it so much that it got infected and she had to go to the doctor and get shots every day for a week, and take two baths a day. Her Mama would then put the medicine on her wounds afterward. It was a horrible experience.

Now, being faced with the toe problem, Lizzy still did not like the idea, but she conceded and sat down on the couch. She opened up her legs giving her Dad enough room to back down and sit in front of her with his head facing outward. He then gently took her right foot and moved it to where he could see it. Her brothers and Mama looked on as the operation began. Lizzy did not watch, but she could feel the pain as he tried carefully to just cut the nail, and not to touch the nail bed. She squeezed with all her might and cried into his shirt as he continued.

"You're doing good Lizzy, we are almost done.....just one more time." he added.

Her father managed to dislodge the entire nail, and then he boasted about how courageous she was. Lizzy never remembered him ever saying anything like that about her before because her Daddy never handed out compliments at all. Mama stepped in, put some medicine on it and wrapped it up. Everyone was very caring to Lizzy that night, even her brothers. A few weeks later, she was back outside barefoot and running through all kinds of trees and debris, and she never thought anything of it. Lizzy had always been that way, a real tomboy.

The following spring one of the hens had three baby chicks. She was Lizzy's special hen. The white leghorn walked with a limp, and Lizzy named her Princess. Princess had always been that way, but she was a good egg layer, and so her Dad said she could keep her. Lizzy understood what it meant to look different from everyone else. She had an eye that wandered off in another direction, and she had a cross-bite that impaired her smile. Lizzy often would pick the hen up when she was a baby and put Princess on her shoulders and walk around the farm with her. Princess would always just stay there, and she seemed to enjoy the company as much as Lizzy did. Lizzy would take her outside of the chicken yard, and bring her inside on the back porch and feed her crumbled bread. Princess got to where she would bust out of the chicken coop, which was not very well secured, and come all the way up to the house and peck on the back door. Lizzy would let her in and feed her bread.

After Princess grew up and had three chicks of her own, she taught them to do the same. They would all come up to the back of the house and peck on the screen door. Lizzy would answer the door in delight and welcome them all in to feed them bread. Her Mama never told her that she could not feed them. Lizzy knew that Princess sure was smart for a chicken.

With the ever growing arguments between her parents, Lizzy sought solitude with her dogs, cats and other animals. There were several dogs. It seemed whenever someone did not want their dog, they would dump them out on the Ryan farm. Lizzy acquired animals quickly. She also named all the dogs and cats, or anything else that wandered up on the farm.

Lizzy's favorite dog was Lily. She was a beautiful Malinois Shepherd. They would play and run around outside for hours. Lily was a funny dog too. She learned how to jump up on the front door, and put her paws up on the doorknob and twist to open it. The first time she did that and came in the house, Lizzy's Mama yelled at Lily, and then she laughed at her ingenuity. Her Mama did not like the animals in the house. The only ones permitted inside was an old cat named George and her three little Jack Russell Terriers named, Samson, Benji, and a girl terrier named Christy. She was named that because she was born on Christmas Day.

Time went on, and Lizzy would walk around the farm making friends with all the animals. She had a horse then too. Her name was Dolly. Dolly was really her best friend. She never told anyone, but many of the evenings after dinner, Lizzy would go out and spend time in the pasture with her. Dolly liked Lizzy just the way she was. Lizzy never had to try to please her or tell her stories to make her like her. She just accepted Lizzy at face value.

Through the years Lizzy and Allen had a mile walk from the bus stop to the farm which was all along dirt roads. They walked in the sunshine, the rain, or the snow. It did not matter.

One day when Lizzy came home, she could not help but notice that her horse was gone. They actually had two horses, Dolly and Sunshine. Sunshine was a mean horse though, so she never missed her. Lizzy knew better than to ask what happened. She became very sad that day, more depressed than usual. It was then she recalled a memory of her and Dolly.

One time, Lizzy had a friend come over, which was rare. She came over with her Appaloosa horse and wanted to go horseback riding. When Candy saw her beautiful horse Dolly, she asked if they could switch horses. Reluctantly, Lizzy agreed. Dolly was her best friend. That horse had weathered many years with her. Lizzy was only six when she got Dolly. Dolly was gentle and seemed to know that Lizzy needed help. The mare would stick her leg out so Lizzy could climb upon her back. The bond between the two was inseparable. Torn between the love for her horse, and wanting to please her new friend, she relented. When she got on her friends Appaloosa named Lightning, she realized right away how untrained and how wild Candy's horse was. He followed no commands and did what he wanted, which was usually running full speed ahead. Candy had a saddle on Lightening, and Lizzy rode Dolly bareback. Then it happened. That Appaloosa took off....just like his name. Lightning ran down the hill from the house and then turned out to go to the main road. When the horse turned, it went right, and Lizzy's body went left at an accelerated speed. At the bottom of that hill was a sand pile. As her body dislodged from the saddle, she landed head first into a sand pile that undoubtedly saved her life.

After getting up and brushing off the sand and spitting out the remaining dirt from her mouth, Lizzy yelled out, "Dolly, Dolly, come!"

She came obediently with her friend who was perched upon her.

"What happened?" Candy asked.

"Your horse threw me off and is headed for the highway! Give me Dolly so that I can go get her!" Lizzy ordered.

Candy dismounted the horse at the same time Lizzy jumped on. At Lizzy's command, Dolly being a quarter horse, took off like it was a race. As they approached the main road, Lizzy saw that the Appaloosa had just crossed to the other side. Lizzy gently instructed Dolly to go after her. Honestly, Dolly had an extensive vocabulary. Lizzy did not know if anyone else knew that but her. She went right across the street, and Lizzy bent down and snatched up the reins of the belligerent animal. Lizzy spoke some colorful words to that horse and later to her friend on the way back to her farm.

When she arrived back at the bottom of the hill where she left Candy, she tossed the reins towards her and curtly spoke, "Never again am I riding your horse."

Lizzy continued brushing the sand out of her curly red locks as she instinctively patted Dolly on her left side and commanded her, "Home."

That is all the direction that Dolly required. Dolly took off up the hill, and Lizzy held on to her long beautiful brown mane proudly knowing that she would never let anything happen to her. Candy never came over again. That was too bad because Lizzy did like her......she just detested her useless horse.

Back then, when her parents would fight, or her brothers would be mean, Lizzy would find Dolly, and they would walk to the bottom of the pasture to their hiding place. Lizzy would cry, and Dolly would put her nose on her peachy cheek and blow air on Lizzy's face. Lizzy would imagine Dolly giving her angel kisses. Dolly was extremely kind and loved Lizzy just as she was. Now her one confidant was gone. The only real creature on earth that knew everything that had ever happened to her and still totally accepted her and loved her unconditionally, had now disappeared. Lizzy knew if she were to say anything about her horse missing that she would surely be punished. In silence, she cried herself to sleep that night, and many nights following. The next few months were extremely lonely for Lizzy.

One weekend Lizzy's Dad loaded up Lily, took her off twenty miles, and dropped her off in the middle of nowhere. He said she had been killing the chickens. Lizzy knew that was a lie, but no one would listen to her. First, her horse was gone and now her favorite dog. Lizzy was heartbroken. Again, no one complained or carried on about anything. Everyone was expected to tolerate whatever came their way.

Weeks went by, and she had forgotten all about Lily. It was Lizzy's way of dealing with the pain of her loss. It was an early Saturday morning, and Lizzy was the only one awake. She took some laundry out to hang on the clothesline. As Lizzy was hanging it up on the clothesline, she sensed something funny…..a feeling that someone or something was watching her. When she turned around to investigate, there sat Lily just observing her as she went about her daily chores.

"Lily?!!"

Her dog all but jumped up in Lizzy's arms and started licking her face and running around and around. Then she took off toward the front door of the house. She did her usual door-opening trick and ran into the house.

Lizzy was yelling, "Lily's back!!!"

With all the commotion, everyone started waking up, and one by one, Lily would run up to them and lick their faces and jump up and down. Even their Dad seemed glad to see her.

"Can she stay Dad? I know she didn't kill those chickens?" Lizzy begged.

He smiled and nodded an affirmative.

"Yeah! Welcome home Lily!" Lizzy celebrated.

Then Lizzy took her outside, fed her, and spent all day with her, just as they used to. Lily looked no worse for wear. She was great at playing fetch and just running alongside Lizzy, and Lizzy loved to run. In school she was a good runner too. Lizzy was actually a great sprinter. She could take off faster than anyone else on the team could. She credited that to having to run away from her brothers when they were being mean to her.

Lizzy was getting older now and in the seventh grade. A neighbor boy took a liking to her. She was still every bit a tomboy as she still climbed trees and ran around barefoot. Shelby and his brothers started coming over to play sports with her brothers. She would watch on the sidelines, never playing with them. That particular time she began to notice how big Max really was. He was taller than anyone in the family, even her Mom and Dad. He was built like a boulder too with broad shoulders and muscles, and all the girls really liked him.

Shelby, the neighbor boy who liked Lizzy, walked up and asked if Lizzy would be his girlfriend.

Shyly nodding, she replied, "Yes."

After he got finished playing ball, he and Lizzy went out to climb trees and to just talk.

While they were up in the tree he said, "Now that you are my girlfriend, we have to kiss."

"What? Kiss? Are you kidding me?" she contested.

"No, that is what boyfriends and girlfriends do," he insisted.

"I ain't kissing you, so that's that!"

"Well, if you don't kiss me, you can't be my girlfriend."

"That's fine with me," she agreed.

He jumped out of the tree and went on home. He never talked to her again. Therefore, that was her first, and very short-lived relationship with a boy. She was slightly perturbed and wondered why he would act so peculiar. She did not let it faze her a lot, because she just was not ready to kiss anyone. When she thought of kissing it reminded her of her Uncle and his beer breath, pressing his lips over hers when she was only five. Though she was interested in fella's, she wasn't interested in getting intimate in any way, regardless that she was now getting older.

By this time, her brothers were older too, and found things to do, usually avoiding Lizzy. She was left alone, except for an occasional ball game, when they needed to even up the sides. The last time she remembered playing ball with them of any kind, was when she was about twelve years old.

"Now Lizzy, you stand here and don't let Max get that ball passed you," Bruce ordered.

Allen threw the football to Max, and Max came straight at Lizzy. She was no competition for his brawny broad shoulders and thickly muscled arms.

"Get him, Lizzy!" Bruce hollered.

Lizzy, not wanting to appear afraid ran towards him and closed her eyes right before the contact happened. Max ran over her like a Mack truck. She cried and got up off the ground, as her Mama called to her.

"Lizzy, come here!"

Max bent down to help her up on to her feet. Lizzy did not put up any contest. She was hurt and did not want to play anymore.

Hobbling over to the porch, she plopped down on the bottom stair. Her Mama came and sat beside her. The lesson soon followed. "You know Lizzy… you're getting too old to be playing football with the boys now. They are getting a lot bigger too, and you are going to get seriously hurt. You need to stop playing sports with them, understand?"

Lizzy hurt so much she did not care if she ever played football again.

As the fighting between her parents progressed, her oldest brother seemed to be at his breaking point. One night their Dad had come in drunk, and he started punching on Mama and Max had enough of it. Max finally stepped in the middle and pushed his father back and told him to stop with the fighting.

"Nothing is worth this kind of torment, and I'm sick of it," Max insisted. Though Max was taller than his Dad, he was no match for what was coming.

His father's fury raised up to such a level that he took his belt off, cussed Max out for interfering and dared him to come at him again. Max did, and Harold beat him so bad with the buckle of that belt that his face was cut up, and his nose was broken, and blood flowed everywhere. Max stormed out of the house, got in his car and did not come home that night. Lizzy was in shock, and so were Allen and Bruce. She looked at her father with so much disdain and fear and then left the room. They decided to go to their rooms without eating, and just stay there. Meanwhile, there was another outburst between their parents but it calmed quickly, and for the rest of the evening, their dad sat in the living room alone, watching a football game and drinking his beer until he passed out.

The next day was Monday, and after-school Max came home. No one knew where he had gone, but he had a bandage on his face, and when Dad got back home that evening, he had nothing to say to anyone. The family sat down to a quiet meal and then all the kids got up and left to go outside. No one wanted to be around their father due to his random outbursts, and now unrepentance. Mama didn't say anything more either.

That year Lizzy was in seventh grade and took choir class because she loved to sing. Mr. Crane was her choir director. He was a bit older, and somewhat a roly-poly with white hair and green eyes. His kind demeanor made all the students love him. He announced one day that Lizzy was to learn a song for state competition.

"Mr. Crane...," she said as she cleared her throat. "I am only a seventh grader. I am too young to go to state, remember?" There was a rule that you had to be in ninth grade to enter competitions.

"Oh, well, we're breaking the rule this year."

Nervously she replied, "Mr. Crane, I cannot do this. I can't sing a solo in front of all those people!"

He insisted, "Lizzy, you have a gift, and you need to use it."

"Mr. Crane, I don't think I can do it."

"I'll help you. We will work together on it after school," he nodded. Other girls sitting by her began to console her, "You can do it, Lizzy. If anyone can do it girl...you can!"

"Okay, but I hope I don't let you down," she replied as she looked up at Mr. Crane who was starting to develop a big smile.

Well, Mr. Crane did as he promised. He worked with Lizzy on that solo many days before state competition. He also had her sing in a trio. She sang soprano in the choir and alto in the trio, as she had a vast vocal range. Though her family could never afford vocal lessons, she was always blessed with incredible, gifted music teachers throughout her life. Mr. Crane helped her so much, and she began to build up some self-confidence. She actually started making friends in choir, and many of them commented on her vocal abilities. She was asked to sing in front of the whole school that year for the annual graduation services.

She went to state that year and received a superior rating on her solo and the trio, as well! For the first time in her life, she realized that all she wanted to do was sing!

When Mr. Crane gave her the medal for state competition, she did not know who was beaming the most, him or her. She had never won anything in her life before, and looking at those shiny medals validated that she had some worth. The entire choir clapped as he handed them to her. It was the first real proud moment in her entire life. She could not wait to get home and show her Mama the pretty new medals and tell her all that had happened.

Lizzy was always singing. When Allen and Lizzy weren't fussing at each other, they could be found every Saturday morning watching *American Bandstand* and *Soul Train* on the television. They would imitate the dances on the television, and she would sing into her hairbrush like a rock star. Lizzy had long, curly, red hair by then and she would fling it around just like the famous Cher Bono did when she and Sonny would sing. Music took center stage in Lizzy's life.

She went through junior high and during the last two years of that, the boundaries of the city were changed, and she had to go to a different school. She met all new people and had all new teachers, and she loved it. The only thing is that she missed Mr. Crane. However, no one knew her or judged her, and that was simply blissful to her, so Lizzy began to thrive. She still was a timid girl regardless, but in ninth grade, there was a tall, handsome dark-headed boy named Carl who got her attention, and he liked her too. So they started doing things together. She had long stopped climbing trees by then and had become a bit more lady-like. They had several classes together, and he would carry her books. He never tried to kiss her, and for that she was glad. Lizzy still had a phobia about kissing anyone. When high school came along, she was forced to go back to her old school district, because the new one had no high school to attend.

But before that, and near the end of her ninth grade year, the bus dropped her off at her bus stop. It was a sunny day, so she enjoyed the mile walk up to the farm. Suddenly, it happened again. She had a vision. This time it was Bruce and Allen. She remembered that Bruce was picking up Allen at school and bringing him home. She saw exactly where the accident was and she also saw that Allen's face was bleeding from being thrown through the windshield. Lizzy began to run home. She was so upset, and she knew that her Mama would be there as soon as she ran in the front door. Her Mama saw that she was out of air, and told her to calm down. But Lizzy was inconsolable.

"Mama! Allen and Bruce have been in a car accident up on the corner of Twelfth and Haney Road! We gotta go!" she cried.

"Honey, how do you know this?" her Mama inquired.

She hurriedly relayed, "The same way that I knew about yours and Daddy's wreck. I saw it in a vision. I got off the school bus, and then I saw the whole thing!"

Her Mama smiled, "Oh Maggie...you have the gift. I will tell you what that all means later... but let's go!"

They jumped in the car and took off. As they drove up on to the accident scene, sure enough, there was Bruce and Allen and some emergency vehicles. Bruce had hit a car in front of him that did not stop at the stop sign to his left. When that happened, Allen's head went through the windshield, and his face had blood all over it. It had loosened his front tooth, cut his nose, and the glass left little cuts all over his face. Bruce appeared to be shaken.

When Mama got out of her car and ran up to theirs with Lizzy trailing, she looked inside, and Bruce asked, "How did you know we were here Mom?"

Mama looked back at Lizzy and then again at the boys. Both of them just shook their heads. "Another vision Liz?" Allen asked.

Lizzy gently smiled and nodded yes. She could not stop wondering how amazing this gift was, as Mama would say it. Later on that night her Mama told her that it was a family blessing. That Papa Adler and her Mama too could see things like she did. Her Mama went on to explain about a time that Papa Adler had fallen off a ladder. Mama was two states away, and she had a vision where she saw the whole thing happen. She hurried to the phone and called Mama Adler to ask her about it. Mama Adler had just hung up the phone and was on the way to the hospital. She said that Papa Adler was painting the capital building when he fell off the ladder. Papa Adler had broken his right leg, but other than that he was relatively okay.

"You see Lizzy... it is a gift that has now been passed on to you." her Mama smiled.

Lizzy wasn't so sure about the gift she had received because every time she had a vision, it was about something terrible or about someone she loved. She did not put much merit in it and tried to forget all about it. However, the following year as Lizzy went on to high school it happened again. This time she was in the last class of the school day and she was getting ready to walk out to the bus when she had a vision. Max was injured. She saw him lying on the gym floor unconscious. He was wearing his basketball jersey, so she knew it happened while he was playing basketball. When she boarded the school bus that afternoon, she looked around on the bus for Max, but he was nowhere to be found. That made her all the more upset.

She asked the driver where her brother was. He answered, "Lizzy, I have no idea."

"I know something awful is wrong with him!" she cried.

"Calm down Lizzy. You will be home soon, and if there is something wrong with Max, I am sure you will know all about it then," he said trying to console her. He realized that his efforts were in vain.

Lizzy knew there was something wrong and nothing in the world could have convinced her otherwise. The bus could not get to her bus stop fast enough.

As the bus driver opened the door, he said, "Good luck Lizzy."

She never heard anything. By then she set off on a full pace run and got to the house in a matter of a few minutes. She was in track, and she was a sprinter, so she started out like lightning, but the adrenaline that flowed due to her concern for Max kept her at that pace all the way home. When she ran up the last hill, she noticed right away that her Mama's car was gone. Since Mama had not told them that she would not be home when they got there, Lizzy imagined the worst.

As she ran into the house, she noticed that Mama had left a note over by the phone. It read, *"Children, I am at the hospital with Max. He got injured while playing basketball, but he is going to be okay. He has a bad concussion. I will call as soon as I know anything else. Supper is in the refrigerator Lizzy. Just put it in the oven at 350 degrees and let it cook for an hour. I should be back home by then. – Love Mama."*

Lizzy cried out loud and then shortly afterward Bruce and Allen came in the door. "What are you so upset about?" Bruce asked.

"Read it yourself," she said as she handed it to them. "I had another vision, and it came true again. I HATE this gift!"

Lizzy was tormented. Why did she keep having these horrible visions? Why did people in her family keep getting hurt? She could not reconcile as to why her Mama thought this gift was such a beautiful thing. She just went into the kitchen and put dinner in the oven as Mama requested, and waited as she tried to concentrate on her homework for that night. At 5:30 p.m. her Dad drove up. After he came inside, he sat down with the kids and told them what had happened to Max.

"Max had just jumped up high to make a basket with the basketball during practice, and one of the athletes behind him had just tossed a ball in the same direction. Well, it hit Max in the back of the head and threw him off balance. When he landed on the gym floor, it knocked him unconscious, and at the same time, he had swallowed his tongue. They had to act fast to get his locked jaws open and the tongue out of his throat because it was blocking his air supply. Max is now in the hospital and will be for a few days. That is mainly so that they can keep an eye on him, as he has what they call a bad concussion," Harold finished.

"Lizzy saw the whole thing in one of those visions she has Dad," Allen blurted.

"Again Lizzy?" her dad asked.

Lizzy nodded. She was visibly disturbed by the entire episode.

Her Dad ignored it and asked, "Is dinner ready by any chance?"

Lizzy nodded again and said, "I just turned the oven off when you drove up."

"Well, let's wash up and eat. Allen set the table, and Lizzy put the food on the table. Bruce get everyone some water, and we will be set." he ordered.

All the kids moved about in the kitchen doing what they were told. Their Dad went to wash his hands and clean up, as he usually did when he came home. He always had grease under his fingernails from the mechanic shop.

During dinner, Lizzy said, 'I'm not very hungry Dad. Can I go to my room?"

"You need to eat Lizzy. He's going to be okay."

He noticed that it did not matter what he said, she just picked at her food. "Go on…," he resigned.

After Max got home in a few days, he was not allowed to go back and play basketball for a few more weeks. So, he sat on the sideline watching everyone else play. Since Max was so competitive he struggled to just sit there, but he knew better than to ask if he could join the team on the court. His coach had received the doctor's order, and he knew his coach would never bend a rule like that. It was his senior year and Max was one of their star players. It hurt everyone on the team when he got injured, but they were all just so glad that he was going to be alright.

The following school year, Lizzy was back at Cherry High School. People were not mean to her anymore. However, no one would really associate with her either unless they were in choir. She concentrated on her music, and she had a music teacher named Shelia Smith. She was so young and pretty, and the boys drooled over her. She also had Lizzy singing soprano in choir and alto in specialty groups. She liked Lizzy a lot, and she utilized her gift as much as possible. Again, Lizzy was chosen to go to state competition with a solo. She also sang in a sextet and a trio, and had received three superior medals that year.

Though her school life had improved, her home life continued to deteriorate. Her parents continued with the weekly brawls and arguments. When those times happened, Lizzy would remember an event when she was younger, and her first encounter with God.

She remembered a time when she was about eight years old. It was about the middle of the week or so when her parents began to fight and throw things at each other. Her Mama got in the first hit. Her Dad reacted as he pulled her down on the floor and stomped on her. He reached for the .22 shotgun and lit off a few rounds in the ceiling, as he usually did. The yelling and expletives were unceasing. Lizzy ran out of the house crying and went to a safe place. She hid behind a huge oak tree in the backyard, feeling so hopeless, so lost, and so all alone.

She cried out "God! If there is a God......will you please help me?!!"

Suddenly, something caught her eye. Looking west she noticed the sun was setting as something strange and inviting happened to her. A sense of peace rushed over her entire body and soul, and though she could not articulate what was happening to her, she credited the feeling of complete peace to God, the one she had just called upon.

Oh, she knew of a place that people would go to pray and talk to God. Her Mama had taken her to the Jewish synagogue when she was only five-years-old. As she was growing up, all of the kids knew when her Mama put a prayer shawl on and lit a candle to pray, that they were to leave her alone. She never said such, but Lizzy had a healthy dose of respect for both of her parents, regardless of their behavior.

When outburst after outburst happened throughout the years, Lizzy's mind would often go back to that night, to that sunset, to that moment when she felt that God heard what she had to say. She was growing older, becoming more and more introverted and insecure about her own identity. The only thing Lizzy had to hold on to for stability was her music. She still loved music, and when she sang or listened to it, all the pain of her childhood dissipated under the melodic notes that filled her life with joyfulness.

It seemed that her Mama's personality had changed too. She wasn't as quiet or relenting when things were said or done that she did not agree with. Her mother's earth-shaking moments increased as Maggie's *Richter scale* seemed to work much differently than other peoples. Lizzy adored her, but much like her father's unsuspecting mood swings, her mother was capable of turning a small mishap into a *sky is falling* event. Unfortunately, her theatrics started rubbing off on Lizzy, and she found herself all the more emotionally unbalanced and unsure of herself as the days progressed. She did not succumb to outburst, but stomach aches and a sense of loneliness crept in that began to control her every thought and feeling.

Lizzy was only a few days short of being fifteen when she had noticed that there was blood on the seat where she had just been sitting. This happened while she was home all alone. Well, her brothers were out on the property somewhere, but she had no desire to speak to them about this. She called Mama at the local bar because it was a Saturday and she knew that she would get ahold of her parents there.

"Mama, I need help. I am bleeding. I think I started my period?" Lizzy relayed a bit nervously.

Gleefully her mother replied, "Oh Lizzy, I will go to the store and be right home."

Lizzy's tummy was aching causing her to wonder why Mama would be so happy to know that she had started her menstruation cycle. Lizzy chalked it up to one of Mama's odd responses, but maybe that was because Mama never talked to her about anything when it came to womanhood. Lizzy supposed it was because she still had some tomboyish behaviors gripping her emotions and will.

Her parents both came home, and Mama took Lizzy in the bathroom and showed her how to use a menstrual pad with a menstrual belt. After she had gotten that accomplished, she stood up and put herself together. Mama was beaming.

"Why are you looking at me like that Mama?" Lizzy asked nervously.

"Oh Lizzy, I am so happy for you. Now you can have babies!" she rejoiced. Then she hugged and kissed her on her cheek.

Honestly, that was the last thing Lizzy wanted to hear about. She knew how babies happened, but she had no desire to start talking about it right then and there, or ever.

"My tummy is hurting too Mama." Lizzy informed.

"I have something you can take for that sweetheart." Her Mama then reached up into the medicine cabinet. She had some over the counter medication designed for women going through such things, and Lizzy was glad because it did work well for her too after a little while. By then, her parents had gone back to the bar.

And so now, as Mama put it, Lizzy was a woman. Lizzy didn't feel any different except for the cramps and now having to wear this uncomfortable wad of cotton between her legs every month for about seven days. That is how she looked at it anyway. It was nothing to get all excited about.

Lizzy began to develop some friendships, but only at school. She was in the choir again, and she usually was selected to be in special music groups too. Lizzy had done very well at the state competition for three years in a row, so she began to get a reputation that her voice could carry others through for a win early on. She had no idea that her talent in singing meant that much to others, as she just loved singing. Even if Lizzy never received a reward for it, she would still choose to do it. It was what she had always loved and what she was resigned to do with her life. She wanted to be a singer and if she kept it up, the pathway ahead would be brighter than ever.

Regardless of her success at school and in the choir, her home life continued to be in great peril. She never shared what was happening at home with anyone. Not even her friends. She was afraid that they would judge her. She never invited anyone over either. If they would have seen her home, which

126

looked like a war zone most of the time, they would surely unfriend her and never speak to her again. She had difficulty keeping them away. Friends always asked her to come over too, but she would make up an excuse as to why she couldn't, knowing that her parents would not let her go. Her parents were strange like that. They never let her go anywhere for a sleepover or out with the girls. She would cover up for her parents too. When they seldom showed up for school performances or when Lizzy sang at local events, it really hurt her heart. She knew better than to share that part of her disappointment with anyone.

As the high school days passed, again, the boys became interested in Lizzy. She too was interested in them, in her own particular way. One young man in tenth grade took a liking to her and kept asking her to go to church with him. She kept making up excuse after excuse as to why she could not go when suddenly, she just had no more reasons. Jerry said that the church bus would pick them up a specific time that Sunday morning. Jerry was a nice guy, or she thought he was. He was tall, had sandy-colored hair, a mustache, and dark blue eyes. His hair was cut allowing bangs to cross his forehead. Other girls seemed to like him too, but honestly, she did not know much about him except that he had an excellent singing voice.

She went home and asked her mom if she could go to church that Sunday. The good thing is that Max her oldest brother was already attending church, so her parents really couldn't say no. Her Dad was not happy about it at all and gave her the silent treatment that Sunday morning.

There he sat in his chair, smoking a cigarette and drinking a beer as he read the morning paper. "You don't need to be going to church. There ain't nothing there for you. You need to stay home…"

Lizzy, replied, "I gave my word Dad, and the bus is already on its way to pick me up."

Lizzy's Dad was apparently miffed at the idea, but he shook his newspaper as to open up the next page and just ignored her as if she was not in the room. Lizzy could see the bus come up the hill and so she smiled at her Mama and went out the back door to get on board. Everyone on the bus was so kind and welcoming. She knew many of the kids on the church bus too. Many of them were in choir class with her. There sat Jerry also, and he scooted over to allow her to sit by him.

"I'm sure glad you came with us today. I wasn't sure you would follow through," he smiled.

Now Jerry's smile was contagious, and Lizzy couldn't help responding to him likewise. Suddenly, some of her friends started singing some Christian choruses she had never heard. She listened and then joined right in as if it was the natural thing to do. She could learn a song only after hearing it one time. After going to church that day, and spending time in the puppeteers' group, she was hooked. She had so much fun. One of the girls there asked, "Isn't Allen your little brother?"

"Why yes.... he sure is my little brother...why do you ask?"

She invited, "You can bring him with you to church if you like. We can pick both of you up if he wants to come next Sunday."

"I'll let him know."

On the way home, Lizzy was so happy...everyone on the bus was delightful. Lizzy could not recall much about the sermon, but she remembered how warm and kind people at that church were to her and she had every intention of going back.

When she got home, her Dad kept up the silent treatment but her Mama asked her all about it, and she told her how beautiful it was and how many of her school friends went to that church. Lizzy explained how they sang on the bus and played with puppets, and had snacks and then went on to church service. "I loved it, mom. They also said Allen could come next week if he wants to, as well."

At the sound of that, she heard her Dad open up another beer to keep up with his weekend ritual of getting drunk. He shot off an expletive or two, but from that day forward, he never stopped her from going to church.

Back at school, and a few weeks before the team left to go to state, Jerry, her friend from choir began to take a fancy to Lizzy. He started carrying her books and walking Lizzy to her locker. He asked if she would be his girlfriend and she said "yes." They would hold hands, but she still did not think that she was ready to be kissed. Unbeknownst to her, he had made that determination for her, and one day he just grabbed her gently and planted a big one on her right in front of her locker and in front of other people. When he finished, Lizzy stood there stunned, not sure if she liked it or not.

Then he whispered in her ear, "See you after class," and then he smiled and left.

Her friend smiled at her and said, "So, how was it, Liz?"

"I don't know, I'm still in shock," she answered as she turned red.

Lizzy walked to her next class, and as she sat there in class, all that she could think about was that kiss and she decided that she liked it after all. She also thought to herself, *"My mother would kill me if she knew I was kissing any boy!"* So, she decided it was best to never disclose that information. Jerry was well liked by many people, and he was also a school photographer for the annual yearbook. Since Lizzie was his girlfriend, he had pictures of her throughout the yearbook that year. She also discovered that year how much she enjoyed drama class. The drama department put on a big musical too, and Lizzy got to act, and dance and sing and had a sense of being in her realm. Jerry and Lizzy broke up the following semester. He took a fancy to another girl, and it broke Lizzy's heart to pieces. She regretted then that she had been kissing someone who did not value relationships in the way that she did.

Eleventh grade came and Lizzy continued to focus on her music and studies. Her oldest brother Max had already graduated, gone off to college, and married. By then Lizzy had become very active in the church. At the same time Lizzy's parents and their alcoholism had grown to become rampant. They were totally disconnected from the lives of their children and seemed to live an existence to only argue and fight.

One day she came home, and her Dad had moved out. He had left her Mama to go live with another woman. Lizzy was actually relieved, thinking the fighting would stop. However, her Mama was depressed but tried her best to manage things. Since Max was gone and Bruce had moved out long before all this, Lizzy was the oldest and left with a lot of the burdens. Her Mama would start yelling at her for no reason at all, and regardless of how hard Lizzy tried to please her, they just could not see eye to eye on anything. She became a bit more physically abusive towards Lizzy, as well. Lizzy told her friend Caroline Bates about it, and Caroline's mother thought it would be a good idea for Lizzy to come live with them if Lizzy needed to. They all went to the same church that Lizzy attended. Lizzy took them up on it. After school one day Lizzy just got on Caroline's school bus and went home with her.

That night, at about 10:00 p.m. there was a loud knock on the Bates' front door. It was Lizzy's

Mama, and she was furious. Johnny, Caroline's father, went to the door, and when he opened it up, Lizzy could hear her Mama cussing him out as she kept screaming, "Lizzy get out here! I know you are in there!"

Shirley, Caroline's mother, ran to where Lizzy was and said, "Stay where you are Lizzy, I am getting help."

Caroline's mother instantly called the police. Lizzy buried her head under the pillow as Caroline tried to comfort her.

"Lizzy it will be okay. You do not have to leave. My mom is calling the police."

Caroline's Dad said calmly, "Maggie, my wife has called the police, and I suggest you leave now."

Maggie spewed out a lot of expletives towards Caroline's father, and he closed the door on her. Afterward, Maggie kept banging on the door and walking around the house banging on the windows and yelling for Lizzy to come out and go home. It was terrifying in a way for all of them, but a few minutes later, the police showed up and made Lizzy's Mama leave the premises. Lizzy was literally shaking and could not stop, as she was so upset about it.

Johnny said, "You do not have to live in that kind of environment Lizzy. You can stay here as long as you need to."

What bothered Lizzy is that she knew that her Mama would keep coming over and keep causing trouble. Lizzy knew that she needed to go somewhere else, but had no idea how to save her friends from dealing with the saga of her dysfunctional life. Since Bruce and Caroline were now dating, Caroline told her that Bruce had been in touch with Lizzy's Dad and that he said that Lizzy could come live with him.

Lizzy thought long and hard about it, and Bruce said that their Dad, even though he still drank, he never quarreled like he did with their mother. After a few days passed, Lizzy agreed to the circumstances. She thought, "*At least, Mama would not know where she was, and since she was with a parent what could the law do?*"

"Thank you, Caroline, thank all of you for your friendship and your hospitality towards me and allowing me to stay here. I will never forget how very kind you have been," Lizzy said as she hugged each of the Bates' family member's goodbye.

Lizzy's Dad was living with a lady named Linda, but by this time she did not care about that. Linda was very sweet to Lizzy, and she would make a chocolate cream pie that Lizzy said was the best she had ever had. The church bus would pick her up every Sunday at her Dad's house, and no one at school knew anything about where she was living now. Caroline kept Lizzy's family problems a secret, and because of that, Lizzy began to excel in school. She admitted later that she could focus on her school work a whole lot better. Her Dad only drank on the weekends now, and she never saw him argue or fight with Linda. He seemed happy and Linda did too.

6

The Unexpected

No one is so brave that he is not disturbed
by something unexpected. –Julias Ceasar

After Lizzy had moved in with her Dad, she kept going to church and even had made a decision because of peer pressure, to follow Christ in baptism. Regardless, Lizzy discovered that nothing had really changed in her life. However, Lizzy was grateful for the great youth group and the big gym that had been made into a skating rink. At that time in her life, she would rather do anything at church than be at home. Home was boring. A few weeks after things began to settle, she noticed as she got off at the school bus that her Dad's truck was in the driveway. He had come home early and was waiting for her arrival.

As she went inside the house, her Dad informed her that there was a warrant out for Lizzy's arrest.

Lizzy cried out, "What? What do you mean?"

Her father was apparently upset as well. "Your mother listed you as a runaway and they are looking for you. The best thing to do is to go turn yourself in. I will take you down there, then I will get you out. I will also get legal custody of you." he promised.

Shocked, Lizzy became afraid, "I have to go to jail Dad?"

Trying to calm her he continued, "It will just be until I can get you out. I promise......*and I will* get you out."

As Lizzy gathered her things, she made sure to take her crucial treasure with her, and that was her bible. Though her life had not changed drastically, she loved reading the passages about Jesus and how He had performed miracles and changed people's lives forever. *"I sure need a miracle now,"* Lizzy thought to herself.

Her Dad took Lizzy down to the police station that night, holding her hand in the car all along the way. She could tell he was as tormented about the situation as she was, so she decided to stop crying.

Honestly, Lizzy thought her Mama just wanted her to come home, and that Maggie would come to get her once she was booked into the juvenile jail cell. However, her speculations were completely wrong, and Dad was right. They locked Lizzy up in juvenile jail because her Mama did not want anything to do with her, but she did not want her Dad to have custody of her either. Lizzy felt rejected, confused and utterly alone.

A woman took her to a cell and told Lizzy to take off all of her clothes and take a shower. She gave her a small pocket sized comb that was no contender against her thick, red curly hair. Lizzy felt ashamed and embarrassed, and at that moment, she developed hate towards her own mother for the very first time. That night, Lizzy curled up on the bare cell mattress and cried herself to sleep.

The next morning after breakfast, she saw a woman from her church. Recognizing Lizzy, Mrs. Brown walked over to her and put her arms out for an embrace.

"Lizzy, what are you doing in here?"

Lizzy received Mrs. Brown's hug and then replied, "I do not know. My mother had me placed here. I was living with my Dad, and I guess she did not like that."

"I will work on this Lizzy. Do not worry. You'll be out of here soon." Mrs. Brown determined.

Lizzy had no idea what all was going on behind the scenes, but it took a few days for her to be able to appear in court. When she entered the courtroom, with Mrs. Brown at her side, she saw her Dad sitting there. Lizzy's Mama was there too, but Lizzy would not acknowledge her. Her Dad, nodded an affirmative in her direction. The judge was already seated on the bench, and he posed a question directly at Lizzy.

"Lizzy, can you tell me which parent you want to live with?" the judge gently questioned.

Without missing a beat, Lizzy said, "My Dad."

It took only a few minutes, and Lizzy was awarded custody to her Dad, and they were told they could leave. She hugged Mrs. Brown and thanked her for all her help. Lizzy was relieved and grateful to be going home.

"See you in church?" Mrs. Brown smiled.

Happily, Lizzy answered, "Yes, I'll be there."

As Dad and Lizzy returned home, Linda had made a chocolate pie to celebrate.

While the three of them sat in the kitchen eating, Lizzy thankfully remarked, "Thanks Dad for getting me out of there."

"It's alright Lizzy. Sorry you had to wait a few days. It will never happen again."

After the commotion calmed down, Lizzy pretty much had the typical life of a teenager. She concentrated on her studies, her music, and school. At this time, her Mama had started going to church, but she never approached Lizzy on the church premises. Lizzy assumed that everyone was upset with her Mama due to the way that she had treated her.

A few months later, it was on a most unsuspecting day, when Lizzy arrived home from school, to find her Dad was already back home for the day. He and Linda were seated at the kitchen table. They asked Lizzy to sit down. It was then that Lizzy's Dad told her that he was moving back in with her Mama and that they were leaving.

"No! I am not going back to live with her Dad! After everything she did to me, are you kidding?" Lizzy exploded.

"Lizzy, I am going home, and I will be with you. I know how you feel, but everything will be okay. You have to trust me in this." he insisted.

Lizzy cried as she went to pack up what few belongings that she possessed. Linda was numb and unemotional. She did hug Lizzy before she left with Harold. Lizzy could not believe what was happening. Dad and Linda seemed so happy. She never saw them argue or anything, so what was the problem? She was almost sixteen, and her mind just could not fathom how all this could be taking place.

There was silence in the truck as they drove to the house. Lizzy no longer considered it her home. Visions of her parents fighting and drinking and guns shooting haunted her memories. The drive up to the house went far too quickly. As they drove up the last road that led to the hilltop, they got out and went inside. Lizzy's Mama reached out to hug her and being the forgiving spirit that Lizzy was, she hugged her Mama back.

"Your room is all ready for you Lizzy. Welcome home," her Mama rejoiced.

Lizzy said nothing as she went to her room and unpacked her belongings. There was no welcome home party, no real cheer in the house, just a lot of silence. Her little brother looked at her and then looked away in a disgruntled fashion. He was probably still mad at her for leaving the way that she did.

The following Sunday, another strange event took place. The entire family all got in the car and went to church. Lizzy did not know what was going on, but she liked it. Her Dad was not drinking and had started going to Alcoholics Anonymous. Lizzy, Allen and their mother went to Ala-non and Ala-teen which were support programs for family members of an alcoholic. Life was different. Lizzy never knew that kind of joy or peace could exist under the same roof with all of them together, but it was great! The following Sunday, her mother, and father got up from their seats and went down the aisle at the church to accept Christ into their lives.

They both started to change and it was noticeable to everyone who knew them.

Lizzy's grades improved at school, and she was just finishing her eleventh year. The following week was final exams and then at last....the long awaited for summer break. Lizzy was looking forward to seeing what this summer was going to bring. Allen and Lizzy went to puppet practice together every week, and choir practice. Lizzy sang solos in church, and people said that she reminded them of her brother Max. He was very talented that way as well. He had been going to church while he was in high school and then he moved off and got married. Since then Lizzy had not seen him at all.

About three weeks after being back home with her Dad, Lizzy was walking home from the bus stop and began planning out the next few weeks of her life. She had decided that she was going to study and pass her classes with good grades, as it was towards the end of her eleventh-grade school year. Her sixteenth birthday was in two more weeks or so, and Lizzy knew that this time it would be different. As she came up the hill, Lizzy saw her Dad's truck screeching down at an accelerated speed. He was home early, and Lizzy was beginning to understand that meant bad news. He met her at the bottom of the hill, and she could tell he had been drinking again. Her heart ached at his inability to keep his promise.

"Get inside," he yelled at Lizzy.

Standing at the driver's door, Lizzy inquired, "What's going on?"

"We're leaving. Get in!" Harold demanded.

"No Dad, I am not going. I can't keep moving like this!" Lizzy said.

He set the gear forward and pulled out spinning his tires, leaving Lizzy in a quake of dust and gravel. She ran up the hill to the house in record time and burst into the front door. There, she found her Mama seated in the dining room weeping.

"You're here?" her Mama asked surprisingly.

"Yeah, well where else would I be?"

She got up, wrapped her arms around Lizzy, and just wept. "He's going back to her," implying Linda.

She consoled her mother, "I could tell he was drinking Mama."

"He can't give it up," as she cried all the more.

Allen came in behind Lizzy, all confused and not knowing what had happened. Lizzy informed him, and then Mama said, as she quickly changed her demeanor, "I need to get you kids to church for puppet practice. Let's go."

Mama drove them there and stayed at the church until evening services began. When church service started, Mama, Allen, and Lizzy sat in the back pew. It appeared darker in the sanctuary and unusually quiet. Lizzy's Mama was so very sad, but she was calm. Right before the end of service the pastor looked at her Mama and said, "Maggie, could you meet me in my study following services?"

Mama just nodded unaware of what was going on, but she remained calm.

They all stood to pray, and then they walked to the pastor's study, but the pastor would only let Mama

138

and the youth director inside. Allen and Lizzy stood outside puzzled at such behavior, waiting on their Mama to come out from behind the closed door. No one could have prepared Lizzy for what happened next. Her Mama was crying aloud and weeping "My Max! No! Not my Max!"

Pastor Gary had received word from Wilmington that their brother had been in a car accident and was killed. Ann, Max's wife, was in critical condition and being flown all the way to Berry for medical help. Then silence fell on the door as it slowly opened. Their Mama asked them to come in, and then she told them the terrible news. Allen and Lizzy just cried and held each other there for a brief moment.

All three, Mama, Allen and Lizzy got in the car and went home and several people from the church came over to console her Mama. Her Mama called the bar and told Harold that Max had been killed in a car accident, but Harold would not believe her. He thought it was a ploy to get him to come back home. Charlene, a church member, had offered to take Maggie and Lizzy to Wilmington the following day so that Maggie could make arraignments for Max's funeral. Allen had plans for the next day at school, so he decided not to go with them.

When they arrived at the funeral home, Mama and Lizzy went inside. Lizzy sat down in the foyer as Mama was asking the funeral home director some questions. Lizzy happened to see the morning newspaper lying there, and on the front of the paper was the car wreck that took her brother's life. She looked at it and then decided to hide it from her mother. This was so her mother would not have to see that terrible picture Lizzy had just observed.

Mama came out from the director's office with tears in her eyes and asked, "Lizzy, do you want to go see him?"

Lizzy nodded yes, and so initially, Lizzy and her Mama both went in the parlor together to see Max. Mama could not stay with Lizzy because she was overtaken with grief. Lizzy had never seen a dead person before, and now she was looking at her oldest brother. He had come so far in life. Max was at the top of his class and graduating that year from college. He was even more muscular than she had remembered and had his hair in an afro. He had bronzed skin and a defined jaw-line that was distinct. Lizzy could tell they had put makeup on his face to cover the big bruise on his forehead from the accident. The impact of the oncoming car had killed him instantly. He and Ann were taking another couple and their sick baby to the hospital on that rainy Wednesday night. A man driving in the opposite lane drifted over the line and hit them directly in the front of their vehicle. Ann was the only one left, now clinging for her life. As Lizzy looked at Max, he seemed peaceful. Max was very popular on campus, and before his body was even brought home, they had a service for him on campus. Lizzy's family did not attend that service, because her Mama had made plans for a service in their own hometown.

After their time alone with Max, Charlene had come inside and they all left to eat. A heavy silence hung over them as Carla drove them all the way back home. Her Mama would reach silently for her handkerchief and press the tears on her face away. Lizzy held her Mama's hand all the way back home. It was Thursday. They never heard a word from Lizzy's Dad or Bruce. Lizzy figured they both knew the truth by now. She was so terribly disappointed in her father. The anger that she once held toward her mother had now been transferred over to her Dad. Lizzy did her best to take care of things around the house. Her Mama was not the same woman that she had known after that Wednesday. Lizzy had never seen her like this. She knew that grief did different things to different people. Her Mama withdrew into herself, staying in her room alone and refusing to eat. Allen and Lizzy did not talk much either. Two days later, on Saturday, the youth at church were going to the zoo, and Allen decided to go with them. Lizzy stayed home to take care of things, and her Mama left to go to the funeral home and make final arrangements and such for Max's body to arrive.

Jean, who had become like a second mother to Lizzy, drove her Mama to the funeral home that day. Before they got back, the phone rang. On the other end was Jean. "Lizzy, do not let your mother out of your site today, she is acting funny. Do you understand?"

"Yes, I will," and then Jean abruptly hung up.

Lizzy was terribly puzzled about the phone call, not understanding any of its meaning, and decided to wait in the dining area looking out the window until she could see Jean's car coming up the hill bringing her Mama back home. Mama got out and thanked Jean for everything. Jean waived at Lizzy, who was now standing on the back porch, and then she reversed her car out of the driveway and left.

About thirty minutes went by, and Lizzy's Mama came out of her room with a bubbly demeanor.

"Honey, I am headed up to the funeral home to see if Max has arrived yet He is due at any time."

"Wait for me Mama, I'll go with you," she quickly responded, remembering what Jean said.

"No Lizzy, you had your time alone with Max, remember? I need to do this."

She then hugged Lizzy and walked out the door. She seemed rational. Lizzy thought that her Mama had just come to grips with everything, and was starting to deal with it. Had she really understood what her mother was about to do, she would have

141

taken the car keys away from her and hid them, but she hadn't an inkling.

Lizzy placed some clothes in the washer and started cleaning up around the house. About forty minutes passed when she heard the phone ring. It was Jean, once again.

Ring…..Ring….."Hello?"

Jean was frazzled, "Lizzy, are you going to be home?"

"Yes….what's wrong?"

"I'll be there in a minute!" Then the phone hung up in silence as the caller disconnected.

Lizzy could not imagine Jean acting in such a manner. She was always calm, always joking, and the one which many of the kids at church went to when they needed some advice. Lizzy lightly paced the floors as she kept glancing out the window and down the long dirt road that led up the hill to their farmhouse. It had already been an unbelievable week as the lurid details of the fatal car accident played out in her head repeatedly. As if that was not enough, her alcoholic father left the family for another woman. Now, knowing Jean was on her way over and sounding a bit panicked, the almost sixteen-year-old girls' heart began to flutter a bit just knowing deep down that something terrible was waiting.

Observing the dust starting to fly up on the country road as Jean's car raced into the driveway, Lizzy ran out to meet her. The forty-year-old woman lost no time getting out and taking Lizzy's arm as they walked into the house simultaneously.

Without losing a beat, Jean continued, "Lizzy, your mother has shot herself at the funeral home. You need to get ready to go to the hospital. She is refusing surgery, but with you going up there, and me signing as the consenting adult, they will start the surgery immediately!"

"She shot herself!" Lizzy cried out in an unbelievable response.

"Yes. Do you remember me calling you this morning and warning you about Maggie being alone?"

"Well, yes....but she was smiling and convinced me that she did not need me to be with her when she left. I do not understand," Lizzy wept in shock.

Jean followed Lizzy as she prepared to leave and kept enlightening her on the details. "When I took your mother up there this morning, she was behaving peculiarly. She purchased three funeral plots: one for Max and one for his wife Ann who is in critical care in Berry, OK, as well as, one for herself."

Acknowledging the information, Lizzy replied, "That is why you called me and told me not to let my mother be by herself?" she posed as she connected the dots. "I didn't know that she would do this Jean...! Honestly!"

"Lizzy, it's not your fault." She responded by hugging her to calm her down. "Let's go.....are you ready?"

Lizzy nodded, and Jean held her hand and led her to the car. Jean drove a bit faster than usual but safely.

"How did you know she did this at the funeral home Jean.....were you there?"

"Will Berry, the Director, and I are friends, and he knew that I was with your mother this morning as she made arrangements for your brother's funeral. He called me when he had no other idea who else to contact."

Lizzy sat quietly contemplating all the events of the week and now realizing that her world was completely shattered. She kept thinking of her father, who refused to answer any of her Mama's calls regarding Max. He supposed it was a ploy to get him to come back home. Hatred began to grow inside her towards her father's irresponsible actions. She did not understand how things had turned around so drastically in only seventy-two hours. She knew that her family had struggles and that no family is perfect, but how she longed for her family to be ordinary, just once. Now with that hope shattered, she concentrated on her Mama and tried to imagine what she would see when she arrived at the hospital.

Jean continued talking, "Your Mom was making funeral arrangements for Max and for herself. I knew something was not right, and that is why I called you."

Jean told Lizzy that Maggie had even picked out her own casket. When they arrived at the hospital, the news press was there, cameras and all. As Lizzy walked in through the emergency room doors a camera light blinded her, and a lady asked, "Are these your father's," as she held out a pair of false teeth.

My father's? What's going on here?" Lizzy cried.

The woman went on, "Your mother shot your father at the bar and then fled to the funeral home where she shot herself. Did you not know?" the reporter continued.

Lizzy looked up at Jean and cried, "Make them leave me alone!"

Jean quickly escorted Lizzy into the bathroom and turned and yelled at the reporters, "Leave her alone!"

Lizzy stayed in the bathroom until the press left and when Lizzy and Jean emerged from there, a doctor was outside the door waiting for Lizzy and Jean to sign the paperwork. Lizzy signed first, and then Jean co-signed. The medical staff immediately got the signal to take Maggie back surgery.

While that was taking place, Lizzy desperately wanted to see her mother, but her mother did not want to see anyone, and Maggie had told the

144

surgeon, "I want to die, leave me alone." These were the same words she had spoken to the director at the funeral home when he had found her in the bathroom after the gunshot rang out.

Jean got the truth about Lizzy's father being shot and taken to the Veteran's hospital downtown. It was a shock to both Jean and Lizzy, and Jean just held Lizzy tightly and said, "No matter what, we will get through this, dear."

Shortly after surgery started, a nurse came out and said they needed to get more Type O negative blood because Maggie had lost too much blood to survive. Somehow, Lizzy remembered that she had the identical blood type, but they refused her blood because she was not sixteen years old yet.

Lizzy pleaded, saying, "My birthday is only seventeen days away!"

Nevertheless, the hospital staff stood their ground due to the state law. Lizzy went around the hospital asking people if they had Type O negative blood they could give to her Mama. She had actually found some people willing to offer, but it was too late.

By then several church members had arrived at the hospital along with Allen. The hospital staff whisked them into a small room off the central waiting area, and everyone piled in. Lizzy knew what was next. She had never experienced anything like this, but she had instincts of discernment well beyond her years. There were about a dozen people in that small room when the doctor entered. Before he could say anything, Lizzy knew what the report was.

"She had lost too much blood, and she just did not want to live. I am so very sorry," the doctor said regretfully.

Lizzy could not even cry. She was numb. Allen wept, and Lizzy held his hand. Lizzy could not remember but was sure many people gave their condolences, but she heard nothing. Everything was in slow motion. By then they had a new pastor at the church, Brother Larry, and he said that he needed to take Lizzy and Allen to the other hospital where their father was now having surgery. Lizzy refused to go but Brother Larry remained persistent. Allen and Lizzy rode in the back seat and stayed silent the entire ride to downtown.

Lizzy silently prayed, "God, please let Dad die. It is his fault all of this is happening, and he does not deserve to live," she angrily thought to herself.

When they walked into the surgery waiting area at the other hospital, there were numerous people there. All of them had been drinking. The story was that Maggie had walked into the bar, shot Harold in the back two times and then left to go to the funeral home. When Max's body had not arrived, Lizzy's Mama asked to use the bathroom, and it was there that she decided to end it all.

Linda was at the hospital, and she cried out and grabbed Lizzy's hand. "Lizzy, will you please pray with me that your Daddy lives?"

That was the last thing on earth Lizzy wanted to do at that time, but Linda took her to the bathroom and Lizzy did what she felt was her spiritual duty, in an unbelieving matter. Afterward, Linda thanked Lizzy and told her that she loved Harold very much.

Lizzy walked off numb and tried to get as far away from the crowd as possible. They were there for quite some time. Bruce showed up too. When they said that Harold had made it through surgery and that he would be okay, Lizzy looked up at the preacher and said, "I want to go home."

Allen said the same, and so he took them to Jean's house. Jean and Johnathan were so nice to Lizzy and Allen. Jean headed up the puppet group, and she really cared about them. Celia, their daughter, let Lizzy share a room with her that night. Jean said if Lizzy wanted to, that she could live with them and stay at Cherry High and graduate. After all, it was Lizzy's senior year. Lizzy thought that would be great. The next day, however, was a blur. Lizzy could not remember anything that happened.

Monday, the day of the funeral came. It had now become a double ceremony with her brother Max and her Mama in the same funeral service. Lizzy never cried insisting she had to remain strong. She also had to sing at the funeral. Maggie had asked her several weeks before when she had heard Lizzy sing a song at church if she would someday sing that song at her funeral. Of course, Lizzy never thought she would have to keep that promise so soon.

The phone rang at Jean's house, and it was someone saying that Maggie's body would not be ready in time for the funeral service because they were still performing an autopsy. Lizzy became frantic, and Jean took over.

"Listen, these kids have been through enough this week. There is no way that they can go through two funerals in one week. You must have that body ready by 2:00 p.m." Jean insisted. "Yes, that is right…," she continued, and before you know it, the story had changed, and all was well.

As Lizzy, Bruce and Allen entered the sanctuary, it was packed. People were even standing in the back. Gary, the music director, talked to Lizzy privately and said, "Now Lizzy, if you find it too difficult to sing, or if something else happens, I will get up and continue, okay?" he stated assuredly.

She smiled, "Thanks, but I will be okay. I need to do this for Mama."

When Lizzy stood up behind the podium to sing she saw so many faces from school and church. The school had allowed many of the students to come to the funeral as well. Right before she sang, she looked out and noticed many of her friends and her high school choir director seated before her. Lizzy started singing, and though she may have mixed up the order of the verses, she made it through bravely, without missing a note.

Afterward, Pastor Gary, who had already taken a new pastorate in another town, got up and shared when Max and Mama both came to know Jesus. He had been the pastor up until the day that Max died. The Wednesday night service that she and Allen and Mama had attended was his very last. Lizzy also held Pastor Gary in high regard. When he preached, she had wished secretly that her own father was like that. Lizzy knew something was different that day. She was listening carefully to Pastor Gary sharing Max's and Maggie's salvation experience, and Lizzy did not want to pretend to be a Christian anymore. She truly desired to give her life to Jesus entirely.   When the pastor used the opportunity to share with the congregation how to accept Christ, he did not know that Lizzy was seriously giving her life to Christ that day. Lizzy was too proud to tell anyone then, because she had gone through all that before and had been baptized in that same church, as well. Because of this, she remained quiet about her decision for many years.

After the service, Lizzy, Allen, and Bruce got in the limo and rode to the grave site. Some of the other "Ryan" family members were there too. The graveside service was short, and when it had finished, Lizzy got up right away and went to sit in the limo. She knew nothing about the protocol for such a thing as this. Her brothers followed Lizzy's lead, and the limo took all of them back to the church. There Jean picked Lizzy and Allen up and took them to her house. Ann's brother, Max's brother-in-law and his father-in-law were there at the funeral and had come over afterward to Jean's house too. Maggie's sister, Aunt Fran arrived with Uncle Charles. Aunt Fran was too afraid to fly, so they drove all the way from Florida and, unfortunately, missed the funeral by an hour. Lizzy was not that close to them so she went out to swim in the pool with all the kids.

Her Mama had made up a *Last Will and Testament*. She left everything to Pastor Gary and gave him custody of both Allen and Lizzy. Now, Lizzy loved Pastor Gary a lot, but Lizzy wanted to graduate the following year from her own school. If she went to live with him and his family, it would mean a new school with strangers, and just one more disruption in her life.

Jean came out to talk to her. "Lizzy, Mr. Butler, Ann's Dad has invited you to go to Berry with them to see Ann and spend a week up there. Maybe being up there will help you make the decision to live here or in Morton, Oklahoma with Allen."

Lizzy agreed to go with the Butler's for a week. She got to ride on the back of Mr. Butler's Harley Davidson with him as his son drove the car back to Berry, Oklahoma. She had never been on a motorcycle, and she knew if Mama saw her now, she would be furious. Lizzy seemed to recall that a good friend of Mama's named Claire was hurt once on a motorcycle, and Mama never got over it. Lizzy hugged everyone goodbye and off they went. Lizzy was confused about staying with Jean and Johnathan, and leaving Allen alone in Morton, OK with the pastor's family. Well, she decided that she had a week to make up her mind, so she relaxed and tried to take in the scenery on the motorcycle. She was enjoying the ride.

Mr. Butler was very nice to Lizzy and kept telling her how much she looked like Max. "I think we are going to hit some rain. Do you want me to pull over?" Mr. Butler asked Lizzy.

"I'll be alright if you are alright," Lizzy replied.

As the rain began to fall, she felt the sting of the raindrops on her legs, as she had changed into shorts and a tee shirt right after the funeral. Regardless, the rain only lasted about three minutes, and she dried off quickly in the breeze created from the windy ride.

"I think Jean was right…I needed to get away." Lizzy admitted.

Mr. Butler smiled, "You are welcome to come up to Berry anytime Lizzy."

Though Lizzy was usually very uncomfortable with grown men, especially after her childhood attack, she felt safe with Mr. Butler. She could not explain it. It was as if they had always known each other. She actually laid her head on his back shoulder and dozed off to sleep for a short distance. When the bike took a quick lane change, it jarred her.

"Oh… I guess I fell asleep Mr. Butler. I am sorry." She apologized very loudly, as the wind carried her voice the opposite direction of Mr. Butler's ears.

"There is nothing to apologize for," he replied back at her. "It has been a tough week for all of us. Rest all you want. I will get us there safely," he smiled.

Lizzy was actually refreshed after the fifteen-minute nap, so she stayed awake the rest of the way into Berry, Oklahoma, where Ann's family lived.

Getting away did clear her mind. Once they arrived, her initial sight of Ann was quite a shock. Both her arms were in casts, and she wore an eye patch. She had lost one eye in the accident. Her broken jaw was wired shut, and she struggled to walk too. She had a fractured left hip. Regardless, Ann was delighted to see Lizzy, and she also said looking at her was like looking at Max. Her family wasn't used to what they called Lizzy's robust hugs. Ann's mother hugged others in a way as if she was distancing herself from them. She never allowed anyone's chest to meet up with hers. It was awkward to Lizzy, but as the week progressed, the family all said that Lizzy had made them laugh and had brought a lot of joy into the house.

On the fifth day of her visit, Ann asked, "Lizzy do you know how to play tennis?"

"Are you kidding? I learned from the best, Max!"

Ann smiled as best she could, "Good, will you take me to the tennis court?"

"You can't play tennis like that Ann. What are you thinking?"

"Just hit the balls to me so I can swing around and hit them back. I need exercise so bad, and it will help me heal better," she insisted.

Even though it concerned Lizzy, she did as Ann asked and they went to the tennis court. Amazingly, Ann was right. She finagled her body, turning the racket towards the balls each time, and gave them a powerful enough hit to make it over the net. Ann was so strong, not just physically, but spiritually and emotionally. Lizzy found it hard to believe that only a week had passed since Ann was in a horrible car accident. Ann was a fighter. She fought for her life, and she won. For the first time Lizzy could see what Max loved about her. Afterward, they went to get ice cream. Trevor, Ann's brother, drove them. He was almost seventeen, and he looked at Lizzy with those big brown eyes, and it just melted her heart. That night, Trevor and Lizzy sat out on the porch and talked. He gently lifted her head up and said, "I'm really going to miss your brother and now you." Then he kissed her. It was unlike any kiss she had experienced thus far. It was sweet and short and tender. She would not have called it romantic. It was not that kind of kiss. They just stood there and held each other for a while like two grieving souls, and for the first time in ten days, Lizzy cried right along with him.

The next morning came, and the phone rang. It was Allen calling for Lizzy. He was weeping. "Lizzy, please come to be with me. I need you here with me. I miss you."

That is all it took. Lizzy's brother needed her, and she was not going to let him down. It was going to be so difficult to tell Jean and Johnathan and especially Celia, their daughter that she was going to live in Morton. Lizzy knew it would not be received well by them, but her brother needed her, and if anyone needed her she could always be counted on to follow through. The next day Mr. Butler drove Lizzy to Jean's home and bid her goodbye.

"If you are ever up our way, please come to see us Lizzy. We love you," he smiled and then kissed her on her forehead before leaving.

"Thank you. I'll do that," Lizzy agreed.

As Lizzy walked in the front door, there was Celia standing with Lizzy's luggage already packed and waiting with tears in her eyes. Lizzy was worried how she was going to tell them all, but they already knew. They hugged each other and Lizzy thanked them for being there for her. Johnathan and Jean loaded their car and took Lizzy to live in Morton with Allen.

When Lizzy walked into their home, there stood Allen with tears in his eyes and a huge smile. Lizzy just held him for a bit and told him she was home now. They both acclimated well to their new life and new family. Pastor Gary and his wife, Debbie, had four children of their own. Two teenage boys and one eleven-year-old girl, who was upset that Lizzy was there because she was the only girl in the family. Lizzy did not blame her for feeling that way.

Lizzy was sleeping in the dining room for a week, in a sleeping bag until she got a bed placed in her new sister's room.

Lizzy was not the same person anymore, mentally, emotionally or spiritually. She had drawn upon the strength of the Lord that she had heard so many others speak about. She had an insatiable hunger for the Word of God. It was all new to her but she looked forward to her daily bible reading and time alone with her loving Heavenly Father.

That next Sunday the entire family went to church. Lizzy met many new people that day. They were very kind to her too. One girl asked Lizzy what it was like to live with such good-looking boys.

She laughed and said, "I hadn't noticed." Sincerely, she really had not. Later on, she pondered on that question and decided that the preachers' boys may have been heartthrobs, but she never saw them that way. Maybe God was protecting her, but she never once had feelings like that for any of them.

A few weeks later Lizzy's birthday came around and Nana, Debbie's mother, made Lizzy a beautiful birthday cake for the event. Lizzy did not remember ever having a birthday cake, but Allen said she did. He and Lizzy had discussed recently that so much craziness was in their home environment growing up, that when their birthdays came along, and if it was convenient, they got to celebrate. It's funny how all the bad memories seem to erase all the good ones. Lizzy had received a birthstone ring for her sixteenth birthday. It was an emerald, and it was so beautiful. She had never had anything that special given to her before.

The next month Bruce got married to Caroline. When Lizzy and Allen arrived for the big event, Lizzy found out that there was no ring for the bride that day and suggested, "That will never do!! Here, take this one," as she took off her new birthstone ring and gave it to her best friend, Caroline.

After Lizzy had returned home and shared about the wedding and the ring, Debbie, realized then that material things just did not mean a lot to Lizzy.

Lizzy admitted after her senior year in high school was over that she really did not remember much about it at all. The only thing she remembers was Mrs. White her choir teacher. She was a bit hefty and had a bouncy spirit. Lizzy loved her and learned a lot from her too. She also remembered that summer when she got to sing at the big church camp south of where she lived. There were 10,000 people there, and at first, she was very nervous, but the music director said, "Lizzy, you have a remarkable voice and I want you to open up our morning service with a solo."

Lizzy was very honored, and when they introduced her to come out on the big stage, her youth group at church hooped and hollered and cheered her on. Lizzy, put that aside and concentrated on what was important, Jesus. She had learned the secret of true worship, and that was that you never sing for a crowd.

Lizzy had an eventful summer, and though boys wanted to date her, she had difficulty being herself and letting her heart be free. It was Lizzy's way of shielding herself from any more emotional pain. She had really learned to love Gary and Debbie, and she started calling them Mom and Dad in just a few months. She always admired Pastor Gary and what he stood for. She decided that one day she wanted to serve the Lord like he did. She learned, however, through a harrowing experience later on, not to put people in ministry up on pedestals.

7

Glass Walls Still Hold Secrets

*Nothing makes us so lonely as
our secrets. —Paul Tornier*

Things went on behind the scenes in her new home that caused great turmoil in Lizzy's life, along with an immense amount of confusion. First, the youngest son, Charlie had come in Lizzy's room one afternoon when she lied down for a nap. Now Lizzy usually slept on her stomach, with a pillow over her head. It was something she had done since she was a young child to drown out the loud fighting of her parents. Charlie came in her room, and laid down over her and reached under her chest area and started fondling her breast. She heard him whisper in her ear, "Now, doesn't that feel good?"

Lizzy was so upset, but she was sure if she ever told anyone about his advances that she and Allen would be kicked out of that house in a moment's time and have no place to live. Living in a pastor's home there was an unsaid rule and that was for all those living there must realize that others are watching them. Lizzy wished someone knew what was happening, but then she realized that Charlie always acted out when his parents were gone. Charlie continued on with this behavior even when they were all on family vacations and anytime she was alone with him anywhere in the house. It made her ill, and it stripped her of her self-esteem once again. So Lizzy put up with it for a few months until she had built up the nerve one particular day to tell him to stop and never do that again. She was grateful that his advances stopped at once without another incident.

As the year progressed, more fearful situations awaited. Debbie had taken ill with an autoimmune disease and Gary was always driving all the kids to school. However, because Lizzy got out of school in the middle of the day, Gary would pick Lizzy up at school and bring her home alone. At first, things were fine, but then one thing after another began to develop. First Gary would start by caressing her arm. It made her feel awkward…mainly since he was her adopted father in a sense, and her pastor.

He would say, "Just relax…doesn't that feel good? I am just trying to make you feel good Lizzy," he tried to speak convincingly.

She knew something was wrong with that, but she was afraid to say anything. Then one day, when she was taking care of the family store in town after school, Gary came to pick her up at the time of closing. First, he walked in and asked, "How did your day go?"

Lizzy answered somewhat disappointed, "The traffic at the store has been very slow today. Only two customers came in during the last four hours."

"That's okay Lizzy. That's not your fault," and then Gary put his hands on her shoulders and pulled her in for a kiss. She did not know how to react to that. Once again, Lizzy knew if she ever said anything about it, that she and Allen would be kicked out of that home. He continued those advances until near the end of her senior year in high school. The truth finally came to her. That though she had escaped one form of abuse she had moved right into a home with another type of abuse. This is why her senior year in high school was a complete blank in her mind. She had read that the body reacts to trauma differently and memory lapses are one way that the brain tries to protect a victim.

His advances toward her kept Lizzy confined emotionally as well. She muddled through that year and graduated with no specific honors or direction for life. She did, however, receive a voice scholarship to college, and everyone seemed to be so proud of her. What they did not understand is that it meant moving again and more change on the horizon. She was grateful that by then all of the abuse had ceased, but the scars of being treated in such a way remained. Lizzy was very excited about her new scholarship but she dreaded yet another move. However, Lizzy put a smile on her face and pretended she was excited at the prospect of college. She had to leave her brother Allen behind to go off to school. Though she was seventeen, emotionally she was younger due to all the trauma in her life.

On her first day at the new campus, Lizzy did her best to pretend that she was all grown up and ready for the new adventure. Truth be told, she cried and cried for almost three days. No one knew the pain that Lizzy was going through. She was literally all alone in a new world without a single soul to call a friend.

As if that wasn't enough agony, under the direction of Gary and Debbie, she agreed to get a foreign roommate. Especially since she felt she might be called to foreign missions. They said it would be a great way to see if she sincerely thought she could handle the responsibility. Her roommates' name was Angela, and she was from Japan. She was nice but she cooked funny smelling food in their room, and she had some strange behaviors to boot. Their room was also located on the fourth floor of the dorm. One day Lizzy walked into the first floor of the dormitory and smelled something grotesque. The closer she got to her room, the stronger the aroma got. The smell resembled that of dirty socks.

When she opened the door, Angela greeted her with a huge smile and said in broken English, "Lizzy, I make you seaweed soup. You need more color in the cheeks, and you look too pale."

Lizzy thought to herself, *"What? She had made this for me?!"* She tried to get her head around that and told Angela that she felt fine, but she did not want to insult her, so Lizzy tried out her soup, all the while holding her breath.

After the first spoonful she forcefully swallowed and said, "That is so sweet of you Angela."

"You like? You like?" Angela seemed pleased.

Actually, Lizzy realized that the soup tasted good if you could just get past the stench. She politely nodded yes, and continued eating until it was all gone. She knew immediately that she was going to have to find a new roommate. Everyone avoided their room and complained of the smell, and Lizzy couldn't blame them. The end of the first semester was nearing and Lizzy, regardless of the rough beginning, had done very well in school. Lizzy also had prepared herself to tell Angela that they needed to go their separate ways, so imagine her surprise when Angela walked into their dorm room that day and made an abrupt announcement.

Angela proceeded in broken English, "Lizzy, I sorry, but I find new friend who is Japanese like me. We are going to move in together on the first floor. I hope I not hurt your feelings."

Lizzy tried her best to look disappointed on the outside while her heart was leaping with joy on the inside. "Awe…really? Well.., I understand, do not worry. It will be okay. I'm happy for you!!" Lizzy consoled.

She gave her a hug before Angela began to pack her belongings. Angela wasted no time and was moved out of their room within the hour. Lizzy sprayed the room freshener everywhere and opened

158

the window. She was relieved and hoping she could make friends now with other girls on the dorm floor.

The very first week of the second semester brought a new kind of roommate. Her name was Mara. She was a happy soul but seemed to be at school for all the wrong reasons. She always slept in, missed classes and borrowed Lizzy's clothes and jewelry. She also stayed out late at night, and Lizzy started thinking that she was a drinker too. She went about her business, but in just a few short months, Mara was gone. On that day, Lizzy had opened up her dorm room door and could see that Mara had moved out, and along with it she had taken some of Lizzy's jewelry and clothing. Lizzy did not care. She decided that Mara needed it more than her.

A few weeks went by, and yet another roommate arrived on the scene. Lizzy derived that Marigold was very much into the party scene. She was a good student, but she insisted that they needed to color code their room and get matching comforters and curtains. Lizzy could care less about matchy-matchy room décor, but as long as Lizzy did what she was told, they got along just fine. Marigold was pushy and a bit of a control freak. Lizzy stayed out of the room as much as possible. She could not wait for spring break to come along. By then, Lizzy was very involved in a singing group called *Light.* They traveled most weekends to go sing at different churches. A girl in the group, named Suzanne, had invited Lizzy to come home with her for spring break. She lived in Florida and Lizzy was excited about the trip and the opportunity to see new scenery.

A week before the trip, a guy walked up to Lizzy in the cafeteria while she was eating and visiting with friends. His name was Bert Hanks. He said that he had heard Lizzy sing for chapel that week and wondered if she would come and sing at a revival at his church. Lizzy accepted his invitation and his friend

Harley came and picked her up at her dorm, and took Lizzy and Bert to the church for the for the evening service. She never thought much of it, but she supposed that Bert really wanted to date her. One night shortly after the revival was over, he called and asked if Lizzy wanted to go out. After she declined his invitation, he kept asking and insisting that he wanted to take her to a Chinese restaurant. His constant begging wore her down, and she accepted. Of course, that date was going to have to wait until after spring break.

"Bert, I have to study, and I need to take tests this week. So we will have to do it after spring break. I am not going to let my grades slip. Understand?" She pushed back.

"Sure, that will be fine...yes, I understand. Bye now." Bert hung up.

What Lizzy did not know about him at the time is that he rarely went to classes. He had gotten sick for several weeks and missed several classes, and she concluded that he never could catch up.

When she ran across him on her way to the cafeteria one day, he said, "I heard you are going to Florida for spring break...I am going there too with Harley. He and Suzanne live in the same town."

Frankly, Lizzy wasn't so thrilled about that, but she smiled and said, "How nice."

Something in her spirit was very unsettled every time she saw him. She could not put her finger on it, but it disturbed her immensely. He followed her to the cafeteria and though he was not invited, he sat with Lizzy and her friends when it came time to eat. Deciding not to let it bother her, Lizzy thought about her trip and that she was going to ride to Florida with Suzanne and three other guys she knew from the singing group. She could hardly wait.

As they were loading up for the trip a few days later, Lizzy was so excited. She had never seen the

160

ocean. Plus, Lizzy really liked Suzanne, and she knew they would have a great time. She would be staying with Suzanne at her home, and the guys would be staying with Bradley's family, located further north in the state.

As they unloaded their luggage in front of Suzanne's home, Bradley yelled out to them, "Hey, you girls have fun, and we will pick you up in a week."

Lizzy had only been in Florida for a few hours when the phone rang. Suzanne's mother named Martha said it was for Lizzy.

"For me?" Lizzy seemed puzzled.

Martha relayed, "Yes, it's some guy named Bert."

"Hello?" Lizzy answered the phone a bit befuddled.

"Hi, Lizzy? This is Bert. What are you doing?"

"Why are you calling me?" she said disappointedly. Frankly, she was getting a little nervous about Bert's behavior.

"Well, I thought I would come over and see you if that is okay?"

"Come over?" she asked as Lizzy looked at Suzanne, but she was no help. Suzanne encouraged him by saying out loud, "Come on over Bert!"

Lizzy was a little put out with Suzanne about the whole thing, but she remained quiet. She began to realize that Suzanne liked Harley, and so she used Bert's interest in Lizzy as a way to see Harley. It was only ten minutes later, and there was Bert with Harley, standing at the front door. Next thing that Lizzy knew is that she and Bert were sitting on the front porch. In her desire to get rid of this guy, Lizzy decided to tell Bert about her life story in hopes of running him away. She wanted nothing to do with him. Unfortunately, it had the opposite effect on him. He told her that he was coming back there the following summer as a missionary at Harley's church. Now that was something that peaked Lizzy's interest. She was thinking of doing some kind of evangelism work or mission work in the area too, so there was one thing they had in common.

Regardless, when Bert left, Lizzy was relieved. In just a few days, Suzanne and the guys that had come to Florida with them were going farther north to see some sites. Bradley called and asked if they wanted to go and the girls agreed that it would be fun.

The day came for them to leave on their short trip. It had been very rainy, and there were reports of many mudslides while they were gone. They all spent the night at a church camp in Keystone Heights, Florida. Bradley's cousin was the camp pastor, so he opened up the dorm rooms for them. The following day they came back to West Palm, where Suzanne lived. When they drove up Lizzy was tired and it was late.

As she walked into Suzanne's house, her mother said, "You better call that Bert guy! He has been calling here all day asking for you!" Martha sounded a little disturbed.

Now, that made Lizzy a bit angry and she said, "Why is he calling me so much?"

Suzanne said, "He likes you, Lizzy."

"I don't care. That is rude to be calling your mother all day and to keep asking for me," Lizzy responded with much agitation.

When she called him back, he explained that he had heard about the mudslides and that he was worried about all of them. Then he asked, "Are you guys busy tomorrow?"

Lizzy said, "Yes, we are all going somewhere in the morning."

Suzanne interrupted again, "We are going to Disneyworld with you and Harley!"

Lizzy did not know that part, and that they had made plans to all meet at Suzanne's house and then

162

leave from there. Suzanne continued, "See you guys in the morning at 8:30 a.m.!"

Lizzy then felt like she was being set up....that is because she was. The next morning came, and Suzanne insisted Lizzy ride with Bert in the backseat of Harley's car, while she sat with Harley in the front seat. Lizzy wanted nothing to do with it, but Suzanne kept pushing them together. She resolved to sit wherever she was told and knew the day was going to be a horrible memory all over again. When they arrived at Disneyworld, everyone got out of the cars, as the guys Lizzy and Suzanne came to Florida with, all had arrived at the same time.

The next thing Lizzy knew was that Suzanne and Harley said, "Lizzy, we'll see you and Bert back here at midnight." Then they ran off together.

They had abandoned Lizzy and Bert. Now the feelings of Lizzy's childhood came back. Abandonment is scary, and she was feeling almost sick. Bert interrupted, "Hey, I'll pay for you, and it will be okay."

'I'll pay for myself, thank you!" she spewed back.

Lizzy was so mad, and she felt betrayed by Suzanne. Because Lizzy had a lot of insecurity, she followed Bert around not wanting to be all alone. All he wanted to do, however, was to shoot guns in the galleries. This was something Lizzy detested, but she never said anything. She was not sure how the atmosphere changed, but he grabbed her hand and asked if she wanted to go on some rides. Anything would be better than watching him shoot guns, so she accepted the invitation and off they went.

She could see that the guy wasn't horrible or anything, but she just did not want to be with him. She accepted the fact that she had no choice and supposed that he enjoyed that part of it. By the end of the day Lizzy thought that Bert was alright, and not surprisingly, he told Lizzy that he loved her. She was confused by that behavior, but at the same time flattered. He appeared harmless and kind, and she went with all of it because of her deep-rooted insecurities.

After getting back to campus the next week she realized that Bert had brought out feelings of insecurity and dependency in her that she was somewhat prone to due to her past life experiences. Bert seemed to want to control every minute of her day too. He would call her at all hours of the night to talk. Lizzy's grades were sliding because he wanted to spend time with her all afternoon and well into the night. She never questioned Bert about his classes or why Bert never studied. He made her feel like he needed her more than anything on earth, and she liked that. Her roommate detested him because he always called when they were asleep. By then Bert started telling other people that they were getting married. That was a surprise to Lizzy, and yet with her codependency, she let it ride.

She was upset about the marriage announcement, and she told him he needed to remain quiet about that until she was ready to talk about it. The truth was, Lizzy had a date with one of the guys from the singing group the next night. She really liked Donald. He was studying to be a pastor, and he was very kind and a bit quiet. He would come over to the dorm sometimes, and they would sit in the dining area and drink coffee and eat ginger snaps. It was great fellowship as they discussed the scriptures and their friendship was growing.

Now, the night had come for the date, and Donald picked her up at the front door of the dormitory. He seemed a little preoccupied that night. As they arrived at the restaurant, Donald asked her to order her meal and then he ordered his. However, before the meal came, she could see that something was disturbing him.

"Donald, what's wrong? You are extremely quiet even for you."

"Are you engaged to be married?" he asked disappointedly.

"Where did you hear that?" she replied shocked.

"From Bert," he answered shortly.

"Well, that is *his idea*. He never asked me," she answered quickly.

She could see the pain in Donald's face. And then she became angrier than she had been in years. Not at Donald, but at Bert. "I will be having a discussion with him. He has no right to go around saying such things," she spouted.

The food came, and both of them picked at their plates in silence. Afterward, Donald took Lizzy home and dropped her off at the dorm. She could tell he was not happy at all. She found out from one of the group members that he had purchased an engagement ring for her, and had hoped to ask her to marry him that night. Lizzy was very disturbed by that news and it broke her heart.

As soon as she walked into her room the phone rang. "Hello...oh, it's you!" It was as if Bert was stalking her. "I do not want to ever speak to you again Bert Hanks. You are a liar, and you told Donald that we were getting married, and you never really asked me and...well, never mind!"

"I did not tell Donald that! It must have been my roommate. He knew about it." Bert tried to cover up.

"No, he described you to a tee....he said it was you...he knows who you are! Good-bye!" Then she slammed down the receiver.

Bert became very angry at his inability to manipulate Lizzy anymore. He did not know what he was going to. Bert truly loved her, but mainly because

165

he could control her. Or, he thought that he could. He walked outside, and as Bert neared the parking lot of Lizzy's dorm, he paced back and forth and looked up at Lizzy's room. He knew she was hurt and she probably would never speak to him again. As Bert walked by a stop sign, he pulled his fist back and hit it. In his anger he had broken his hand.

Lizzy got word of what he had done, and that scared her all the more. His violence was coming out, and she thought, "*For a preachers' son he sure had a hefty amount of anger in him.*"

A few days later, Bert came up to her in the cafeteria and sat down across from her at the table. "Hey, how are you?" he asked as if nothing had happened.

Lizzy noticed Bert's right hand all bandaged up and looked down at it. "I got angry the other night. Mainly because I do not like people spreading lies about me. I did not tell anyone about us, Lizzy. I kept that promise. It is just that I do not want to lose you over something as silly as this. Does it matter how Donald found out…really? I love you, and I want to marry you."

Lizzy could not understand the grip this man had on her. There was something wrong with him and she knew it. Yet she felt like if she stayed his friend, or his fiancé like he wanted, that she could help him find himself and be set free from whatever his troubled soul was chained to.

She just put her head down, prayed silently for her food, and then looked up. "I can forgive you, but you are going to have to work hard to build my trust again."

The following week she had juries in the music department. She had three songs to prepare for the judges, and she told Bert to let her alone so that she could pass her music juries. He still called all hours of the night and kept showing up wherever she was on campus. She began to think he must really care about her or he would not be acting this way. The day before juries he ran up to her and handed her some flowers…flowers he had picked from the campus gardens… the ones that bore a sign that said, "Do NOT Pick" on a stake placed beside them. She thanked him, and when she got into the building, she trashed them.

It seemed liked rules for everyone else did not apply to Bert. He got by all of the time doing unacceptable things without any consequences. She still did not ask how his classes were going because she soon figured out that he wasn't in classes. Her grades had slipped some because of the constant interruptions by Bert. She never understood why she was drawn to save him…but she was.

One night, about 2:30 a.m. the phone rang. When she answered, he said, "If you are going to marry a minister, you are going to have to learn how to wake up in the middle of the night, at any time."

Lizzy never once thought about how he never slept. But later she realized that he must sleep all day while she went to classes, so he was never tired.

Lizzy told him she would marry him, but she did not even know why she had agreed to doing so. Lizzy assumed it was her insecurity and him making her feel like he could never make it through life without her. He said that he would rather die than not have her as his wife. She felt like something was controlling her, causing her to stay connected with this guy, but she never put two and two together until many years later. Lizzy wanted to be in love, and so she made up her mind that she was going to be in love, regardless. By the end of the semester, she had agreed to go home to California with him to meet his parents. Afterward, he was to fly out to Florida to become a missionary at Harley's church. The following week Lizzy flew out to Keystone Heights to meet up with the Director of Evangelism teams for the state. She had been accepted to be on the summer evangelism teams, and she was so excited. Lizzy was the only applicant from out of state ever allowed on the Florida evangelism teams. She traveled all summer long with two guys....Larry, the music man, Lonnie the preacher, and herself as the fellowship director. It was a great experience. Only one thing.....she could see something developing that was wrong, but she had no power to bring it to an end.

Every time they arrived at a different church, the pastor or secretary would often ask, "Are you, Lizzy? If you are, you need to call Bert, because he has been calling here all day long asking for you."

She then recalled that she had given him her summer itinerary. He knew every church that she was going to be at that summer. She realized now that it was a grave mistake.

"I'm so sorry," Lizzy sheepishly responded. She would then call him and let him know she had made it to the next meeting place. Lizzy knew now that Larry and Lonnie were getting irritated at Bert's behavior, but they never said anything about it. She wrote Bert every day, and any money she made through love offerings given to the team, she sent on to Bert. He convinced her that he would put it in a bank and that Lizzy could get her money out after the summer months were over. Like a fool, she honestly believed him. She kept a very minimal amount out for toiletries and sent the rest onward as he requested.

After the summer ended, Bert had made arrangements for Lizzy to stay with a family in West Palm because they went to his church. Lizzy felt as if she had no say so in the matter at all. And the money...well, Bert insisted he needed it to live on while he was in West Palm, so he knew she would not mind. There was absolutely none of her money left. He had squandered all $2,600.00 of it. She did not know what to do but to follow his instructions. After all, they were going to get married that Christmas, and she thought he was just doing what was best for both of them. Lizzy was ashamed and irritated, and once again, she felt all alone. She had told Gary and Debbie that she would be back home after the summer teams concluded, and now Lizzy had no money for the trip, and she was too prideful to tell them what was actually going on.

Before she went on evangelism teams, she had found room in her heart to completely forgive Gary for his behavior and she realized that something had changed in him too. Maybe he had a spiritual encounter that enabled him to grow more in the Lord and realize that his previous actions toward her were out of line. Lizzy realized that no matter what someone did for a living, that people are just people and that no person is perfect. She also knew she had faults of her own and that she was struggling to overcome challenges in her life, as well. This left no room for her to remain judgmental of others if they truly showed repentance, and Gary had done just that. Debbie never knew anything about it. So, when she would go home to visit the family, she usually just visited with Debbie and Allen. Their relationship had been reconciled and she knew that she had forgiven Gary completely. She was so grateful that God had taught her to do that, and though she was soaring spiritually, emotionally she remained in bondage because of Bert's actions.

Due to their engagement, the plan was to go back to Oklahoma for the wedding in December, but now Bert was asking if they could move the wedding to Florida. Gary was going to do the wedding, but now Bert wanted his pastor father to perform the wedding. She had no real say so in the matter. Lizzy had no way to get home for the wedding anyway, and that was mainly due to him squandering her money, so all she could say was "Why not?"

Bert had finally found a way to sever her relationship with Gary and Debbie and the rest of her family and friends. She never realized how very controlling he indeed was. Lizzy hid behind her faith and just told others that this was God's will for her life. It sounded spiritual enough, but she did not think those who knew her well swallowed the deceit.

Suddenly, Bert announced to her that they were getting married in October instead of December. It was nothing that was discussed. It was presented as a more reasonable time for his father to come down and perform the ceremony, and so that was it. She had no money for a wedding, and she bought a used dress for $20.00. The man from the family she stayed with agreed to give her away as the *father of the bride*. She liked Abel, but he was not a real father figure in her life. Her brother Allen did manage to come to the wedding and surprise her. She had no one to help plan the wedding with, so she had actually forgotten all about the reception, except for the cake. Suzanne's mother agreed to make the cake as a kind gesture, and Lizzy thanked her immensely for the beautiful gift. Lizzy called the ladies at the church crying the very day of her wedding. She was so upset, and they went into high gear and said, "Do not worry Lizzy. We will get the reception hall all ready for you. Don't be upset. It will be fine."

Actually, the day of the wedding, she thought of calling Gary and Debbie and asking if they would help her fly home. She just did not feel that she could go through with marrying Bert, but she felt so trapped. She knew what others expected of her, and she did not want to let them down, even if it meant marrying a man she really did not love.

Her mind went back to the ill-prepared reception hall. What else could she do? She trusted the ladies would handle all of it, and they did. Bert was now the youth pastor at the church, so they were glad to pitch in. She convinced herself that everything would be just fine and that getting married was the wise thing and that it must have been God's will because she had no other options. Looking back, she realized that her excuses were not a reason to get married, but she was young, and yes, immature emotionally for her age.

They married without a hitch and spent two days at Disneyworld before coming back to Bert's apartment. After returning, Bert's friend who took wedding pictures had lost all of the film cartridges. They had no pictures of the event, whatsoever. She thought something was wrong with her when she wasn't even upset by his incompetence. Lizzy did not even know what to do about birth control, and so she spoke with Bert's mother about it, who suggested at that late date to purchase something over the counter. She was nowhere near ready to get married, much less have children, but on their honeymoon Lizzy had gotten pregnant, and nine months later she gave birth to their first son Adam.

By then they had moved three times. Once from their first apartment, and then to another apartment when Bert took a job at another church. Lizzy was not happy about all the changes that took place on a consistent basis, but she took her wedding vows seriously and that mean that she would have to honor her husband's wishes. After moving twice, they then moved into a small house that was closer to that church the very week Adam was born. It had already been an eventful pregnancy, with toxemia and bed rest, and Lizzy was exhausted. She had tried to be the kind of wife she thought Bert wanted, but his constant making fun of her cooking and her mannerisms was wearing her down. It seemed she could do nothing right, and Bert was a constantly there to remind her of her shortcomings. She then began to rationalize it. After all, maybe she was not as smart as she thought she once was, or capable of doing anything right. By then she was glad Bert had taken control of everything in their lives.

Adam was five days old when Bert went off on a retreat with the youth from the church, leaving her home alone with their first born child and the responsibilities of unpacking. The church always came first and so it was throughout their entire marriage. Right before he went, he brought home a new puppy and said that it would keep her company. Lizzy knew that she did not need that kind of company. That puppy cried all day and night, and Adam had problems nursing, sleeping, and everything.

That same week, Lizzy opened up a book on how to give a baby a bath and stood it up beside the kitchen sink. Lizzy got the water ready and went to get Adam. Gently undressing him, she put him on the towel lying on the counter and started bathing him the best way she knew how. That poor child was just screaming at a high pitch cry. Adam and Lizzy both cried, and they went back and forth like that for several minutes until an angel appeared. Well, she wasn't an actual angel, but it was Harriet, a woman who had become very motherly to Lizzy during her time in West Palm.

She came inside after Lizzy hollered when she heard a knock at the front door and said, "Come on in!"

Harriet took one look at Lizzy and then at Adam and asked, "Can I help?"

Lizzy was relieved when she took over the duties. She began bathing Adam without the use of the baby manual and Adam seemed to like her, as well as the bath. Harriet showed Lizzy how to bathe him and how to care for him. Lizzy did not have a house phone because Bert had not paid the bill, though he insisted that he had. This became the norm throughout their marriage. It would have been helpful to be able to call Harriet in moments like this. Lizzy thanked Harriet for the much needed help as she put Adam to sleep. Harriet said that she would be back the next day to check on Lizzy. Lizzy must have looked so helpless, and frankly, she was.

Lizzy had no car, no phone and no way to communicate with anyone. She spent many years like this after marrying Bert. It was another way to keep Lizzy isolated and to remain in complete control of her life. When he wanted to talk to his parents, he would call home collect from a pay phone, and that was two or three times a week. He said to her, "My family is your family now. You will have to get used to calling my folks mom and dad."

When Lizzy thought about the scripture passage in Ephesians 5:31 that read, "*For this reason a man will leave his father and mother and be united to his wife, and the two will become one flesh,*" she realized immediately that Bert was always going to cling to his parents.

As if things couldn't get any worse at the moment, Bert, during that youth retreat, had severely injured his knee and now needed surgery. Harriet had received a call from the pastor at the church and drove over to let Lizzy know. They gathered the baby up, and Harriet took them to the hospital. Lizzy was in no shape to go through this, but here she was at the hospital waiting for Bert's surgery to be performed.

Harriet asked, "Lizzy, would it be helpful if I took Adam with me to my house and took care of him for a few days while you stay here with Bert? It really would not be much trouble, and I would be happy to do it for you," she smiled.

"I don't know…are you sure it is okay with a newborn to be away from his mother that long?" she asked.

"It's better than trying to stay in a hospital with him dear. I know the Lord understands. We just have to give it to Him."

At that, Lizzy agreed that it would be a better circumstance for her and Adam, and so she snuggled her little boy and told him to be good for Grandma Harriet. Harriet had stepped in like a grandmother, and she seemed proud to be called Adam's grandmother too.

"You can call anytime dear and check on us. Please try to not to worry and try to rest as much as you can while you are up here. You look very pale Lizzy," Harriet added.

Everyone at church, and now Harriet kept saying that she looked pale. The lack of rest and proper nutrition wasn't helping. Before she left, she gave the dog half a bag of dog food so he would not be hungry. She knew he would be howling in the garage, but she couldn't do a thing about it. Not now anyway.

After the surgery, Bert was in the hospital for a few more days. Harriet decided to loan Lizzy her car so that she could go back and forth between home and the hospital. Meanwhile, Lizzy had awakened one morning to pounding on the front door. She could see through the peephole of the door that it was a policeman. She was afraid to answer the door, being that she had received notice while Bert was in the hospital that they were being evicted. This would be the first of many times throughout their marriage that a crisis would come upon them in such a manner. Lizzy could see the policeman trying to look inside the windows, and so she hid in the dark hallway. She was so afraid, and Lizzy knew something was really wrong, but she could not call anyone, and she had to protect Adam.

The next day she went to the hospital to get Bert and then when they came back home she told him what was going on with the police. Bert claimed that he knew nothing about it and that he had paid the rent the week before he left for the youth retreat. It was another lie. Lizzy knew that to be true, because she had caught Bert in many lies before. They usually had no phone, and often, the electricity would be turned off too. Her husband would always claim innocence or ignorance. A few weeks later his parents had sent them money to come to California and stay with them until they could get a place of their own. For the next few weeks, life was miserable. Every night, multiple times in the night, Lizzy had to get up and make the dog shut up. He would start howling, and then the baby would awaken. After that Bert always needed something, a pillow or medication, or water, and she was going insane with no sleep, not eating, and feeling trapped, desperate, and once again, all alone.

They sold off everything they had acquired, which wasn't a great deal, and took the bare essentials in the back of a station wagon that they were making payments on. Well, at least Lizzy was told Bert was making payments on it. They were able to give the puppy away to someone who really wanted him and could take better care of him. They stayed with his folks for several weeks, and then Bert's cousin in Washington State called. He said that they could come there and that Bert could look for a job. So Lizzy, Bert, and Adam moved into his cousin's home and Bert got a job working for a car parts place. It would not matter much, because he would soon quit. He did that a lot, always saying how it was the company's fault or whatever. Bert never took into consideration that he had a family to provide for when he quit his jobs. He just got mad and walked out on so many different jobs throughout the years. This was due to his inability to be held accountable for anything.

More than one pastor throughout the years queried Lizzy about her husbands' strange behavior. So she knew that she wasn't alone in her thinking that something was terribly wrong with him. She just did not know what she could possibly do about it. She could not call any family members and tell them about the situation because she was estranged from all of them. She had way too much pride for that. She could not talk to anyone about his behavior, or he would find out, and when he showed anger, it was terrifying to her. At times he would push his fist through a wall, or take Lizzy by her arms and shake her while he yelled at her inability to do anything.

Years passed, and they continued to move excessively. There was always *greener grass on the other side of the fence* is how Bert would put it. She gave birth to their second son in Washington State, then they moved immediately to Oregon for a part-time church position. She was already eight months pregnant with her third son when they moved again and he was born prematurely. Two months after he was born Bert started looking for another move, now to Oklahoma. They never stayed anywhere very long, and it was a puzzle to Lizzy as to why.

Bert had taken a job at a church in Beaver, Oklahoma. Again, he was gone all day, and she had three children to care for in a tiny trailer house.

During that time, she had begun writing music, and she was really feeling confident about her songs. She had sung one at their new church, and the pastor had requested for her to sing it again at the night service.

As she continued to write, Bert made a comment, *"You better let me play that for you 'cause you're gonna ruin it.*" From that time on, whenever she sang, he insisted he had to play and to sing harmony with her because he did not want all of the attention to be on his wife.

The new church paid for their rent and a telephone. She was grateful for that because she knew it would not get turned off, or that they would lose their home again. However, when Bert was home, he was either taking long baths or watching television and entirely ignoring the family. He was emotionally disconnected and it did not seem to bother him in the least.

His boys hungered for their father's attention, but he would pat them on the top of their heads like a dog and say, "Go to mama."

A few weeks passed, and Bert was asked to go hunting overnight by some of the men at church. By that time, Lizzy did not care whether he went or stayed since she had all the responsibilities with the children and taking care of the home, anyway. However, something happened to her that had not occurred in decades. After she got the children down for a nap, she closed her eyes and she had a vision. She could see Bert and that he was walking in an open field, and that he was limping. All that she could tell was that he was using a stick to help assist himself in walking. There was no way to get in touch with him or the men that had gone with them, but they would be home the following day, so she would have to wait to see what happened.

The next afternoon, Bert walked into the living room limping, just as she had seen in that vision. "Are you okay?" she asked.

"Yes, I put my foot down in an open hole in the field that we were walking in yesterday, and it twisted, wrenching my bad knee again. I think it will be okay, but I will need to get my knee brace out and wear it for a few weeks," Bert explained.

177

Lizzy told him that she knew he had been injured and that she had a vision of it. He shrugged it off and said, "That's nice dear." Then he asked her for dinner in the living room that night so that he could prop up his leg. The strain of keeping three children all by herself and now taking care of a husband full-time for a few weeks was starting to get to her.

Lizzy started not feeling like herself. All that she knew was that she was weak and not up to doing all of the things expected of her on a day to day basis. Lizzy also had frequent migraines, something Bert had no sympathy about whatsoever. She started getting migraines when she turned twenty one. The doctor at that time had given her medication for them, but though the medicine worked, it left her unable to do much for several hours. She had to sleep off the drugs. Bert did not like her lying in bed with migraines. He took her medicine and flushed it down the toilet. Bert told her she was addicted and that she was making it all up to get out of housework and from taking care of the family. She had remembered his reaction to her getting ill before, and so she dreaded if anything was serious this time and what his response would be.

Lizzy made a doctor's appointment, and one of the women in the church asked if she could watch the children for her when she had to go. She was very grateful for that.

As she walked into the doctor's office that day, the doctor did a complete physical on her. He also drew blood so that he could run several lab tests.

The doctor informed her, "Mrs. Hanks, I will call you in a few days with the results, but I think your body is under an immense amount of stress. A short getaway may be a great solution for you if you can manage it."

There was no way that Bert was going to let her go anywhere alone, but that is what the doctor was implying. She just remained quiet about all of it and went on not feeling well most days.

Several weeks later, after all the children had gone to bed, she walked in on Bert while he was taking one of his baths and he was reading a Playboy magazine. That was enough for her to do whatever she could to get away from this deceitful man. He had no idea that she had seen him. This was a good thing because she could put her plan in motion and she did. She had just discovered that her brother Allen was living in Tinsley, Oklahoma at that time and she called him and told him of her dilemma.

She finally spilled the beans enough, not everything, but enough for him to ask, "Do you want me to come to get you, Sis? I will! You tell me when and I will be there."

That is all it took. Lizzy thought about it and planned her escape for three days later, knowing that Bert would be at church all day. She planned on calling a babysitter for that day, and when the children were gone, Allen could come and pick her up. She could then escape. It tore at her heart to leave her sons behind, but she was so beat down, so lifeless, and so hopeless.....she would be no help to them right now. She also had no way of providing for them. Bert had worn her down to nothing while constantly telling her that she was useless.

The day came and also the babysitter, who was a sweet lady in the church that had agreed to pick up the children. She was going to bring them back when Bert got home. As the lady and her sons drove away, she wept and wept, not knowing when she would ever see her precious children again. Lizzy had no place to keep them at Allen's, and she needed to get a full-time job to support herself. After that, she would hopefully be able to provide for them.

Allen came, and she loaded her belongings in the car and left and never looked back. While she was in Tinsley, she got a full-time job, began supporting herself and was paying rent for a room. The house belonged to a seemingly friendly couple. She was missing her children terribly, but she did not know what she could possibly do. By then, Lizzy and Bert had divorced. They both had custody of the children, but she lived too far away to see them. He moved way south in Oklahoma at the time of her departure, taking yet another part-time ministry job at a church and pretending all was well.

After she moved to Tinsley with Allen, she called Jean and told her what had happened. Allen had just seen Jean and Johnathan a few months prior. When she explained what had happened to her and Bert, Jean said, "Honey, I am glad you are not with him anymore. We just never felt right about him, especially when we heard from Debbie everything that was going on."

Lizzy was surprised that Gary and Debbie knew anything, but she found out that the pastor in Oklahoma knew Gary and that he had spoken to him about Bert and Lizzy.

Lizzy had rented her room from a couple in her new town. Six months had passed and she was working full time and making a pretty decent living. She really missed her boys, but at that time she had no idea just where Bert and the boys were living. Also, by this time, David the husband of the couple where she lived had started making advances towards Lizzy, and she would push him away. He had a bad temper too, and she was already making plans of getting out of the house as soon as she could. David forced himself sexually on her one night all while holding a gun to her throat. He became very controlling of her time and would show up at her job, as they both worked at the mall. Now, she felt trapped once again.

Lizzy started making plans on how to get away from David and his wife without them knowing. After a week had gone by, Lizzy planned an escape. She just discovered where Bert had been living, and she called him at his work because he had no home phone. Lizzy asked if she could visit the children. He agreed to her coming and so she planned her escape.

Before leaving, she packed up and got her vehicle loaded, but David came home early that day. He asked, "Where do you think that you are going?" David was a cop, so he placed his hand on his side arm when he posed the question.

Lizzy felt the anxiety rise up in her but answered nonchalantly, "I am going to visit my kids."

He was not at all too happy about it, but his wife Cynthia had just driven up into the driveway. Now David could not make a big scene over Lizzy's decision, because Cynthia had no idea what he had done to Lizzy. Lizzy was grateful for her timing.

She left her mother's china cabinet and the hope chest that Max had made her when she was a little girl behind in their home. She had just picked up the items because she had gone to visit Debbie and Gary and they said that they were holding them for her all this time. She thought she could come to pick them up one night when David's wife Cynthia was home. He would not make such a big fuss about it then.

When she arrived in southern Oklahoma, Bert had brought the children to a local park. They played together and then they all went out to eat at a local restaurant.

Bert asked, "How are you doing?"

"I am fine, I really miss the kids though." Lizzy admitted.

"Well, you are welcome home whenever you want to come home. I know that I messed up pretty bad, but I am not that same person you left in Beaver," he gently replied.

Lizzy was quiet. She did notice something different, but because of the way her gut led her in the last year…she could not trust herself anymore.

Noticing her look of debate, he added, "You'll pray about it?"

Lizzy nodded and agreed to do that. She was going to stay in the area for a week. During that time they went on family outings, and that had become a priority. Bert brought her flowers and seemed to be a changed man. The local pastor said that Bert had been counseling with him and that he believed Bert had changed. When Lizzy looked at her options, going back to the rented room or staying with her kids, she decided to move to where Bert and the children were. However, Bert said that he was moving back to California again to his parent's house for a short while, but that Lizzy was welcome. She knew then that she had no love for the man, but she loved her children…so she agreed to go. The truth was that Bert had just quit his job again over something petty. But she did not know that until a few months later.

Before they moved Brother Mike came over and said, "You two need to stop living in sin," he teased. I can marry you tomorrow night at the church if you are willing."

Bert said, "We'll be there." So that was that.

Afterward, she had to help pack up again for yet another move. On the way out of the state, they did go by David and Cynthia's and Lizzy got her hope chest, but left the cabinet behind. There was no room for it. David was livid but he could do nothing about it. She was glad to be out of his control, yet she understood fully that she had basically jumped from one frying pan into another one again.

Bert and Lizzy moved back to California and then Washington State once again. Bert went from church to church getting worship pastor jobs. Lizzy got pregnant again with their little girl. Lizzy was so excited. She got the nursery all ready as they had actually bought a home. It was a mobile home, but they were making monthly payments on it. She dressed up the nursery for a little girl. Meanwhile, Bert had decided to go into business with another man and sell mobile homes. Something did not sound right, but once Bert made up his mind to do something, that was it. No one dared try to convince him differently. It wasn't long before their home was foreclosed on and Bert promised to get them another one as soon as possible. He had bought a brand new top of the line luxury car though. He said that it belonged to the business. Lizzy thought to herself, *"The business that did not help him save his house?"*

It did not matter, because Bert never stayed long anywhere and Lizzy could never figure out why they had to move so much. And as expected, the following months brought a few more moves, and then another long haul out of state and back to Oklahoma, as the vicious circle continued. There was one more separation, and then another agreement to live together again. No matter how hard Lizzy tried to get away from this man, he always sucked her into giving in and moving back together with him.

During their time in Illinois, Bert was arrested for passing a hot check, and Lizzy had to go bail him out of jail. All of a sudden Bert said they needed to move to Arkansas. There was nobody and no job in Arkansas, but whenever he got a whim to move, she had to go along for the ride. They moved there and eventually he took a pastorate at a small church. By then, Bert's parents had moved to Arkansas too, and they did not live too far away. During that pastorate, Bert once again got caught passing a hot check, and he was arrested. This time he called his father to get him out of jail, and the whole church knew about it. A lady in the church worked for the bank where he passed the bad check, and she had informed the deacons at their church. It was an embarrassing time for Bert and the entire family. Although Bert kept his pastorate, things never were the same. Shortly afterward, Bert started looking again, and that meant a move was on the horizon.

Bert had a cousin in Colorado, and they invited Bert and Lizzy and the family to come out for a vacation. Bert took them up on the offer and two days before they left for the trip, Bert drove up in a new family van. He said that he had just bought it. Since Lizzy had no control of the money, she had no idea if Bert had actually bought it or not. More than one vehicle had been repossessed during their marriage, and Bert would always insist that he had paid the bill. He would never man up and confess about anything. She dared not even ask about this vehicle, and the children were all excited, so she let it slide.

The next morning they loaded up and took off. The family slept in the van the first night on the trip, and the second night, they were in Colorado. They stayed with Bert's cousin and somehow in the midst of that visit, Bert had manipulated yet another congregation to take him as their pastor. It was unbelievable to Lizzy, but each time they moved she secretly hoped that Bert would find a church home and stay there. Well, things were looking promising at the church, until Bert asked the church to sell the parsonage and pay for them to rent a bigger house. The church could not afford that, but they sold it and struggled to pay for their rent on a month to month basis. Comments would get back to Lizzy through members of the congregation that Bert wasn't following church procedures. The church treasurer was not happy with Bert at all. Lizzy did not know much about what was going on, but the low grumble in the congregation was getting louder and louder.

Bert was also buying stuff in the church's name without their approval. Lizzy had actually developed a close relationship with a few women in the church. One of her best friends was Becky. Becky seemed to understand the undertones in Lizzy and Bert's marriage without Lizzy ever saying a word. Becky would come over and pick Lizzy up so that they could visit. When Lizzy would go over to Becky's home, Bert would call every twenty minutes asking if she was coming home yet. Eventually, Becky would say, *"I better get you back home."*

It was becoming more evident to Lizzy now that this was a huge problem and others were picking up on it too. Also, when Bert preached, he would always look for sermon examples that would humiliate Lizzy. In his illustrations, she would always be a bad example of how not to do something. However, if church members called in the middle of the night, mainly if they were in a hospital, he would send Lizzy. He would moan and say, "I don't do hospitals."

Lizzy eventually got a full-time job as an Office Manager at a manufacturing plant and was quickly promoted to General Manager in a matter of months. Her new boss, Avery, was about ten years younger, but very keen on business and owned the company she was working for. Lizzy was the only woman in the manufacturing plant, but Avery would leave her weeks at a time to run the place. He trusted her, and she never let him down.

Many things had transpired in the church within the following year, as the congregation purchased a new building, changed its name and things appeared to be getting better. The children were now all teenagers and so their lives were busy as well.

One night, when Lizzy could not sleep, she came out of the downstairs bedroom to find Bert watching an X-rated video. She knew he rented movies, but he never showed her the names, and always said he would wait until she went to bed to watch them because they were horror movies and he knew she did not like them. On another occasion, when Lizzy came out of the bedroom, Bert was upstairs on the computer and talking to someone.

Bert said, "I think your body is beautiful… are you kidding me?" to whomever he had on the other end of the phone.

Lizzy heard every word, and he had no idea that she was half way up the stairs within hearing distance. She just stood there and listened to him make plans to get together with the woman soon. She slowly backed down the stairs and went into her bedroom and cried out to God, "Lord, I do not know how much more of this I am supposed to take. Please give me wisdom. I don't want to run but I need out, and I need help! Amen."

A few nights later Lizzy awoke at 1:00 a.m. to find that her husband Bert was nowhere in the house to be seen. She looked in the den and the computer room. When Lizzy looked outside the front window, his SUV was gone. She knew deep down what was going on but did not want to admit to it. Lizzy was up for the rest of the night. She pretended she was asleep when he snuck into the bedroom quietly and got in bed. It was four-thirty in the morning.

As soon as he got settled, she asked, "Where have you been?"

Startled he replied, "Honey, I was up on the computer preparing Sunday's sermon, that's all."

"No, you were not. I went up there at one o' clock in the morning and looked for you. Your vehicle was gone…so where have you been?"

Realizing he had been caught lying again, "Well, honey. I am a pastor, and sometimes I cannot share with you what is happening to anyone in the congregation. You know that," he half smiled.

Lizzy turned over without a word and pretended she was going to sleep, but she was weeping silently inside. When Bert got up to take a shower that next morning, she looked in his wallet to see if she could find out any information on his shenanigans, and found a wad of cash so big she did not know what to think. He always had money, but not money like this. *"Was he dealing drugs, or what? It would certainly explain his random mood swings."* These were thoughts she kept to herself. On her pay days he would show up as if on cue, and take her check and say he was depositing it in the bank. She never had more than five dollars at a time in her purse. They had bought a house a year before, and now she was hoping that he was making the payments because she could not reason as to why he carried thousands of dollars of cash in his wallet.

That night the arguments ensued. In the midst, Bert forced himself sexually on Lizzy. She was profoundly wounded and afterward, she got up, went to the bathroom and got sick to her stomach. If there ever had been any kind of love between them, he had successfully destroyed every ounce of it.

Lizzy had enough. She could not stand to be in the house with the same man who stood behind the pulpit asking others to repent yet never changed his own evil ways. People actually liked him because they did not know the Bert that Lizzy knew. One day she told him that she was aware of his Playboy magazines and movies and the large bundles of cash in his wallet.

Lizzy got brave enough to insist, "You need to come clean now, or that's it!"

What happened next was something she never thought could happen. Bert got very angry with her. She was standing at the top of the stairs, and he shook her so hard and then just let her fall back as she lost her balance.

Bert yelled, "You don't know anything Lizzy...you're crazy!"

After she fell, the kids that were in the basement asked what happened. Before she could even answer Bert replied, "Oh, your mother just lost her balance on the stairs...right dear?"

Because Lizzy had confronted Bert, he started carrying his gun. In fact, one night he was in bed, and she was laying there reading, and he took his gun out and pointed it right at her. He knew all the while that she was terrified of guns and he used it as another form of control.

"Don't worry honey, it's not loaded," he said as he tripped the trigger. The gun was pointed at Lizzy's head. She began to sweat and then weep. He laughed it off and growled at her, "You need to get a grip!"

Bert began to feel insecure because Lizzy did not want to have sexual relations with him anymore. That was because the previous month before, she had actually contracted a sexually transmitted disease from him and had to take medication to get over it. Lizzy told Bert that he needed to take the medicine too. The truth was, she was so naïve about all of that, and she did not understand what the nurse was saying to her until way after the fact. The medical staff is never allowed to tell or insinuate that a spouse is unfaithful. They simply said that it was sexually transmitted disease.

Bert had enough rejection from Lizzy and started saying things out loud in front of the kids. "If you leave me Lizzy, I'll kill myself!" Then he would carry his gun openly to the car and act like he was leaving.

It terrified the children, and her youngest son Aaron said, "Mom, do something...he is going to kill himself!!"

Lizzy told Aaron, "Don't worry honey, he will never do it."

That made Lizzy appear heartless and cold in front of her children. They had no idea the torment Bert had put her through all those years. Now, he was turning their children against her, and it was more than she could bear.

8

The Last Straw

*Time flies over us but leaves it's
shadow behind –Nathanial Hawthorne*

The following morning Bert informed Lizzy that he would be taking her to work and picking her up from now on. The tension between them had become so horrible that all they did was bicker. He was now, once again, smothering her in every area of her life. She withdrew inside of herself because she did not know how to defend herself against his actions. He called her job about every hour to check on her. Sometimes, he would just show up periodically throughout the day. He was trying his hardest to get her fired, but his antics were only making her boss mad at him, not Lizzy. Bert also insisted that she was not going to drive anywhere by herself, and that he would take her wherever she needed to go. So, he would drop her off at work in the morning, and call five minutes before picking her back up at the end of the day, just to let her know that she had better be ready.

All that time, he was packing a gun. Lizzy had no idea why he started carrying that gun, but she was sure it wasn't for a good reason. One late afternoon, when Avery and Lizzy were working up until the clock, Bert called.

Lizzy picked up the phone, "You better be ready. I will be there shortly!" Then the receiver went dead.

That was Bert's usual way of warning her that he was not going to wait one minute in the parking lot for her. What Bert did not know is that Avery had picked up the same extension and heard the entire conversation.

Immediately Avery came rushing into her office. "Are you okay Lizzy?"

Lizzy looked at him and put on a fake smile, "I'm fine."

He got serious, "No, you're not. I heard that conversation. I know more than you think I know Lizzy. Do you need help?"

Lizzy did not know how to respond. She just started crying. "I don't know what to do Avery. He is getting more violent as time passes and I have done nothing but try to get him to see the truth."

"I know what to do." Avery answered. "Do you want help? That is all I am asking." He waited for her reply.

Lizzy paused and then nodded, "Yes."

"Listen closely, as we do not have much time. Turn around right now, and cut yourself a check for five-hundred dollars. Afterward, go out the back way, tell Pete to give you his cell phone and the keys to the company van. Find a hotel over the weekend, and I will see you Monday," Avery persisted. "All that I want you to do is call me and tell me that you are okay. Understand?"

"What if Bert comes in here? And Avery…, he is packing a gun!!" Lizzy cried.

"I know he is packing, and that is why I have been packing my gun for three weeks." He pulled back his Levi shirt and showed her his gun mounted on his side belt. I told you that *I know more than you think I know Lizzy*. Now hurry!"

Lizzy cut herself a check and walked out the back way to retrieve the phone from Pete and the van keys, and then she asked Pete to go see Avery. Pete smiled and said, "Sure thing boss. Have a lovely weekend!"

"You too Pete…see you Monday."

Just as Lizzy pulled out with the company van, she could see Bert pull in to the front of the office building. She worried for Avery and all of the crew there, but Avery had also mentioned, "Lizzy there are sixteen men here…I think we can handle a wolf in sheep's clothing. Don't worry."

As she drove across the street to the bank and cashed the check, she could see Bert get out of his vehicle and go inside. That is all she had seen. By then Lizzy was on her way down the road and headed to a hotel out of town. She knew he would be looking for her, but he would be clueless as to where she was since she was in the company van.

After she checked in to the hotel, she went straight to her room for the weekend and did nothing but order in food. She was too afraid to even go out, knowing that Bert would probably kill her if he saw her in town anywhere. It was awful to think that your husband was capable of such a crime, but it had become her reality. It brought back terrible memories from her youth, and she wondered how things had ever escalated to such a point in her life.

When Monday rolled around she was hesitant about going to work but she had called Avery, and he assured her that he was keeping guard and not to worry. She had no plans to go out that weekend after all, however, she had bought two changes of clothes at the local charity store, but otherwise, Lizzy stayed put.

By now Avery had told the crew at the shop about Bert and how dangerous he was. Avery had also told Bert that previous Friday that he did not know where Lizzy went. Bert got angry, pushed over a rack in the front office and slammed the door on the way out. Avery had actually told some local sheriffs about the incident, as well. They were good friends of his. He said, "If anything ever happens to my employees or me, Bert Hanks is responsible."

So she went on in to work that Monday, only after calling Avery to make sure things were alright.

"Lizzy, we are all keeping an eye out for Bert, so do not worry. You will be safe."

Only a few minutes after she had arrived there, Bert drove up in a moving truck. He had been parked across the street waiting until he saw her open the office door. Avery told her to stay inside. He stepped out with all of the workers lined up in front of the building.

Lizzy did as Avery suggested and stayed inside with a window view of what all was happening. Bert walked up to Avery and showed him his side belt. There was no gun.

"I came to say goodbye to Lizzy. We are moving. Me and the kids," he informed.

"I will let her know," Avery responded.

Avery signaled for Lizzy to come out. Bert looked fearful with all the workers lined up in front of the office. He knew that he was outnumbered. Lizzy came out, and Bert yelled, "Are you going with us, or staying?"

"I'm staying," she answered.

"You'll be nothing without me!" he spewed as he turned around quickly and walked away.

Lizzy could hear the children and how upset they were. He let them get out of the truck to come to say goodbye to their mother.

Adam said, "Mom, he said he would kill himself if we did not go with him. Understand?" he relayed sadly.

"Yes, I understand son. I cannot live with your Dad one more day. I love you."

All the children were visibly upset, but Lizzy had no control over the situation. Later on, she found out that Bert had stood before the church and accused Lizzy of an affair. He said he needed to resign and go move to Arkansas with his parents because his children needed a godly family around them. Out of pity for him, the entire church came over and loaded up the moving van and wished him well.

After Bert and the children drove off, one of the deacons showed up and approached Lizzy. He said, "Lizzy, God can forgive you and heal your marriage. All you have to do is repent."

"You have no idea what is happening here Robert. Please leave." And so the man left.

Lizzy, was terribly confused, as she had not done anything to repent for in her own eyes. She was protecting herself. Three weeks later, while Bert left and Lizzy stayed in town, another event surfaced that shed more light on Bert's character. The office phone rang, and it was a bank in the city looking for Bert Hanks. They said that he had written hot checks all over town and they were trying to find him.

Lizzy played it cool and said, "We do not have an employee by that name, Ma'am."

She pushed back, "We *know* that you have an employee by that name because we tracked his social security number to your business."

Lizzy calmly asked, "May I have the social security number?"

As the lady on the other end continued speaking and telling her the numerals, Lizzy began to physically shake. By then Avery was in her office and noticed her demeanor.

"Thanks for the number, ma'am. Let me do some investigating, and I will get back to you at once." Then Lizzy hung up the phone very distraught.

As she hung up, Avery stood there. "What's up Lizzy?"

"Oh Avery, I have no idea what Bert has done, but I am starting to realize the depth of his devilish deceit. I believe that he opened a bank account in

194

town with my social security number and then he wrote checks all over town that bounced. They traced that number to our plant, but they are asking for him, not me. What do I do?"

"I know what you need to do…follow me," Avery said gently.

Avery went into his office, looked through his business number rolodex and started dialing a number. "Yes, may I speak to Charles? This is Avery."

The receptionist put the connection through immediately. "Charles? I got an employee who needs some wise counsel. Can you get her in today….? You can….? Great! Oh, and send the bill to me, alright?" Avery hung up.

Avery looked at Lizzy, "You need to go in at 2:00 o'clock."

"But I can't pay for that…and you should not have to do it either," she shamefully replied.

"Oh, don't worry Lizzy. You'll pay me back. A little bit every week….but you will pay me back…so do not worry. Just get over there…okay?" he smiled.

"Yes, sir," she smiled back and thanked him for everything.

After going to see the lawyer, Charles told her the only way she would not be held responsible for the checks or any other problems associated with Bert was to divorce Bert and make him responsible for all the bills, checks and everything else. She followed legal counsel and did just that. She was so scared that she would go to jail for his actions and that he had ruined her credit. It was more than she could bear. She found out later that their home was being repossessed too for non-payment. It was for the last six months of non- payment.

One day, as she was going through the project management jobs for the plant, three men approached the office door. She recognized all of them. They were deacons from the church that Bert once pastored. It had been three months since Bert left and she had no idea why they were there, but she stood up at her desk and invited them in to have a seat.

"Please have a seat. How can I help you all?" Lizzy offered.

She looked in the oldest deacon's eyes, and he had tears welled up inside. She did not understand anything that was happening.

"Lizzy, we came to apologize to you. We know what Bert did now. The police have been to the church as he had written bad checks all over town, long before you left him that Friday. Bert had stolen that last car you all had, though he insisted that it was paid for. He also charged thousands of dollars to the church without permission and now we discovered that a woman he had an affair with came looking for him at the church. It appears everything he accused you of was exactly what he was doing."

Ben chimed in, "Lizzy, we have spoken with the church members that are left, and we want you to come back to the church. You have always been so loving and caring, and really, you are the one who has pastored us in so many ways."

"Uh...Ben....? There is no way that I can do that. I am in counseling, and I am trying to heal right now. Since you know what he has done, you know that I need a lot of healing," Lizzy exclaimed.

Tony responded, "We understand now. Bert told us that you were having an affair so that he could look spiritual and pretend that he was making wise choices for his family, when all along he was the one running around on you. We are so sorry for believing him Lizzy. Why did you not come to us and talk to us? You just disappeared," the oldest deacon sadly remarked.

"Well…. I am not trying to sound spiritual, but I truly sensed God speak to me and tell me not to try and defend myself. That he would battle for me. It has not been easy, believe me...but I am getting stronger. I know there will always be people in this town believing what they want to believe about me. I am not perfect and I have made mistakes, but God is healing me, and I am trusting Him with my future. I know now that my future will never be with Bert Hanks ever again."

The oldest deacon put his arms around her shoulders and continued, "We love you Lizzy. Can we pray for you?"

"Of course...and when you leave, please don't stop praying. Okay?" She gently smiled as a tear ran down her cheek.

At that word, the rest of the deacons stood, and Lizzy came to each of them and gave them an embrace and thanked them for their love and concern. They then laid hands on her and prayed fervently for her. After that sincere prayer, her heart felt lighter than a feather. The truth had come out, and she had been redeemed in the eyes of these godly men.

"And now let me pray for you all.....," she insisted. And so she did.

Avery came in right before the men finished praying for her, but she had no idea at the time as he slowly slipped out once he saw what they were doing. When they all left, he walked into her office again. "So, you all were having a little church in here I see," he smiled.

Avery wasn't a church-going man, but he had a healthy respect for the Lord. He was careful about his language and his actions around Lizzy as he respected her and he knew she was the real deal when it came to walking out her faith. He had seen it in action.

The week before the deacons came in to see her, one of the workers had gotten injured on the job.

He had accidentally cut his finger off, and he came running to the office for help. Lizzy called 911 and then jumped up and got a towel. The man had fallen in her office floor overtaken with the pain. She wrapped his hand up, applied pressure and started praying for him immediately. Something happened because the worker, Juan, just stopped moaning. He was completely alert, but he stopped moaning. Avery knew all about it because he had heard about the accident from Peter and came running into the office. There he found Lizzy in the floor with Juan. She asked Peter to go get ice while blood was dripping all over her and on to the floor. Regardless, she continued ministering to Juan. Lizzy also had the common sense to tell Peter to retrieve the finger from the saw blade and put it in a container with ice. Avery watched in amazement. Lizzy did not mind getting dirty if it meant she could help someone else and Avery never had forgotten that scene. During that time he was speechless and at a loss as to what to do, but not Lizzy. She was taking authority and shining in the midst of crisis. The emergency vehicle arrived and took over, but Juan did not feel any more pain. They asked if she had given him anything for pain, and Lizzy just smiled and shrugged. "We had nothing to do with it, sir."

The EMT looked puzzled, but he turned to help Juan into the ambulance and then they left. Lizzy got up, tried to clean things up the best way she could, and Avery said, "You got blood all over you. Do you want to go get checked out at the hospital too?"

It's not necessary, I know I will be fine. However, I would like to leave early now, and go get out of these clothes," she requested.

Take the rest of the day…you're a hero Lizzy!"

"I'm not a hero Avery…I just did what anybody in my place would do." she smiled.

Sometimes, when Lizzy came in early, she would play her worship music as she was working. Avery started coming in her office, and he would sit through a song and then get up and say, "Okay, I had church today," and then walk out.

Lizzy would just laugh, but she kept praying that one day, he would find Jesus. She knew that God had put Avery in her life too. Avery admitted later on that he had been keeping a notebook of the days Lizzy would show up distressed, bruised on her upper arms and other things. He had already warned his friend, a police officer about Bert and what he suspected of him, as well. That is why when Bert called that last time and basically talked to Lizzy like she was a dog, Avery had-had enough.

Lizzy was now doing very well. She had been in counseling for two years. When she started seeing Sharon Wright at her new church downtown for counseling, it helped Lizzy so much. In the beginning, she was not sure how Bert pulled it off, but he found out she was in counseling at that church and he called Sharon and grilled her over the phone about Lizzy. Sharon told Bert that she could not say anything about anyone she was counseling and that he needed to go get help for himself.

Sharon almost laughed, "Bert tried to sound all authoritative calling himself a pastor, but I put him in his place and assured him that he did not have a right to stand on when it came to any of my clients."

During counseling, a lot of things came out. Sharon told Lizzy that the problems she had faced were not about her, but about Bert. Bert had blamed her for everything instead of seeking help and admitting that he was incapable of telling the truth. He was not willing to own up to the fact about how many people he had hurt in the fallout.

"You have nothing to feel shame for. You may not have done everything just right, but you did not cause this Lizzy. Bert is a control freak, a passive-aggressive control freak with narcissistic tendencies. I only had to speak to him on the phone a few minutes to know that. People like him rarely change. Lower than half the percentage of people who have those traits ever stop being controlling. God can heal, but they will need to stay in counseling their entire lives due to accountability issues. They always blame others for their faults. Just know this Lizzy, this is *not* your fault," Sharon said again in an affirming way.

Then she smiled as she reached over the desk and took Lizzy's hand. "I am glad you are here and that God is healing you. I am also glad that you got away safely from that man. I credit the Lord and your boss for that."

A tear released down Lizzy's face as reality set in. It was if Sharon had known Lizzy her whole life. She seemed to understand every emotion and feeling of shame that Lizzy had harbored for decades, and when the dam of Lizzy's fears finally released, she cried uncontrollably for fifteen minutes as Sharon held her and prayed for her deliverance.

During the ongoing counseling sessions, Lizzy felt like that she could share anything with Sharon. She had a question to ask, especially after the previous week's sermon.

"Sharon? I have Christ in my heart, and I know this is true, but I have something my mother called a gift that I am starting to think may not be a gift at all, but a curse. She went on to speak with her about the visions and how they always brought about bad news, etc.

"Oh, I see," Sharon agreed. "This can be a problem."

"Pastor Luke was saying in his sermon last Sunday that there are generational curses, and I sensed something in me, perhaps the Holy Spirit reminding me of this "gift" and how it is not a gift at all, but a possible curse. Am I right?"

"That's very observant of you Lizzy. Yes, I believe you are talking about being clairvoyant. Would it be alright if I asked Pastor Luke to come in and join us for a few minutes? He could probably add insight and help you with this too," Sharon asked.

"By all means! I don't want this thing over my life one more minute," Lizzy added.

Pastor Luke came in and sat with Lizzy and Sharon and listened as Lizzy explained some of her childhood incidents and one as an adult where she had these bad visions.

"Lizzy, we can pray and ask God to take that away right now. You will have to denounce this curse upon you, and I can lead you through that. It is simple. I believe that once you do that, you will never be bothered by this clairvoyant spirit ever again. Are you ready?" he smiled.

Lizzy looked at Sharon, who was smiling encouragingly at her, then all three of them took hands as Pastor Luke began to pray. Then he asked Lizzy to repeat after him, ensuring that she would denounce any ties to witchcraft including clairvoyant activity. Afterward, Lizzy looked up, "I felt something inside of me---- let go of me....you know like.... break!" She cried and rejoiced.

"Amen, Pastor Luke said. That is called freedom! Who the son sets free is free indeed Lizzy! I want to tell you something now. God has a word *just for you*. I sensed Him wanting me to tell you this while we were praying. Lizzy, God sees you as a virgin, pure, white and clean. Your past no longer has a hold on you. You have a very special anointing, not only in worship, as we have all witnessed, but in everything that you do. God is going to open doors for you that you cannot even imagine right now." He rejoiced with her.

Since that day in that office, Lizzy had never again had a bad vision like that. In fact, she started having spiritual visions. They were visions from God. They were totally different. Always uplifting and encouraging. She spoke with Sharon about them, but she was afraid to say anything to anyone else, because she had never known anyone else who had godly visions, except men in the Bible.

Sharon had told Lizzy months later, after Lizzy admitted that she was having godly visions, that Pastor Luke too had visions. She could talk to him about it anytime. He would be excited to hear what God was showing her. Then she read a passage in the Bible about visions,

> "*Then, after doing all those things, I will pour out my Spirit upon all people. Your sons and daughters will prophesy. Your old men will dream dreams, and your young men will see visions.*"
> (Joel 2:28) NLT

"Yeah! I am still considered young according to that passage," Lizzy giggled.

After Bert left town, and Lizzy had started getting her life back together, she called Debbie in Oklahoma. She wanted her to know exactly everything that had happened and why it had happened the way it did. Debbie was very supportive too.

"Oh Lizzy. We had no idea of all that was going on, but Gary and I agreed that Bert was not the man for you. In fact, Gary has never ever said anything bad about anyone, but he made a comment about Bert one time. He said, *"That is one lazy man."* He said that after he was in a conference up north and had met with the pastor from the church there, an old friend of ours. Anyway, they had a long talk several years ago about Bert. We know more than you think Lizzy. You always have a home here too if you need it," Debbie added.

202

After developing a better relationship with them, she discovered in her absence that Gary had experience throat cancer. Now for a pastor to do so might as well be a death sentence. He was unable to work for the longest time. Debbie shared how that moment indeed had broken him and how he came out a stronger man than ever after going through that storm.

"That's what storms do honey...they make us stronger if we let them. I wish that I was half as strong as you are Lizzy. You have been to hell and back more times than we can count, but every time you have come back stronger. Now is no different," Debbie bragged.

Debbie stayed close in touch with Lizzy from that moment on. They talked on the phone every week, and Lizzy came to visit a few times every year. While she was in town, she always found time to see her brother Bruce, as well.

One time, she, Bruce and Allen all got together in Illinois where Allen lived. He had invited them there. The last time they were together in a room was at Max's and Mama's funeral. Her brothers were really put out about her disappearing on them, but after she explained her marriage to Bert, they understood and forgave her.

The three of them went out on the town in Chicago. Allen showed them around as they went to eat and then to a museum and then to a dinner club. She wasn't too comfortable about the club, but since she was with her brothers, she figured they would take care of her, and they did. They found a quiet corner and started talking. During that conversation, her brothers learned about things that went on in her childhood that they never knew about. Lizzy shared what their uncle had done to her too.

Bruce rose up, "You should have told me Liz...I would have killed him!"

"Bruce, you were only seven. I do not think you could have done that, but thanks for saying that," she said proudly.

Bruce reached over and put his arm around her for the next hour as the three of them sat there and reminisced and caught up on each other's lives. From that moment on they agreed that they would get together regularly and stay in touch.

9

New Beginnings

*Failure is simply the opportunity to begin
again, this time more intelligently. –Henry Ford*

It wasn't too long before the members at Lizzy's new church discovered her worship music abilities and asked her to join the worship team. Within six months, she was asked to be the Wednesday evening worship leader. She had been writing music and also traveling to other congregations to minister. It appeared that God was opening new doors of opportunity in her life once again.

As the days moved on and Lizzy really began to spread her wings, she took a new job in Denver, Colorado as a manager over four-hundred and fifty employees. It was challenging, but Lizzy loved it. Lizzy had undoubtedly recovered well from her past wounds, and her new job responsibilities showed that she was more than capable of running a company successfully, as she received recognition awards for her outstanding abilities. Additionally, everyone there knew she was a committed Christian who loved the Lord. At times employees would just show up and ask to come in and talk to her about their life problems and not necessarily business problems. She would give them wise advice and always pray for them.

During this season in her life, Lizzy would take time off to travel east and see her children. Sometimes the kids would come to visit her too. God was healing their relationships, though it was difficult at times for the children to really understand everything. Two of the children had moved out away from their father. One was in college and the other had moved to Florida. Her youngest son Aaron was graduating from high school and headed for college as well. Michelle, Lizzy's daughter was very involved in her high school activities and had no desire to move to a new school, so coming back to Colorado was not even an option. Lizzy did not want to tell them negative things about their father, but if they pointedly asked her, she would not lie.

The first night Lizzy was in her own apartment after Bert left town, she had no furniture or household goods, being that he took everything. Because funds were tight, she went to the dollar store and bought, one plate, one cup, one bowl, one fork, one spoon, one knife, one frying pan and a vegetable pan. She also bought a mat to sleep on and a blanket. In her new place, she got ready for bed and laid down in the living floor on the mat and covered up.

As she was lying there her thoughts went upward, "Lord, I want to thank you for everything that I have. I know it is not much but it is suffice and more than others have. I have a roof over my head, a good job and something that has been missing from my life for decades, *Your* peace. You are the Prince of Peace and I praise you Lord!" Then she drifted off to sweet sleep.

Daily, there was a constant reminder of the past and all that had been stripped of her. If she allowed her mind to wander, she would become depressed and start feeling useless again. One night when she was studying the Bible, she sensed God had a word just for her as she was reading in the book of Joel.

"I will repay you for the years that the swarming locusts have eaten.....the young locust, the destroying locust, and the devouring locust....my great army that I sent against you." (Joel 2:25).

It was a comfort knowing that God was now in control of her life. She still made mistakes, but God was always right there with her and providing for her in unexpected ways.

Meanwhile, she had met someone. His name was Joe Dumais. He was so different. Joe was a French Canadian with a terrific sense of humor and he was a gentle soul. Oh, on the outside he could come across crass and contentious if you riled his feathers, but anyone could see through his teddy bear demeanor. She met him through a mutual friend, and they started corresponding via email and telephone calls.

When he was telling her some of his favorite things, she decided this was the type of man she wanted to get to know better. He had written in an email once, "*One of my favorite things to do is walk on fallen leaves and listen to them crunch under my feet.*" To anyone else that might have sounded childish and perhaps not manly at all. But Joe put up no pretense. He was a gentle and perceiving soul, and he genuinely cared about her and others. To Lizzy, it sounded whimsical and charming, and after her life of nothing but drama and trauma, a little whimsy was more than welcome.

Joe was the real deal. He never cared about impressing anyone, and so when they met for the first time at a restaurant, it was a safe public place and she instantly felt at ease. They had a lovely time together, and she knew then that he might be what the book of Joel was talking about the previous week. God may be using Joe to restore her too.

After dinner they walked the plaza, went to a bookstore and enjoyed the evening. Lizzy was taken aback by his attractive looks. He looked very similar to Kenny Rogers, and she loved his bright blue eyes. They were filled with wonder and stories to tell, and she wanted to hear every one of them. Though Joe was nine-years-older than Lizzy, they connected in a real way.

She invited Joe to go to church with her the next Sunday. Since she was still in counseling, Sharon wanted to meet him. Lizzy agreed to it, as she never wanted another control freak in her life ever again. So, Friday night came, and Joe decided to meet with Lizzy in her group meeting and to also meet Sharon. Fridays was a good time for husbands or dates to go to group. That way Sharon could give her female clients her professional insights about their relationships. Sharon liked Joe and thought he was a perfect match for Lizzy. Sharon was also impressed that Joe asked her for books about abuse as he had never experienced anything like that before. Joe wanted to learn more about domestic violence so that he could understand Lizzy better.

One could say Joe came from good stock. His father was the Mayor of a small town in Canada for several years. When they moved to the states, his father worked for a New York newspaper. Joe was the youngest of five children. His family appeared very close and caring. After Joe graduated from high school he went into the service. He served in the Army at the end of the Korean War. What Lizzy loved about him most was that he was such a good listener and always had great advice to render. Especially when a situation was pressing or hard for her to navigate through all alone. Eventually, they became best friends.

It wasn't long before Lizzy and Joe knew God had put them together. They were like two peas in a pod. They spent as much time together as possible. Joe had bought her a portable keyboard so that she could stay up all night and worship and write or whatever she wanted to do. Lizzy was deeply touched by the gift. She never had anyone give her such a wonderful gift without strings attached.

One night Joe called and asked Lizzy if she would like some herbal tea. She wasn't even sure what herbal tea was, but she was willing to try it out. So Joe asked, "What flavor of tea do you like?"

"Um, all I have ever had is ice tea, so I do not know," she laughed.

"Well, do you like peach or raspberry...or.....?"

Lizzy interrupted him and said, "Peach sounds like something that I would like to try."

A half an hour later Joe was at the door with a big grocery sack. He had bought fifteen different herbal teas. She supposed that meant that they were going to have a lot more tea time if he had anything to do with it. She didn't mind. She loved spending time with him. During their tea times they learned so much about each other and God.

The upcoming summer was at hand, and she was going back to Oklahoma to visit family. It was a Ryan family reunion. By then she had forgiven everyone who had ever hurt her, including Bert and her father. She had actually gone by her Dad's home a few years earlier and visited with him and Linda. It mainly involved small talk, but it was a start.

She was going to stay at Gary and Debbie's house and then her daughter Michelle was going to come there too and stay with her. From there, they would go to the reunion together. Lizzy got an idea...since she and Joe were seemingly getting serious, she wanted her folks to meet him. She asked him if he would like to come with her to Oklahoma and meet Gary, Debbie, and Michelle.

"Sure...that would be nice," he said. Lizzy had no idea as the day got closer why Joe seemed so particularly happy to go, but he was.

They drove the thirteen-hour trip in one day from Denver, Colorado to Morton, Oklahoma. When they arrived, Gary and Debbie invited them in and hugged both of them. Gary really liked Joe, and he said as much.

Debbie said, "Oh Lizzy….that is one special guy that you got there. He really cares about you, and he's not lazy. Look at him in that kitchen cooking a feast for all of us!"

"Oh Mom, I am so glad that you approve. Yes, he has made me very happy during the time we have been together," she added

"Any plans yet dear?" her Mom smiled and winked.

'We have spoken about it Mom, and we are waiting on the Lord for the timing, but I think it will happen," she smiled back.

Debbie reached over and put her hand on the top of Lizzy's, "Honey, you deserve some happiness after everything that you have been through."

Later that evening they all sat down to a lovely meal made by Joe. Lizzy was beaming with pride and Joe was full of joy. He loved cooking for others and family togetherness. He was the one convincing Lizzy of how important family was. He insisted that she need never abandon family because of fears of how they felt about her. He had become such an excellent example of that too.

Joe had been divorced, but the marriage split was amicable. He was married to a lawyer in New York when they divorced. Joe was not a Christian at the time. He had moved to Colorado to take a new job with the government. He never missed a single day of work. He was always punctual, always reliable and won award after award for his diligence and expertise.

The previous New Year's Joe had invited Lizzy to go to his mother's home for the holiday. He and his entire family would come in every New Year's to have a family get together. It was such a delight to be in New York, and Joe made one of Lizzy's dream come true. They took a Ferry over to Ellis Island and Lizzy got to set her eyes on the Statue of Liberty. At Ellis Island, Lizzy was able to locate in the logs her grandparent's names. They had come over to America and had to go through Ellis Island like so many immigrants did back in the day. Anyway, she had met his family and they all were so kind and loving towards her. Now she was excited to introduce Joe to the rest of her family, as well.

The following day Michelle showed up, and Joe and Lizzy all had a great time together reminiscing and making new memories. Then the family reunion day approached. Lizzy's parents were thrilled that day too. Mom had insisted that they stand in front of the backyard tree for a picture of Lizzy, Joe, and Michelle before they left for the day.

After they arrived at the family reunion, Lizzy's cousins, aunts, and uncles all came around her and embraced her. She had not seen them in decades. There was Bruce too, walking in with Harold, her Dad. Harold saw Lizzy and smiled. She walked over to him and hugged him. Lizzy had indeed forgiven him for everything, and deep in her heart, she knew that was how it was supposed to be. She could tell that he had already been drinking that day, but he was not drunk. There would be no booze on the premises either, so chances are he would remain somewhat sober for the event.

As the day transpired it was time to come inside and eat. The family reunion was being held in a church fellowship hall. What happened next is something that Lizzy will never forget...nor would she want to.

As they were sitting at the tables, she began looking around for Joe. He had apparently disappeared, as well as Bruce. Then out from the stage curtains came a man dressed up as Henry the Eighth. Everyone was laughing. Lizzy too until she realized that it was Joe. Now, Joe was the director of drama at their church back home, and she figured that he must have found a costume in the back room and now he was hamming it up on stage. She turned red, and somewhat embarrassed...until he blurted out.....

"*Hear Ye, Hear Ye!* I have come here today to speak to you about something very important. Can anyone tell me what the name Ryan means?"

Everyone in unity shouted, "King!"

"That's right! What a smart crowd you are," he added as he winked.

"Well, I am a king, and I am in search of my queen," he said as his eyes perused throughout the room. Then when he spotted Lizzy, he called out, "You....please come here," he commanded with much authority as he waved her forward.

Everyone was politely giggling now, but still chuckling at his theatrics. By now, Lizzy's face was so red that her Aunt Larrain said, "Lizzy, your face is as red as your hair!"

Everyone laughed all the more. When Lizzy got to the front of the room, she had no idea what Joe was doing or thinking. They had done skits together at church, but he had not given her the script this time and she was very nervous.

He took her hands and sat her down on the seat placed next to him on stage as if it was a throne. After she sat, he pulled out a ring, bent down in a grandiose manner before her and said, "I have come from afar to ask you a most important question. Will you be my queen?" Then he bowed down before her majestically, and awaited her answer as he held up the ring in view.

Everything was in slow motion by then...as Lizzy was trying to figure out what he was saying. She was so surprised at his performance that she looked at the ring, then she looked at him and then back at the ring.

Finally it had dawned on her that he had asked her to marry him.

The smile grew on her face and tears filled her eyes as she said, "Yes, I will."

The room burst out in applause as the couple embraced and he placed a gentle kiss on her lips and escorted her back down to the table that she had left moments earlier.

At that time, Lizzy was asking, 'Where did he get that costume? And how did he pull this off without a hitch, and…" then she was interrupted.

"I have all the answers to your questions Sis." As she looked up, Bruce was videoing the entire affair.

Later that evening Michelle's ride came to take her home, and Joe asked Lizzy out for a dinner celebration. She found out then how he had gotten Bruce's email off of her desktop one evening when she had left her email server open, and he was working on her computer. He then emailed Bruce and told him what he wanted to do, and Bruce and Joe put the plan into action.

Additionally, Debbie had told Lizzy that Joe had asked her and Gary that morning when she was getting ready for the reunion if he could marry Lizzy. They were pleased, and he showed them the ring. That explained them being so very happy right before the three of them left to go to the reunion.

The following eleven months were busy months too. Back in Denver both Joe and Lizzy had started going to another church, and she was very active in the music ministry there. Joe facilitated her outside ministry opportunities as well. She could always depend on him to take care of the sound and keyboard set up and to encourage Lizzy in her ministry. Together, they planned the perfect wedding, and he paid for her wedding dress and the lovely reception at the hotel afterward. She had never seen or owned such a beautiful dress in all of her life. Joe encouraged her to get the dress she wanted, not what she thought he could afford. Lizzy had a knack for creating flower arrangements, so she made all of their silk flower arrangements including her stunning bridal bouquet. The people at the wedding thought it was real flowers. She really did a great job, and she enjoyed every minute of it. All of her children were coming too. Gary and Debbie were going to be there, and Gary gave her away at the wedding.

There was a huge dinner and dance afterward, and everything was more than Lizzy ever could have expected at this time in her life. She had written a song to sing to Joe at the wedding as well. During that song, she saw tears well up in his eyes, making it difficult for her to look at him until she finished. He was pleased, and that made her feel that the day was all the more special.

Their lives together would not be trouble-free, but they had a good firm foundation built by God, and they knew that no matter what came their way that He would see them through. That was a good thing too because, in just a few hours, they would have to lean extra hard on God in faith to bring them out of an unexpected trauma.

That night after the wedding reception they had gone up to the honeymoon suite in the hotel. Many of their family members were staying in the hotel too before flying out the following day. The kids had all come into their room, and they wanted Lizzy and Joe to open up the wedding gifts. Lizzy got some comfortable clothes on and so did Joe. Adam, Travis, Aaron, Michelle and Travis' girlfriend, Samantha, were all there. They laughed and enjoyed the next hour together as they opened gifts and teased each other. Lizzy's heart was full.

Soon the children all left, and it was late. Lizzy mentioned, "I know it is late sweetheart, but I am famished. We had such a lovely dinner, but I was so busy visiting with everyone that I barely touched it," she relayed.

"No problem love. We will just order something from the hotel kitchen," Joe mentioned as he handed her a menu he had just located on the table in the room.

In a matter of minutes they both ordered a late dinner and waited. They snuggled up on the couch in front of the fireplace and looked each other in the eyes, "Is everything else alright Mrs. Dumais?" Joe smiled proudly.

"Why Yes, Mr. Dumais. It has been a most perfect day." Then his lips gently covered hers, and he kissed her with more love than she had ever sensed before. When he had kissed her, she became a little lightheaded. She absolutely adored this man. She had for once in her life understand what true love felt like and what real love does. Joe always watched out for her, and though he was protective, he was not in any way possessive or controlling. He just wanted her life to be perfect. She had made him the happiest man in the world becoming his bride, and he intended on spending the rest of his life deserving of her great love.

The food came, and they both curled up on the bed and ate it as if they were starving. "Do you want a bite of mine dear?" Lizzy asked. "It's delicious!" she added.

Joe looked at Lizzy's plate of food and responded, "I don't think so. It doesn't look that good to me."

Lizzy was so hungry that she did everything but lick the plate. Afterward, she became very sleepy. When the two had finished the lights went out, and they both looked forward to some good rest. They would leave the following day for the mountains to spend three days there before going back to work. In four months, they would take a three-week honeymoon and spend more time together traveling the east coast and going up to Canada. Those were the plans, but for now, they were going to enjoy the time they had together at this moment.

Lizzy woke up several hours later with a tremendous stomach ache. She had no idea what was going on, but she felt very ill. She quietly got out of bed and went into the bathroom. Whatever was wrong was severe. She could barely stand up, and her face was pale, and her hands were shaking. She sat in the only available seat in the room and suddenly the stomach cramps were unbearable. She wondered if she had a stomach bug or something. She was in the bathroom for close to an hour when she heard a tap on the door.

"Honey, are you alright?" Joe asked in a concerning manner.

"I will be," she insisted in a weak response.

"Lizzy, what's going on...?"

"I don't know...I am pretty sick."

"Can you open the door please?" he asked worriedly.

"Oh honey, please...no. It's not good in here," she admitted. Lizzy was too embarrassed for him to see her that way.

"Sweetheart, please open the door. I will get you a drink of water," he convinced her.

Lizzy reached over with all of her strength to open the door and when she did she passed out. Joe was scared. He called the front desk, and they called an ambulance. She would drift in and out of consciousness, and it appeared that she had food poisoning. She was extremely pale and very weak.

Lizzy did not remember anything as to how she got to the hospital. All that she knew was that she was in a room hooked up to an IV and had awakened in so much pain she could not take it without saying something. "Help me…," she cried.

Joe was there, and a nurse came running in and realized that Lizzy was getting worse. The nurse put a morphine injection in her IV, and when Lizzy could catch her breath, she realized the pain diminished. "Thank you….," Lizzy whispered as she fell back into unconsciousness.

The doctor walked in and spoke to Joe. "We are going to take her down the hall for some tests. She is passing blood. This is not good, but we will do everything that we can," he said tenderly. Then two nurses showed up, and in a matter of seconds, they took the gurney that held his precious bride out and down the hall.

Every fifteen to twenty minutes they had to give Lizzy another shot of morphine. The pain in her abdomen was overwhelming. After the test, they discovered that her colon had swollen up to be three times bigger than it should be. This was definitely a severe case of food poisoning and the most dangerous type anyone could have.

Joe remained calm but very concerned. He called Lizzy's brother at the hotel and told him what was going on. Joe asked him to meet her parents for breakfast and just tell them that Lizzy needed to sleep in but that she would call them later that day. He knew that they were much older and flying back the following day and he did not want to upset them. He also knew that Debbie's immune system did not handle stress at all. He did, however, tell the children what was going on though, and they came to the hospital to see her. He knew Lizzy would agree.

"You are right hon…Mom and Dad do not need to see me like this." She said faintly.

The doctor came into the room right behind Joe. He took Lizzy's hand, "Mrs. Dumais, you have a bad case of food poisoning. Your colon is very inflamed, and your bladder is shutting down as well. Also, your liver numbers are way too high. Your heart is beating irregular too. We are going to admit you and put you on strong antibiotics and other meds to ward off any more damage. You just rest, and we will keep the pain medicine also coming Ma'am. You just hold on and we will get through this," he promised.

After the doctor left Lizzy started worrying about the medical bills, but Joe told her it was not a concern. That as of midnight on their wedding day, she was on his medical plan. He was always thinking ahead like that. She got to where she called him, *Mr. Preparedness.*

Joe bent down and looked at her carefully in her eyes, and said, "Honey, we are going to get through this, you and me and most importantly, *Jesus."* Then he prayed over her with great intensity. *"God, you gave me this woman as my wife, and I am going to do everything that I can to do right by her....but Lord, I need your help. We need your help! Please touch her Lord. Please help the doctors and nurses who are caring for her as well. Lord, we said for better or for worse. So, if we have to get the worse part out of the way first so that we can enjoy the better, so be it. Thank you for healing my wife. We love you Jesus. Amen."*

The next day looked even grimmer. Lizzy continued to get worse and weaker. She was losing blood, and the doctors had given her a transfusion. By that time the doctors and nurses found out that it was the couple's honeymoon. All the medical staff worked exceptionally hard and carefully to ensure that Lizzy was getting the best of treatment. Pastor Mike and Cindy from their church showed up and prayed over them. Cindy assured Lizzy and Joe that a prayer chain had already gone out, and that people all over the city and in other states were praying as well.

When Lizzy did not call her parents after they got home, her parents called Joe the following evening on his cell phone.

"Joe, Lizzy is not answering her phone. Are you two alright?" Debbie carefully asked.

"Oh, Debbie, we are okay. We did not want to worry you. We are glad that you made it home safe. Lizzy was hospitalized on Saturday night with food poisoning. It is pretty serious, but God will get us through this. I will keep you updated. If you can get more people praying, that would be a help," he requested.

"Is she awake right now?" Debbie asked.

"I am on my way back up to the room right now. Hold on, and if she is, I know that she would love to talk to you." He replied.

As Joe made his way down the hall and into the room, Lizzy had just come to again. She smiled weakly at him. He grinned and said, "Someone here wants to speak with you sweetheart," and he handed her the phone.

"Hello someone…" she softly giggled. She could keep a sense of humor anytime now. She had learned that from Joe.

"Oh Lizzy, How are you sweetheart. Joe told us everything…Your Dad is already emailing people all over the world to be praying for you." "Thanks, Mom. It's gonna take that kind of prayer to get me out of this bed. I love you, Mom," she said as she handed the phone back to Joe and closed her eyes.

Joe took Lizzy's hand and held the phone with the other. "Don't worry. I know God is with us Mom. Just keep praying, and I will let you know of any updates. We love you!" He thankfully added.

"We love you too! Take care of our girl for us Joe. We will be in touch," Debbie relayed and then she hung up.

Lizzy's room was filling up with flowers and cards from people in the church and friends from afar. Allen had come to the hospital to see her before he caught a flight back to Chicago. Other church members came sporadically to check on her too. She never knew so many people cared about her.

At that moment she had a morbid thought. *"I just got married, and now I am going to die... it isn't fair... but life just isn't fair is it?"* Lizzy thought to herself. She was so weak and really not getting much better. Between Joe and the doctor they believed she got the food poisoning from the late night dinner they had in their hotel. Joe recalled that he thought the cheese on the top of Lizzy's entree looked off, but Lizzy said it tasted good, so he left well enough alone. He'll never do that again he thought to himself.

The next day brought promise. Lizzy's bleeding had stopped, and she began to feel better. Her liver numbers were improving, and her bladder started working again. Her heart was still not functioning as well as they had hoped but it was progressing. She was getting a little stronger too. She had asked Joe to go to work and not worry about her. He could come up after work and see her. By then Lizzy knew that she would be alright.

When Joe left and the room was quiet, her mind went everywhere. Then suddenly she let out a big cry, much like Lucy would do from "I Love Lucy," and the entire hall could hear it as it was followed by, "This is my honeymoon!"

The nurses came running in, "Oh honey, it's going to be okay. You two have a lot of love for each other. We have witnessed it. You have an exceptional man there too. You will have days to look forward to, I promise. You are getting better by the hour Lizzy." they comforted her.

The nurses suspected that the medication that she was taking was causing some depression and anxiety too, so they told the doctor. Lizzy had always had issues with any pain medication or anesthesia. It took her weeks to get it out of her system and usually the doctor would have to put her on anti-anxiety medication to help her for short term until the medicine was all depleted from her system. That usually took three weeks for Lizzy.

Later that day Joe arrived around 4:00 p.m., after he had gotten off work. The nurses came in at the same time and said, "Lizzy, it is time to get out of bed. Do you feel like taking a walk?"

"Anything is better than looking at these four walls day in and day out. Yes!" she smiled surprisingly.

"That's the woman that I married. I love that smile!" Joe proclaimed.

"We are going to have to keep you hooked up to everything, but I think we can manage it. You and your husband and this pole can take a stroll," the nurse giggled.

They double gowned Lizzy so that she could feel completely covered and then put anti-slip socks on her and helped her up out of bed. That was the first time she had been out of that bed in four days, and it felt great. For a free spirit like Lizzy it might as well had been four years.

"How are you feeling?" the nurse inquired.

"A little weak, but not too weak to walk a bit." she admitted.

Smiling, Joe held the pole with one hand and offered his other arm to Lizzy. "You are doing great lovey," he encouraged her. "You actually have some color back in your face."

Lizzy smiled and walked onward down the hall. Joe stopped the stroll when he noticed the large picture of the mountains on the wall ahead and an eagle in flight. "Look honey, it's just like we imagined it would be," he smiled and then kissed her cheek.

Lizzy busted out laughing. When she laughed the whole world laughed with her. Her laugh was so contagious. Joe laughed along with her as they continued the stroll. Down the next corridor, there was another picture of a field of flowers and a mountain behind with the sunset reclining. Again Joe pointed out, "Look honey, and there isn't any wind to bother us either."

She laughed again. "You know what Mr. Dumais, you are the best husband a girl could ever have. I am sorry for ruining our honeymoon plans," she sadly responded.

"Don't you worry your pretty little dimples over it, sweetheart. We are going on a honeymoon in a few months, and you can make it up to me then," he replied with a sexy, sultry voice.

She stopped right there, and turned and kissed him. Afterward she softly stated, "I love you so much Joe."

"I love you more," he responded.

They made their way back to the room, and she felt tired and hungry at the same time. "I wonder what kind of broth they are going to bring me today. You want to go get me a hamburger?" she winked. She wasn't sure that she could eat what she called real food as of yet since no one had spoken to her about it that day.

As if on cue, the dietary aide showed up, and Lizzy couldn't believe her eyes! There on her dinner tray was a hamburger and a salad. She looked at Joe, and then she looked at the plate of food, and only in Lizzy style, raised her head and hands to the sky and said, "*Ask, and you shall receive*!!"

The dietary aide laughed along with the rest of them. They brought Joe a tray too, and they both gave thanks that Lizzy could finally eat regular food.

Lizzy was off her pain meds and finishing up her antibiotic drip when the doctor came in the next morning. As he approached her bed, he said, "Lizzy, all of your blood tests are perfectly normal. I do not know if you realize how very remarkable this is after everything that you have been through the last five days. It is a miracle. That is all that I am going to say. It appears that you will be able to go home this evening." He smiled and patted her hand.

He then walked out of the room, and Lizzy reached over for the phone and called Joe at work immediately. "Hi hon…guess what…I am free to go home this evening! Praise the Lord!"

Joe was thrilled, "Seriously! That is such wonderful news sweetheart and a true answer to prayer. I will see you after work. Love you!" he said.

"Love you more," she answered and then hung up.

Lizzy got up out of bed and sat in the chair beside her bedside. She refused to get back in the bed the rest of the day. Joe had already brought her up some clean clothes so when she got discharged they would be there. As usual, he was always one step ahead of anything that she needed.

Then Lizzy looked up at the sky outside the window, *"Thank you, God… thank you, thank you, thank you for healing me! I knew you would never let me down. I know that You are for me, so who can stand against me? I understand now more than ever that you put Joe in my life. The devil obviously did not like that. I realize now that we are under attack. You must have wonderful plans for us. Thank you that no weapon formed against will prosper! Please help us to trust you and listen to your voice sweet Jesus. I love you. Amen."*

That afternoon Joe showed up at 4:00 p.m. like he did every afternoon, and by 5:00 p.m. Lizzy and Joe were on their way home, but not before Joe made a stop at the nurse's station. He was so impressed with all of their care for his Lizzy that on the way to the hospital he had stopped by a bakery and picked up a sheet cake. He had some words put on it too that read, "*Thank you from the Honeymooners.*"

The staff gathered around and thanked them and clapped as they left the hospital. It was quite a send-off indeed. Everyone knew the seriousness of Lizzy's condition, and many of the nurses knew that a divine hand was at work in her case.

As they drove up to their home, Joe ran around and opened the car door, and they slowly walked up to the front porch.

"Wait just a minute!" Joe requested.

Then he unlocked the front door, opened it and turned quickly to bend down and sweep her off her feet. He carried her across the threshold and gently kissed her and said, "Thank you Lord, my bride is home!"

10

The Greatest of These is Love

Being deeply loved by someone gives you strength,
while loving someone deeply gives you courage –Lao Tzu

Two months later, Lizzy received a phone call from her doctor late at night. He lived across the street, and he had noticed her light was on, so he had hoped she was awake. He had just received a medical report that night, and it was about her.

Lizzy answered the phone, "Hello?"

Dr. Sayre answered, "Lizzy, this is Doc Sayre. I hope that you are still awake, as I have some news for you."

"Yes, I am still up. What's wrong?"

"Well, when you were in the hospital a few months ago for that food poisoning episode, they ran a test, and I just got the results in my office today. You have a gallstone, a large gallstone and it is getting ready to pass. This is dangerous, so I have called Dr. Simon and set up an emergency appointment for you first thing in the morning to see him. He is right across the street from the hospital. Understand?"

"Uh …yes. I will be there. How come you just got these reports Doc?" She asked.

"I am not sure why they did not address this when you were there, but we need to address this now. Just go at 8:00 a.m., alright?" He insisted.

"I'll be there," Lizzy agreed.

That morning, Dr. Simon's nurse called Lizzy at 7:30 a.m. and requested that she go over to the hospital first for an ultrasound then bring the films over to Dr. Simon right afterward. She said she had already scheduled the emergency ultrasound. Lizzy told Joe about the medical report, and they prayed. She told him to go on to work and that she would call him with any other news.

He gently kissed her forehead and gave her a gentle embrace then said, "Aren't we glad that we have a doctor who calls after hours when needed? It will all be fine...you will see," he said as he left for work.

Lizzy arrived at the hospital on time, and they rushed her right back. She still could not understand the scope of seriousness about the issue. As the ultrasound tech was performing the scan, he inquired, "Mrs. Dumais, do you feel alright?"

"I feel completely normal," Lizzy insisted.

Then he remained quiet as he continued scanning. Again he asked, "Are you *sure* you feel okay?" he asked again.

Annoyed she answered, "Why? Is there a reason that I shouldn't?"

He smiled, "Well, most people who have a stone this size in this location are in a lot of pain. I am surprised that you are feeling well. I am done for now. Give me a few minutes, and I will get the films so that you can take them across the street."

After she got dressed, and as promised, the man came in and gave her the films. She decided to walk across the street to the doctor's office since it was only two blocks away.

When she walked in, the receptionist asked, "Are you Lizzy?"

"Yes Ma'am," Lizzy replied.

"Dr. Simon will be right with you. Just sign here," she directed as she handed her a clipboard and a permission form for Lizzy to sign.

Before she could sit down, a nurse came into the waiting room and asked her to come on back. Everyone seemed so serious. Lizzy just tried to shake it off. She felt just fine, and she could not understand the concern in everyone's faces.

Dr. Simon came in and introduced himself and then turned to put the films up on a reader so that she could see what he was talking about. "You see this right here Mrs. Dumais? This is a serious gallbladder attack getting ready to happen. I have scheduled you for emergency surgery tomorrow at 11:00 a.m. We have to take your gallbladder out. You must have had symptoms before because it looks like it has been traumatized. I won't know much more until I get in there. This surgery is pretty routine, and you will get to go home tomorrow night if all goes well. Do you any questions?"

Thinking of her commitments, she answered, "Um…yes…I am scheduled to sing the National Anthem at the Airforce base tomorrow at 8:30 a.m. So can I check in after that?"

"Mrs. Dumais!" Dr. Simon responded in an exaggerated manner, "You have no business singing, jogging, or doing any activity until we get this taken care of. It is a dangerous situation. People have died with this kind of attack," he elaborated.

She smiled and assured him that she would be fine, and would see him in the morning. She had no intention of breaking her promise to sing the following day. After all, she felt completely normal even if everyone else thought she should be feeling otherwise.

After telling her husband about the report and surgery, Joe said, "You pray about it. If you sense you need to sing for them, then you do as God tells you to do. I will meet you at the hospital either way," he consoled.

The next morning came, and the July 4th ceremonies were going to start soon. She felt completely normal and sensed after praying that she would be safe going to the base and then going on to the hospital. As she sang that morning the sun was bright, the flag was raised high, and the Airforce base was filled with military personnel anticipating the ceremonies of the day. As Lizzy sang her voice was clear and strong.

Afterward, everyone let out a huge cheer, and the Lieutenant General who was standing behind her walked forward and thanked her heartedly for her performance. "I have not heard that song sung like that in decades. That was a lovely job, Mrs. Dumais. It's so nice when an artist like yourself kept the anthem to its original form. I tire of hearing people wreck it over their showmanship," he offered.

Lizzy thanked him and others who had asked her to come and sing and then politely dismissed herself. She drove home, took a shower, put on comfortable clothes and left for the hospital. Lizzy arrived at 10:00 a.m. as promised. When Dr. Simon saw her he asked, "How are you doing this morning?"

"All is well," she smiled.

"I am so glad you listened to me and stayed put today," he added.

"Um…," she cleared her throat. "Dr. Simon, I am a woman of my word. I did go to the base this morning and sang, but I am here now and I feel completely normal. Sorry to disappoint you," she reluctantly admitted.

He patted her on the hand, "Alright…some of my patients…..," and then stopped himself before he said anything else and just smiled. "See you in surgery shortly."

Joe just arrived in the room when the doctor was leaving. Lizzy introduced them and the doctor said, "You're French Canadian, huh? Well, so am I and it's nice to meet you," he said as he left the room.

The nurse rushed back in, got the IV drip going, and before long Lizzy was in surgery. When she awakened in recovery, Dr. Simon was there along with Joe.

Dr. Simon smiled, "Hi Lizzy. You did really well. I want to tell you that in all my years of removing gallbladders…., well, how do I say this….yours is the nastiest looking gallbladder that I have ever seen. It had scars on top of scars which means you have suffered from gallbladder attacks for decades. See this stone?"

Then he held up a small glass jar with a round charcoal-colored stone in it a little bigger than an almond.

Lizzy inspected it, "Yes sir."

"This was the stone that I was worried about, but you also had numerous other stones in your gallbladder too. Because of the extent of the damage, I want to keep you an extra night to make sure that you do not have any complications." he added. "How are you feeling?"

"Just the same way I did before I had surgery," she smiled back.

"Well, you should expect a little pain after the medication wears off, but you will bounce back in about a week. I will see you in the morning. Let the nurses know if you need anything else and just try to rest now," he ordered.

"Thank you doctor," Lizzy added in appreciation.

He gently patted her on the top of her arm and turned and shook Joe's hand, "You better keep an eye on that one….," he laughed as he left the room.

"That's my intention," Joe laughed back.

"God sure protected you sweetheart. Think of how bad it would have been if you had that attack.

The nurses are coming now to take you to your room upstairs. I am going to get something to eat and go back to work for a few hours. You just rest, and I will see you this afternoon," Joe relayed as he kissed her goodbye.

Several months later she was thinking back on what the doctor said about gallbladder attacks, and she realized that a pain she had contended with since she was about twenty years old was gone. She would have a pain in her upper abdomen and feel nauseated and sometimes feel faint when it hit her. She always just would breathe calmly and pray for it to pass. Since that surgery, Lizzy noticed that the particular pain she had often experienced had not returned.

The following month her brother Bruce called. He said that Linda had passed away and that Harold, her Dad, needed someone to come stay with him for a week. Though Lizzy had started being on talking terms with her father, they were not close whatsoever. Harold still smoked heavily and drank heavier, and she had no desire to go live with him for a week. But that is what Bruce was implying.

"I can't do that Bruce. I am allergic to cigarette smoke, and well, you know Dad and I are not close at all. I have forgiven him for everything, but there is no way that I can stay with him for an entire week," she added.

"You're all the hope I have. I am working full time, and Allen is too. You are not working full time right now, and I would even be willing to pitch in for the airplane ticket. Please tell me that you will at least think about it and call me back tonight?" he begged.

Bruce was the type of person that never took "No" as an answer. "Okay, I will call you tonight," Lizzy promised.

When Joe arrived home, she spoke to him about the situation and how she did not want to go.

Joe said, "Maybe this is a God opportunity for you honey. Maybe God wants you there to witness to your Dad." And then he gave her his usual response to things like this, "Just pray about it. I know you will do the right thing."

Frankly, that irritated her all the more, but she promised to pray and she went into her studio and closed the door. Once she started seeking God's heart on the matter in an honest fashion, she too also sensed what Joe was implying was correct. She recalled how her father did not like Joe that much and was disappointed at the family reunion that she accepted his marriage proposal. Her father always had a way of putting a damper on anything that made Lizzy happy. It reminded her of someone else in her distant past.

"God, I guess I still need to work on some forgiveness here with Dad. Please give me the strength to do so, and strength to go if it is your will," she prayed earnestly.

Afterward, she emerged, and by the look on her face Joe knew what the decision was. "I am proud of you honey. Your dad needs you, and I know that God is going to use you in all of this…keep the faith," he encouraged.

That evening she called Bruce and let him know that she would be willing to go. He said that he would purchase the entire airfare and see her in a few days. She insisted on one thing, "Make sure you get the biggest air purifier that you can find and put it by his smoking chair."

"I sure will Sis. See you soon!" he said and then hung up.

A few days later the plane landed in Oklahoma and Bruce was there at the airport to pick her up. As they rode into Blossom, Oklahoma Bruce filled her in on their Dad's condition.

"Lizzy, Dad cannot do anything much for himself. He needs someone to cook for him, do laundry, clean house, etc. I just cannot do all of that right now. I am working on getting him someone to help, but you being here will give me time to find the right person. Thanks for coming," he affirmed.

As they drove up to the small mobile home park where their father lived, Lizzy remembered the trailer all too well. She could not believe that her Dad still lived in the same old trailer all of these years. When they knocked and walked inside, her Dad seemed delighted to see her, but he was reserved. The house wasn't too smoky as Harold had kept the air purifier on and only smoked in his chair. She noticed right away the dirty condition of the house. Linda had been very ill the last year and had succumbed to a heart attack just a few days prior. Her funeral was in a few days. Lizzy was almost overwhelmed with the amount of housework that needed to be done, but she bid Bruce a farewell, rolled up her sleeves and got to work. Bruce said that he would bring Amy over for dinner that night if she would like that. Lizzy said that would be fine.

As her father sat in his smoking chair, Lizzy tried to make up her mind as to what needed to be done first. She took one look at the dirty clothes her Dad was wearing and his unshaven face, and it did not take long to figure out where to start.

"Dad, let me run a bath for you," being that they did not have a shower. While you are taking a bath, I will get some clothes out for you and if you need help with anything, just let me know," she insisted.

He looked at her like she had lost her ever-loving mind. He had not taken a bath in months, and now she wasn't giving him a choice. He grunted and cursed as he walked down the hallway to the bathroom. "They'll be none of that while I am here

Dad. I would appreciate you watching your language in my presence."

He said nothing else as he entered the bathroom where the tub water was already running. When he emerged, he had put on the same old clothes, even after taking a bath. She also noticed that he still had dandruff flakes and dry hair. "Dad, did you even take a bath?" she asked.

"Yes," he miffed at her.

She shot back, "Then why are you wearing those dirty clothes again?"

"Because my other clothes do not fit me. I've lost too much weight." he snarled.

"Oh, so we need to go get you some clothes for tomorrow too," she realized. Lizzy got to moving in high gear and said, "Dad, go ahead and get ready to go to the store with me so we can get you some clothes, and then I need to get groceries for tonight. We should get back here around 1:00 p.m. That will give me plenty of time to clean up the kitchen and prepare a meal."

He got his boots back on that she had struggled in helping him remove, and then she grabbed her purse and they took off. Her dad still had the same old car he had twenty years ago too. It was like stepping into a dirty ashtray though. She was somewhat disgusted but insisted she was going to drive. He gave her the keys without a single remark. As they drove up to the department store, she was slightly embarrassed to be seen with her Dad like this, but she would have been more embarrassed at the funeral the next day if he had no other clothes to wear. As they walked in, she looked at the size of the shirt he was wearing then and decided that he probably needed the next size down. She picked out a white shirt, gray slacks, a tie and black sports jacket. Her Dad went into the changing room and tried them on. When he emerged, he almost looked like a new man except for the whiskered face and hair standing on end.

Lizzy turned to the clerk and smiled, "He'll take them."

The clerk looked at her like she was trying to clean up a bum on the street, and frankly, she had seen some bums on the street that look better than her Dad did that day. She decided he needed a set or two of everyday clothes as well. Since she knew his size, she got him another pair of slacks and a few extra shirts. "We'll take these too," she said as she handed them to the cashier.

"Yes ma'am," he said without another word except for telling her the total of the clothing and a mere "thank you," before they walked out.

By that time she did not even care what others thought. She saw a bit of pride come back into her father's eyes when he saw himself in the mirror with the sports jacket on, and that was worth much more than the price of the clothes. Her Dad seemed surprised at her actions too and a smile became a permanent fixture on his face, a face that usually had a hard set jaw and a suspecting eye. Now it was softening, more relaxed and he even started laughing as Lizzy tried to strike up a conversation with him.

"I guess that guy hadn't seen anyone who really needed clothes before, huh Dad?" she laughed.

Harold reached over and laid his hand on her shoulder and squeezed it gently then withdrew it as if it was a mistake. He then rested it on the back of the seat. Lizzy understood his body language. Her Dad wasn't one to tell you that he loved you, but if he did love you or approve of your actions, you usually got the shoulder pat or gentle squeeze of affirmation. It was enough for Lizzy to reply, "Your welcome Dad."

They arrived at the corner grocery and both went inside. "Dad, what do you want for dinner?" she asked. Immediately he answered as if he had been contemplating it for a while. "Fried chicken," though when her Dad spoke he struggled because of the stroke, and so it sounded like, "Fwide Chikn." And then he smiled with hopeful eyes.

"That sounds good to me too Dad. I can make us up a big batch," she smiled back. He followed her slowly through the store, and she deliberately calculated her steps so he would not have to walk too much. As they got up to the checkout, the cashier said, "Hello Mr. Ryan. How are you today?"

"Good," Harold smiled. After the groceries were rung up, her Dad reached for his checkbook. "No, Dad, I will get it, don't worry," she stated.

He looked at her, ignored her plea and handed the check to the cashier after trying to sign it. "I got money," he said in a prideful manner then struggled to articulate the following sentence, "I jus didn't hab clobes," he blurted out in Harold Ryan fashion. She noticed that his penmanship looked like chicken scratch. The cashier was all too familiar with him though and immediately started filling out the check for him before asking him to sign it.

When they left, her Dad picked up a bag with his good hand, and she got the other two bags of groceries. The clerk smiled kindly at her as they left. In a matter of five minutes they were back at his house. After carrying in the groceries, Lizzy put them away, and then she rolled up her sleeves and got to work. She decided if she was cooking dinner that night that the kitchen was a priority. Lizzy removed a mixture of stuck on grease and nicotine from everything. She stripped the windows of their curtains and washed them, and when she saw Harold just sitting in his chair sipping beer, she approached him, "Hey Dad, can you take these outside and hang them up to dry?" she asked as she was holding a basket of wet curtains.

He smiled, "I sure can." And then he hobbled a bit to get up due to a bad back, but once he stood he could walk fine. He took the basket under his left arm, and she opened the door for him. The stroke that he suffered years ago, when her mother shot him, had left his right arm weakened. He seemed extremely happy to oblige Lizzy. When she noticed how well he managed to hang the curtains on the line, she got an idea.

After he walked in, she asked, "Dad, if you can and would like to, after a rest of course, will you vacuum the living room and the back two bedrooms while I finish up cleaning the kitchen?"

He smiled again and said, "I don't need to *west*." Her Dad struggled trying to pronounce the "r" in rest, but Lizzy understood.

"I can do that Lizzy." And then he walked down the hall to the back room and got the vacuum out and started cleaning. Then something dawned on her. As long as she gave him tasks to do, he did not care to smoke or even drink.

She thought to herself, "Maybe he is doing that because there is nothing else to do! Well, I can fix that!!" she secretly acknowledged as she laid out a plan in her mind.

When her Dad finished vacuuming she had him take the trash out after a short break. When he was done, she asked him to go get a clean set of clothes on and brush his hair for dinner that night. Surprisingly, Harold seemed to do anything that she asked.

She finally got the kitchen in working order and began preparing dinner. When her Dad emerged in his clean clothes, she told him that he looked nice in them. He smiled and went to his smoking chair and picked up a cigarette.

During the next hour, he watched news, and she made ice tea and offered some to him. He took it and drank it. She quickly hung the living room drapes back up after he retrieved them from the clothesline. The house looked about 80% better than it did that morning when she walked in. When Bruce and Amy arrived, they seemed shocked at how clean it looked.

"You did a lot today Sis," Bruce replied.

"It smells good in here too, in more than one way," Amy added as she hugged Lizzy. Amy and Bruce had been together for about eight years. They had not married, but they were committed to one another.

"Look at you Dad... you got new clothes?" Bruce asked.

Harold half smiled, "Lizzy got 'em."

"Good for you Dad. I don't even know what size you wear now. The clothes I bought you a few months ago are in the closet and too big." Bruce replied.

Lizzy added, "He said that he had been losing weight. We got him some clothes for the funeral tomorrow afternoon too."

"Nice," Bruce smiled.

When dinner was ready, everyone gathered around the table and immediately Harold reached for a chicken leg and put it to his mouth.

"If you don't mind, I would like to give thanks before we eat, alright Dad?" Lizzy asked.

He let out a disgusted grunt and put his chicken down. "We don't pway here!" he exclaimed once again as he struggled to say the word.

"Well I do," and she bowed her head and put out her hands for everyone to join her. Everyone held hands and Lizzy offered up a simple prayer of thanks. When she finished Amy spoke up, "Now that wasn't too painful, was it Harold?" she teased him. He relaxed, smiled and picked up the chicken and started eating.

A conversation ensued at the table....something that never happened when she was a child without consequences. It was rather pleasant though, and everyone mentioned how good the meal was. Lizzy even had time to bake a peach crumb cobbler. Her Dad had second helpings on everything...even dessert.

Bruce looked at Lizzy and said, "I haven't seen him eat like this in a long time."

"Well, he must have worked up an appetite. I had him out hanging clothes, vacuuming, taking a bath, shopping, and just about anything I needed help with. He was a great help," she added as she looked over at him.

Their Dad just smiled and got up from the table to go sit in his chair again. Amy and Bruce helped her clear the table and clean up after dinner before heading home. That evening her Dad looked at her and said, "I need help, Lizzy."

"What's the matter Dad?" Lizzy inquired.

"My feet are killing me. My toenails are long, and I need them cut. Will you help?"

The thought that went through her mind was not as bad as the reality of the situation she was getting ready to face. Harold struggled to get his boots off by himself, but what she did not know is that he would sleep in them because of it. Even though she helped him take them off, he was able to get them back on by himself.

She bent down, and he raised his leg to assist her in getting his boots off again and then he raised his other leg in a like manner. After she had gotten the boots removed, she took off his socks and what she saw would make any medical personnel panic. His toenails were about two inches long, thick, green and gnarled with fungus, and curling underneath his toes. She had no idea how to start.

Nervously responding, "Oh my goodness Dad. That has to hurt. Let me think."

She got up and got a large pan, put warm soapy water in it and took it in the living room. She gently lifted his feet into the pan and let them soak for several minutes before tackling the task. She found a pair of scissors and nail clippers. She wasn't sure what would cut those nails, but she had to try. There were no gloves in the house either. "Lord help me," she said under her breath.

Lizzy reached for her Dad's left foot and slightly lifted it out of the soapy water. At least the smell of dirty feet was subsiding. She looked up at her Dad, "You know what Dad…I would never do this in a million years for anyone, but the Bible says in *1 John 4:7* that we are supposed to *love one another*. After all, *love* is the greatest gift of all. So, I am going to show you that I love you and do this." Lizzy relayed compassionately.

He sat there without any reply, and she assumed it was because he was probably embarrassed by his toenails.

She tackled the task head-on, and little by little she cut away the nails on his feet until they were at a reasonable length. About an hour later, she took alcohol to his nails and then her hands, as it was the only thing in the house she could find that was even close to an antiseptic. His face looked relieved. She was sure that his feet felt better. She went to his bedroom and retrieved a clean pair of socks and handed them to him. He struggled to get them on so she bent down and put them on for him.

Afterward, she managed to help him get ready for bed, although he was going to sleep on the couch as he had for years. She went to lay down in the back room where Linda once slept. She had enough strength to change the linens and take a bath before turning in. Of course, Lizzy would have to bleach the tub before she would be willing to get into it. So it was after midnight before she laid down to rest, but she finally drifted off into a peaceful sleep after calling Joe and discussing the events of the day.

The following morning when she got up, her Dad was already up and had made coffee. It was about 6:30 a.m. She made a quick breakfast for them and then announced that she was getting his tub ready. He snapped back, "I al-weddy took a bath yesterday!"

"I know that Dad but your hair is really dirty," she answered carefully.

"*I can't wash it in theh.*" he insisted.

"I will show you how Dad." They traipsed back to the end of the hall, and when they approached the bathroom, Lizzy showed him that she had put a cup on the side of the tub with shampoo. She told him to use the cup to get his hair wet, then wash his hair and then rinse it the same way.

Harold did not look thrilled at all and said, "*Anothu bath an two days in a woh!*"

"Dad, you need to take a bath every day." And then she closed the door.

Lizzy then went into his closet and laid out his new clothes on the bed. She had taken his boots and cleaned them up as best she could by polishing and buffing them and spraying some foot spray in them, that she managed to find by accident the night before. Then she tapped on the door, "Dad, I have laid out your clothes in your room. Just letting you know," she said as she slowly walked away.

About forty minutes later he emerged and then went to his room. Lizzy was in the kitchen just finishing up washing her long hair in the kitchen sink. As he walked down the hall, she could smell men's cologne. "Woo-wee! Somebody sure smells good around here!" Lizzy laughed.

When her father entered the kitchen he had a huge smile on his face. His hair was clean and combed back like he always wore it in earlier years. He had shaved, and now he had his clean clothes and boots on.

He lifted up his left arm to her and asked, *"Wood you button my sweeve?*

"Gladly handsome," she said.

He then sat at the kitchen table and had another cup of coffee while she was getting ready. When she came out of the hallway, she noticed that he had gone in and put his new jacket on and they met in the hall.

"You look good Lizzy," he said. And then Harold put his hands on her upper arms and looked her into her eyes, and then pulled her in for an embrace. After a long moment, they stood there again as Lizzy fixed his necktie for him. Tears came to her eyes as she could not remember her father showing that kind of compassion to her except for a few rare moments in her childhood. Lizzy then brushed off the sleeve of the coat as it had a loose string on it.

"Thank you," he tenderly commented. Lizzy felt her heart melt with that sincere thank you and the previous embrace. She thought to herself, *"My father is getting soft in his old age, that's for sure!"*

Bruce came by and picked them up for the funeral. He noticed how good his father looked too. "Dad, I think it has been years since I have seen you look so good." he commented.

Their Dad just kept smiling and got in Bruce's pick-up truck. They drove a good forty minutes before they arrived at where the graveside service was being held. Linda's sister was there along with about thirty-five family members. The service was not very long. Harold was understandably emotional.

When the service ended and everyone bid their farewells, Bruce took Lizzy and their Dad to lunch before bringing them back to the trailer.

The next day, Lizzy started doing deep cleaning in Linda's room and the bathroom. She had to wash everything from ceilings to floors. Her Dad asked if Lizzy would be willing to pack up Linda's things and call the Veterans of America to pick up the items. Lizzy was willing and so she called them, and the company said they would be there the following morning. She worked very hard making sure she got all of the clothing and shoes packed. Linda really had very few material things. She was a reader and she had Louis L 'Amor books that Lizzy donated too. She placed it all right outside the patio door since the weather was clear and there really was no other place to put it.

Once she got Linda's room so clean that it was shining, with a new bedspread and some other updated things that she went out and purchased, Harold came back to look at it. "*This looks w-eel nice. I think I am going to sweep in here from now on,*" he smiled.

Lizzy was pleased with that comment. "You can start tonight if you wish Dad. I can take the other bedroom." In that room was a new bed that had rarely been slept on. That was her father's room. He just never got adjusted to that bed, or so he said that was the case. She pulled back the cover, and the sheets looked like they had never been slept in. "Would you like me to move your clothes back there too Dad?" she asked.

Harold gently answered, "No, I will do that Lizzy."

That night they had a good time watching the football game. They were both Sooner fans. Her Dad smoked very little, and she never saw him drink

242

another beer the rest of the time she was visiting with him. He either wanted iced tea or Dr. Pepper.

Lizzy had only a few days left before she had to go back to Colorado. She was telling Joe how her Dad was changing and getting soft in his old age. Joe replied, "I am so glad that you went on to Oklahoma Lizzy. Just imagine how good this has been for both of you."

"I agree. We are having some good times now. I think tomorrow I am going to take him out to eat, and then ask if he wants to do anything special while I am in town." Lizzy responded excitedly.

The next day, her Dad said that he always wanted to see the Oklahoma City Memorial where the bombing of the federal building took place. Lizzy had not been there either, so she made a day of it. Her Dad got up on that day, drew his own bath and got cleaned up without her saying a word. He also was getting used to her praying before meals and did not contest to her doing so anymore. As they walked the Memorial, her Dad needed to rest so she rested with him. He never said much, but judging by his actions Lizzy could tell he was deeply moved over the exhibits. He wept briefly, trying to hide his tears from her.

That night when she cooked dinner, she set the table and called him over to eat. When he sat down he put his hand out and asked, "Pway?" She nodded, and he gave a prayer of thanks for the food and for Lizzy. It was one of the sweetest prayers she had ever heard, and she had to pinch herself as she realized that it had flowed from her father's lips.

After the dinner, they went in to watch another game on television. After sitting down, he asked her, "Lizzy, you want a drink?"

"I can get it, Dad," she answered as she started to get up.

He motioned with his hand for her to stay put and asked, "You want a Peppuh?" meaning Dr. Pepper. She smiled and said "yes," and then when she reached for the lap blanket, he walked over and unfolded it and placed it over her legs. Then he turned and came back with two sodas. He opened hers and handed it to her. She could not remember her Dad ever offering to serve her like this. It was a lovely memory that she would hold in her heart always.

As she left for her flight the following day, her Dad hugged her like he did not want her to go. Their relationship was surely improving and becoming something better than it ever had been before. "Dad, I will be back in a few months to see you, okay? Meanwhile, I will call you once a week, and you can call me anytime too." Lizzy smiled.

He hugged her again and patted her shoulder. That was a final goodbye until next time. As she got on the plane and headed home she felt such a sense of peace and had such a thankful heart that God had restored her relationship with her father. As Bruce picked Lizzy up to take her to the airport, Lizzy filled Bruce in on the kind of services that their Dad would need to maintain the quality of life that he enjoyed while she was with him. Unfortunately, Lizzy later on discovered Bruce did not check on the woman who was watching their Dad enough due to his hectic work schedule. It saddened her deeply to know their Dad started looking rough around the edges again, and that he had gone back to drinking.

Her Dad, however, did speak with her about every week or so on the phone. His voice was sounding weaker and weaker, and she began to think that something else was going on. She mentioned it to Bruce, and he promised to go over and check on him that next day. Bruce went over that weekend and found their Dad in the bathroom unable to stand up. He called the ambulance, and they took him to the hospital. They told Bruce that his Dad's cirrhosis of the liver was severe. He would need to go into rehab when he was discharged from the hospital as he could not go home in that condition.

Bruce called Lizzy and let her know, and the following week Harold was admitted to the rehab center in Oklahoma City. It was a perfect place where the nurses were especially attentive, and Bruce liked that. So did Lizzy when she drove down to see him. Harold did not know that Lizzy was coming for a visit, so when Lizzy walked into his room, he was sitting in a wheelchair watching television. He was pleasantly surprised to see her, and she asked him if he wanted to go for a stroll. He agreed that it would be a good idea.

Outside of the facility there was a rose garden and since the day was beautiful, Lizzy took him out there in his wheelchair. Once outside he decided that a cigarette was in order. After leaving the garden, Harold wanted to show her around, so he kept pointing to different places he wanted her to push him. First the therapy room, then the sitting room, then the cafeteria, and so forth. He seemed to really like living there and that surprised Lizzy. When they rolled by people that Harold knew, he took time to say hello to them. She never knew that her father was a social butterfly. When they went by the soda machine, she asked if he would like something to drink.

Harold said, "Sp-wite pwease." So a Sprite it was. She put some change in the machine and when the soda came out, she handed it to him after she opened it. He took a big drink and then started choking. She knew that liquids sometimes caused him to do that, but this time he was really struggling. Ever since his stroke he had that problem. Finally, he settled down and took smaller sips and did alright.

When Lizzy looked up, she saw Bruce and Allen walk in the door. Allen came to surprise her and their Dad. They all sat there for a few hours and talked and just visited. It was a great visit, and Allen was especially moved by how affectionate their Dad had become. He hugged Allen and patted him on the back of the neck. Allen had not had any affection from his father that he could ever remember, so it particularly affected him.

When dinner time came, Harold rolled his wheelchair into the dining hall and Bruce, Allen and Lizzy bid him a pleasant evening. They knew that soon he would be going to bed. Their Dad was so happy. Happier than any of them had ever recalled him being, and the people at the rehab seemed to like their Dad too. The move there was undoubtedly a good one for Harold.

Lizzy stayed in town and spent time with her brothers and took a short trip to Morton to see Gary and Debbie. It was an enjoyable visit before she headed back to Colorado. The day Lizzy left to head home, she drove by to see her Dad one more time. She told her father that she and Joe were going to Africa on a mission trip the following month, but Lizzy promised to come by and see him when she got back to the states. He seemed to understand. Meanwhile, she gave him a book she had written, and he promised that he would read it.

11

The Land of the Forgotten

Being unwanted, unloved, uncared for, forgotten by everybody,
I think that is a much greater hunger, a much greater poverty
than the person who has nothing to eat. –Mother Teresa

Joe and Lizzy had such a full and abundant life. They both had jobs and played as hard as they worked. They enjoyed riding the bike trails around the park and lake nearby, and they were very active in their church and community.

About six months prior, Lizzy and Joe were invited to join a team to go to Africa for missions. They both knew God was calling them to serve in this capacity and so they accepted the call immediately. It was a short term mission trip; nevertheless, it was an opportunity to serve the Lord in Rwanda. This was an area of Africa where the people had encountered enormous loss in the previous years due to a heinous genocide.

Both Joe and Lizzy would be teaching conferences and Lizzy would be singing in the evening worship services. Additionally, they would take the nationals out into remote areas and evangelize. It would be an excellent opportunity to meet international pastors and to work with other ministry leaders from the area.

Upon their arrival, there was a very intense moment at the Kigali airport. If this was a sign as to the kind of warfare they were going to encounter during their month-long stay in Africa, it was going to take every ounce of their spiritual energy and focus to stay alert and protected.

As they disembarked the small plane that carried them into the Kigali Airport from Kenya, armed guards were awaiting their arrival. Suddenly, there was a misunderstanding of sorts that happened in customs as their team was being processed, and rifles were drawn. Joe, being the only one who could communicate effectively with them, was taken back into the interrogation room while the rest of the team was forced to stay in place under extreme surveillance. Local pastors were outside the airport with a bus awaiting the teams exit at the airport so that they could take them to the hotel. However, the expected wait of fifteen minutes turned into a couple of hours.

There seemed to be a concern about the luggage and extra cargo that was being brought in to the country. Joe kept his cool while Lizzy and few of the other missionaries started praying silently regarding the situation. Then, as if nothing had happened, Joe emerged from the interrogation room with a smile about an hour later and with permission for the team to proceed through customs. Rifles were pulled back, and security relaxed as the team moved out of the airport. Though the moment was very concerning, they were much relieved when they were allowed to go.

Later on, they found out that the local pastors waiting on them started praying with great fervency. They understood having to wait that long for the team meant trouble, and it caused apprehension among them. The nationals were most gracious and rejoicing to see the team emerge from the airport. There would be over 300 pastors and wives at the week-long evangelism training conference, and some that had traveled by foot for over a week just to attend.

The hotel accommodations were advertised as a four-star hotel, but in all sincerity, they would be fortunate to be classified as a one-star hotel.

Sometimes Lizzy and Joe had electricity, and sometimes they went without power for days. The same was true about running water. The atmosphere around the city was somewhat hostile, though the hotel staff was most accommodating. Lizzy and Joe walked into their room and immediately were overtaken with fumes of mosquito spray, a necessity but not a pleasant one whatsoever. The bed was sagging in the middle, almost like a hammock, and the electrical box was above the shower with electrical wires dangling loose at the end of tub.

They looked at each other and laughed, "Well, at least we have indoor shelter, which is better than living in a tent in the jungle for a month," Lizzy grinned.

There would be days without water, and then all of the sudden, about two o'clock in the morning they would hear the water running. They would jump up out of bed quickly and take their much needed showers, avoiding the electrical wires. It was a challenging time with the lack of rest. Outside their hotel windows, and on a nightly basis there would be street brawls and the sound of broken glass and yelling disturbing their sleep. So long days that started at 6:00 a.m. and ended around 10:00 p.m. was seemingly getting longer and longer without adequate rest. None of the other team members were experiencing this kind of interruptions at night. Their rooms were on the back side of the hotel. Lizzy and Joe kept praying every day and every night for God to protect them and allow them to rest. They began to quote Psalm 91 on a consistent basis.

"Whoever dwells in the shelter of the Most High will rest in the shadow of the Almighty. I will say of the LORD, "He is my refuge and my fortress, my God, in whom I trust." (Psalm 91" 1-2) NIV

About two weeks into the mission, Joe was tossing and turning and moaning very loudly in the middle of the night as if he was being tormented. Nightly drums were being beaten offsite in the hills behind the hotel. They assumed it was demonic but now, Lizzy became very concerned. She decided to awaken Joe after seeing him being so distressed in his sleep.

"Honey, honey...wake up! You're okay! "Lizzy spoke with urgency.

Joe had broken out in a sweat, and when his eyes opened, he replied, "Thank you. I was in a spiritual battle. I was fighting Satan over souls. He was dragging them to hell, and I was pulling them out!" he cried.

Lizzy put her arms around Joe, and they both prayed to bind the enemy from their lives and from their mission. The following day they received answered prayer and began to understand more deeply as to why God had brought them to Africa.

In the morning their team, along with forty nationals, drove into a remote jungle area, and they unloaded from the bus on the opposite side of the common area. They had to cross a river to get over to the common area in the jungle before setting up for an evangelism meeting. All the local women proceeded onward standing on stones that formed a pathway on top of the water, so that a person could see them and avoid possibly getting their feet wet during the crossing. Lizzy watched the locals began to cross, and so she stepped out on the top of the smooth stones, following after the others. About halfway through the shallow river crossing, she lost her footing. What happened next caused a great outburst among the nationals.

Lizzy began to fall, and she began to scream out, "Oh no....!"

Immediately, one of the African pastors came out of nowhere, and ran and caught her in his arms right before she hit the water. "I got you Sister Lizzy!"

he laughed as he gripped her slim body and tucked it into his massive arms.

The pastor's wives all let out a big laugh and the enormous African pastor who had caught her was laughing so hard that tears rolled down his cheeks. He carried her safely through the river to the opposite bankside. His arms were solid, and he held her up over the water as if she was precious cargo. Joe and one of the other missionaries watched the entire scene from the rear as they were the last to make the crossing, ensuring that everyone else was safe. The whole party had such a good laugh over it, and even some of the community that lived in the jungle there were nearly howling at the American woman's inability to cross a river. It became a successful icebreaker for them to get into the common area and set up. Of course, Lizzy was so embarrassed, but it didn't stop her from laughing at herself. She was just grateful that she did not fall into the river.

They had over forty national pastors with their team, so they felt safe knowing that these local pastors were familiar with the people. Once they arrived in the common area, little children started running up to Lizzy and running their fingers through her long, curly red hair, something they had apparently never seen before. Her freckles also were something that the African children had never seen, so they lightly rubbed their hands up and down her arms and giggled. She felt like a spectacle on display at a zoo for a short time, but she allowed the children to come near, and after they inspected her differences they began to smile back at her and then hug her. Before she knew it, the children were taking her hands and leading her throughout the common area. She had been accepted and that was a great sign that God had prepared the hearts of the people for what was coming next.

One of the local pastors had an old truck, and he had set a large board across the back for a platform, and a microphone up on that platform. He used a generator to power the minimal microphone system. After a hasty set up, he asked Lizzy to come over and get on the platform. She looked at him questionably.

"Sister, I want you to stand up there and just start singing. Sing whatever the Lord leads you to sing and then watch what happens." he said with a broad smile.

Lizzy was a little hesitant, but she followed his lead and started singing an old hymn, "How Great Thou Art." What happened next was nothing short of a miracle. She started seeing people walking out of the jungle areas and hillsides, and they were coming in from all around. It was like an instant congregation of people formed in a matter of minutes before them. These people literally lived in the jungle, under trees, in caves, or wherever they could find shelter. When they heard her singing, God drew them out in curiosity to investigate it. There was a rope strung across the front of the platform about two feet away preventing the natives from coming right up on the truck. Lizzy could not believe her eyes. In a matter of minutes, about seven thousand natives had gathered right in front of her.

"That was beautiful and so anointed," the African pastor relayed as the crowd and missionaries all started praising God afterward.

Then as instructed, Lizzy stepped down, and Joe stepped up on the platform. Alongside him was an interpreter on another microphone. Joe gave a simple gospel message with much clarity and power that late afternoon. As he preached, the crowd was utterly silent except for the distant sound of drums that came from the Muslim leader. He wanted to disturb their efforts but he was unsuccessful. Joe had never preached with so much love and yet authority and power. God was enabling him to reach these people, and before the afternoon was finished, over three thousand natives were born into the kingdom of God.

Lizzy thought about what she was seeing with her own eyes. Many times, when missionaries came back to the states and told stories of how many thousands of people received Christ on their journey's, Lizzy would doubt. She always suspected that they were exaggerating the numbers. Now, that she saw the hunger of the African nation to know Jesus, she understood how extraordinary this moment was and how God can still lead thousands at a time to Him in just a few moments. It was very much like the New Testament example of when Peter preached in the book of Acts. She was so humbled to be a part of something so miraculous. After all of the converts were recorded by the nationals who were with them, the local pastors and the missionaries all gathered around for a prayer. It was time to assign a pastor to these new converts in this village. So the team fervently prayed until God told them who the new pastor was to be. After the decision was made, the new pastor was given the names and locations of every new believer, and he was then called the pastor of that church.

Joe and Lizzy stood in amazement as they witnessed so much faith in action that day. When those who desired to ask Jesus to be the Lord of their life came forth, the joy from the camp was so loud that it must have matched the joy in heaven.

Lizzy was reminded of that passage where Jesus says in Luke 15,

"In the same way, I tell you, there is joy in the presence of the angels of God over one sinner who repents." (Luke 15:10)

She closed her eyes and began to rejoice with heaven that day over the three thousand people who trusted Jesus. She was in awe of God, and she was giving Him all the glory. The pastor's wives who were with her joined her in high praise as they all began to sing praises to God.

As the men broke down the platform and readied to leave, the women took Lizzy's hands and said, "*We are going to make sure you get across the river safely this time dear sister!*" they laughed. Lizzy had developed such a good rapport with them that she had grown to love them dearly in the short time she was in the country. She became especially fond of one of the pastor's wives named Maombi, and they had become great friends.

That night when the team got back to the city, they cleaned up, ate dinner and then went to the campground for their camp meeting. That meeting place was full of pastors and pastor's wives so hungry to learn how to evangelize, and that they were never tired of hearing more about the Word of God. The building was located on the top of a hillside. As the services began the team led in worship, however, the nationals had requested Lizzy to sing again before the preaching started.

Lizzy stepped up to the microphone to sing, and in the middle of her song the power went out. They were all sitting there in the dark. Nevertheless, she did not miss a note, she just kept singing. Lizzy had a big voice anyway, and probably did not need a microphone to assist her, but then something miraculous happened. The testimony of one of the pastors on her team got back to her later, and it was something that genuinely humbled her and caused her to give thanks to God all the more.

One of the pastors told her later that night that when the power went out on the hill that he could hear her voice singing across the valley, and that people were coming out of their homes or wherever they were just to listen to her. He said, "Lizzy, it sounded like an angel singing over the land. God has truly anointed you to carry worship wherever you go!" he wept.

After Lizzy finished singing, the nationals began to rejoice and praise God for a good five minutes. Some of the women hugged Lizzy with tears in their eyes. Joe stepped up to preach, and he opened up his Bible and started reading from Genesis. *"And God said, let there be light,"* and then….as if on cue, the lights came on! The crowd burst out into joy again and started clapping and dancing before God. It was quite a sight, and it took a few minutes to get them back into their seats for the remaining of the service.

The following evening, one of the local pastors insisted that he wanted one of the women to come to his church and preach a message to his women. So the twelve women gathered together to pray and seek who God would want to speak the next night. Immediately, one of the other leaders spoke up and said, "I have a strong sense that Lizzy is the one who is to bring the message. I keep hearing something else in my spirit too. Does this make sense to you Lizzy? I keep hearing that you are our Esther." she exclaimed.

Lizzy had not shared anything that her prayer warriors back home had prophesied over her, so she just started gently weeping and praising God. "I will tell you later why those words are in your spirit sister." she smiled.

"So, I take it, you are willing?" the woman asked with a returned smile.

"Here I am Lord…send me!" she answered as she looked up to heaven.

The women clapped and laid hands on Lizzy and prayed for God to empower her for the upcoming evening.

The next night Lizzy and the entire team arrived at the church. The atmosphere was filled with excitement and the house of worship, that held about sixty people comfortably, had over one hundred and fifty people inside and about three hundred people outside on the hillside listening in through the open portals throughout the building. What was also supposed to be a women meeting turned into a community meeting. There were women there alright, with husbands and children. No one wanted to miss out on what God had to say to them that evening.

The church leaders, all men, were standing upfront on the left and right and rejoicing at the outcome. The pastor got up to introduce the team and then Lizzy. Afterward, they had a time of worship and praise. Now, Lizzy was a worship leader back home, but she had never worshipped God in the manner these people were doing. They came and got her and started dancing around the sanctuary singing songs to Jehovah and rejoicing with great shouts of praise, hands clapping, and praises that were so loud that the entire city could hear them. The dancing was so intense, and Lizzy caught on pretty quickly to the movements. It was worship…much like when King David was bringing the Ark of the God back to Jerusalem. This went on for a good hour or so before she ever returned to the platform. By the time she was asked to start the message, she had to gather herself and try to look a bit dignified, as well as catch her breath.

"Praise the Lord!" she exclaimed as she stepped up to the microphone. The interpreter was off to her right. Now the one thing that she had learned early on was to never run over the interpreter because his message might be better than her own.

"You will have to give me a minute to catch my breath," she laughed, and the crowd roared along with her and started clapping.

Lizzy raised up her hands to silence them and continued, "I want you to know that the name of your land is a great misnomer. Rwanda means "*Land of the Forgotten.*" But I want you to know that I came over 8,000 miles to tell you this great truth; God has NOT forgotten about you!" she shouted with joy. The room lost all composure as they stood to their feet and started praising God and thanking Him for sending Lizzy to them. It took several minutes to calm them down before she could continue.

Lizzy shared her testimony and how she came to know Christ. She shared about some of the stories that she had heard in her short time of being there in Rwanda, and she assured the people that God listened to their prayers and understood their pain. Lizzy gave simple analogies as to how God uses times of trials to make us stronger. She then shared the simple gospel message of why Jesus came in the first place and that because of His great love for mankind, He would never abandon them if they just put their trust in Him. She led them in a prayer of repentance and during the alter call over sixty people gave their lives to Christ that night. Also, several others admitted that they were coming back to Christ and dedicating their hearts once again to Jesus. During the altar call the pastors, about seven of them, were all up front either praying for those who responded or praying for one another.

Afterward, Joe looked at her and nodded pleasingly. Then, as the meeting had begun with jubilant praise, it also ended the same manner. The people started rejoicing and singing and praising God and yes, dancing again. There was much joy in the house and on the hillside. Lizzy said to Joe, "*It is a wonderful thing to be doing what God has called you to do,"* she exclaimed. She felt so much peace and joy while ministering to these people, that she lost all appetite for worldly food or riches. She merely wanted to see more people come to Christ.

Now, before Lizzy and Joe went to Africa, they were told that the culture in Africa was different than America, besides some of the obvious things they already knew. One of the cultural behaviors was if a man honored another man or highly respected him or his teaching, he might come up and hold hands with that man. Well, during the first week, when Joe was teaching Bible classes to the pastors and during times of fellowship, some of them would approach him and hold his hand. It was a well-known sign that they highly respected and loved him. Because Joe had salt and pepper hair and a white goatee, to them his white goatee was a symbol of God's favor on his life. Lizzy was so proud to know that out of all of the team members, the local natives there were honoring her husband in such a way. No other man on the team had been bestowed with that kind of honor. Likewise with Lizzy. The pastor's wives spent every moment they could get with Lizzy. She had developed such close relationships with them that it was difficult for her to leave them behind.

Before they left Africa, something that had been prophesied to Lizzy by two of her prayer partners actually occurred. Two prayer partners, who lived in the USA and in two different states, had called Lizzy and told her, each within a week of each other, that they both had a Word from God for her regarding Africa. Now, these two women did not know each other, so what they said was validated.

One of them had called her, and then the other called with almost the same message for her within a week. "Lizzy, when you go to Africa, you are going to go with the favor of Esther. The kings of the land are going to receive you and honor you, and they are

258

going to want to lavish gifts on you. You will not want to receive the gifts knowing how poor the people are but you must, or you will dishonor them. You will go with the favor of Esther," Anabelle prophesied.

During their last week in Africa, Lizzy had some beautiful experiences. One time, she was walking along in a remote area with Maombi as her interpreter, going out to share Jesus with whoever crossed her path. As they entered the area, a woman walked out from the jungle and began to approach her. The native reached up on her own head, took off her handmade headband and placed it on Lizzy's head as if it were a crown. She was showing great honor to Lizzy. It was so humbling that Lizzy was holding back tears. Through the interpreter that day, Lizzy shared why she was in Africa and that she wanted that woman to know that God loved her so much that he sent Jesus to die for her. As Lizzy explained the pure gospel truth, this woman was ready to receive Christ. She knelt on the ground and Lizzy and Maombi knelt down with her. There in the middle of the field, that woman surrendered her life to Jesus. It was such a moving moment that Lizzy never forgot it.

The following day, Maombi and Lizzy went to another remote area to witness. After they had walked about a mile, they saw a woman working in a field. As they approached, they introduced themselves and asked the woman if she had a moment to talk to them about the things of God.

The woman asked Lizzy to follow her. Maombi stayed right by Lizzy's side interpreting. After they walked another mile, they saw an actual building. It was a cement building that this woman lived in with four generations of family members. When they got to the door, an older woman answered it. She was in her seventies, or so Lizzy surmised. There were also other women in the home including the daughter of the woman who had answered the door. She was in her fifties. There was also several children with ages ranging from ten down to a one-year-old girl.

After Lizzy explained who she was and why she was there, the woman at the door said, "I have been praying for someone to come speak to us about God…I just did not know it was going to happen today…come in….please… come in!"

Lizzy then replied, "I pray for divine appointments every day and God hears!" Lizzy smiled as she and Maombi entered the humble home. Here was her divine appointment, another answer to prayer.

As Lizzy visited and got to know a little bit about the family, she found out that during the Rwanda genocide that all of the men of the family had been slaughtered in front of their wives and that all the women in the home had been raped. It was a sobering moment for her. Together, nine people were living in this simple two-room home, though the accommodations were nicer than most natives in the area could afford.

Lizzy explained how much God loved them and why bad things happen to good people. She spoke of Jesus and his sufferings, ensuring them that Jesus understood their deep pain and agony better than anyone. She finished by sharing the gospel truth and asking them if they wanted to allow Jesus to be the Lord of their lives. Three out of four generations of women gave their lives to Christ that day. Lizzy prayed with and for the women, and invited them to the common area for a worship service that was going to happen later that day. The women were rejoicing and said they would be there, and several hours later, the women had kept their promise. Their faces were shining, and they were filled with hope and joy as they arrived at the common area outside the jungle region.

It was evidence that the Holy Spirit was in control of their lives.

Maombi asked Lizzy if she would come back to Africa sometime and stay much longer. Lizzy said, "Joe and I are always open to where and what the Lord wants us to do. We will pray, and if God says *yes*, we will be back." she smiled. "Meanwhile, as you have watched me share the hope we have in Christ, I want you to take the lead now, and teach others how to share this glorious hope, dear sister!" Lizzy encouraged.

"I will Lizzy…I love you so much!" she said, then gave Lizzy the biggest embrace. "You and your husband can stay with us, if and when you come back to Rwanda." she added.

As if Lizzy's heart was not full already, when she arrived back to the hotel that night, the hotel clerk waived her over to the desk. "Mrs. Dumais, there are several gifts here at the desk for you!" he smiled with excitement.

"Gifts?" she asked.

"Yes. Women and men have been dropping them off all day." he finished.

"Oh my goodness…God is good!" Lizzy exclaimed. She gathered them in her arms and took them to the room with her. Lizzy couldn't wait to see what they were all about. Many of the local natives she had worked with and met had dropped off tokens of appreciation to her. Some of the gifts were for Joe too. Her mind immediately went back to the words her prayer warriors had prophesied over her, "*You will go with the favor of Esther.*"

The following day, Maombi approached her and gave her a handmade shawl, and one of the other women gave her a beaded bracelet. She was so humbled by their expressions of love that she got an idea on how she could bless them back.

She had eight outfits on the trip, and she decided, since the pastor's wives wore the same clothes every day, that she would pick seven of the women to come to her hotel room the next night and have a fashion show. All of her dresses were basically new, and they were light and summery attire which she seldom wore in Colorado. So the following evening the ladies showed up at her hotel room and she invited them in. She had the hotel staff wash and press seven of the dresses that she had been wearing during her visit. As the women entered, all in smiles, she had them try on the dresses. The women were beaming with pride that they were given a dress by Lizzy, whom they had grown to love as a mentor and friend. All of the women left that night donning their new attire, and Lizzy's heart was full of joy knowing that God had sent her and Joe to Africa for such a time as this.

Now, Lizzy had room in her suitcase for the gifts that were given to her. For the next four days, she would be wearing the same clothing but it did not matter to her. She not only was overjoyed to leave the clothing behind for women who truly needed it, but her heart was filled with much love and joy over her experience, and with the people of the land. Lizzy was assured of one thing.....in her heart, these people would never be forgotten. Her faith was increased, and she knew that a part of her would always remain there in Rwanda, Africa.

12

The Unbroken Circle

*But I say to you, Love your enemies and pray for those who
persecute you, so that you may be sons of your Father
who is in heaven –Jesus Christ*

After arriving home from Africa, Lizzy and Joe
received a phone call from Bruce. Lizzy's father had
taken a turn for the worse and had hours to live. She
did not have much time to think or pack. She put
together a few outfits, took a shower and Joe prayed
over her for safe travels as Lizzy left at 3:00 a.m. to
go to Oklahoma.

The drive was smooth, and Lizzy arrived 12
hours later in Oklahoma City, at the rehabilitation
center where her father lived. As she walked in the
nurse led her to the room, and told her that he had
been on Hospice care for a few weeks now. As Lizzy
walked into the room, she saw that the television was
on a Christian station. That was surprising to her, and
she inquired.

"Your father really got into Christian preaching
on television a week before he started declining so
rapidly." the nurse added.

Lizzy turned to her father, who was
unconscious, but she sensed that he knew she was
there, so she started talking to him as if he heard
every word.

"Hi Daddy, it's me, Lizzy. I just got back in the
states about 30 hours ago. I promised you that I
would come to see you." She put her hand on his
already modeled arm. It was cold and lifeless. He was
breathing, but she noticed something very beautiful.

The skin on his face looked more youthful than she remembered. She even touched it, and it was soft and easy on the eyes. She definitely saw something there she had never seen before. His face was peaceful. It was if a total peace had washed over him. It brought tears to her eyes, and as she looked across the side table, she noticed something. There was the book she had written that her dad had promised to read. She took it up in her hands and opened it to where the page marker was displayed. He had read the chapter titled, "How to Become a Child of God."

Lizzy was elated, "Oh Daddy! You read it... and you believed it! I just know it now!

Since the shift change was happening, a new charge nurse came walking in the hall. It was about 9:00 p.m. She was gruff and obviously in a bad mood. She passed the room where Lizzy and her dad were, and as she looked in, she commented, "Ugh! He's still here? He should have been dead by now!!" and then she walked off in the most uncaring fashion.

She immediately noticed a change in her father's breathing. It became somewhat more profound, and the breaths were slowing down. "Daddy, it's okay. I have forgiven you for everything..., you *know* this. And I know you love me Daddy, even though you never said it in so many words. Daddy, you can go. This old body has petered out... you go now...and get your new body... and I will see you again.....I love you Daddy."

A tear rolled down her face as the room resonated with her last words spoken to him. She sat there just holding his hand, and his breathing seemed to calm. She was very fatigued. Bruce said that he could not stand to see their Dad that way, so he did not come back up to the rehab center after their father's rapid decline, except for one more time.

All kind of thoughts went through her head...but now they were good thoughts of Lizzy and her father. One time, when Lizzy was about seven years old, they were in the garden picking peppers, and she saw her Dad pop one in his mouth. She asked if she could try one, and though he warned her that it was hot, she wanted to do it.

"Here goes nothing Daddy!" she said as she popped the hot chili in her mouth. It was so hot but so good! The heat from the small pepper brought tears to her eyes, but she really liked the flavor. Her Dad ate another one, and then she followed, and they both busted out laughing at themselves. Afterward, they went inside and got a tall glass of milk to wash down the fiery, hot pepper residue.

There was another time when she was graduating from ninth grade, and she was wearing a maxi dress, and Lizzy had her hair all done up and ready to go to the big event.

Her Dad said, "I need a picture of my beautiful daughter." So, she and Mama and Daddy all stood in front of the wild rose bush in the yard, and Max took a picture with his new camera. That was the only picture she ever had with just her and her parents.

Lizzy's mind was everywhere, and she was thinking to herself, "*I guess I do have some good memories of my father. I suppose I let all of the bad outweigh any of the good in our relationship. Thank you Lord for reminding me.*"

Then her mind drifted off to their most recent memories. She recalled taking him to get new clothes, his appreciation of her cooking, and how served her a Dr. Pepper and covered her up when she got chilly. To some people, she realized those things would appear mundane, but to Lizzy every moment was a special one, rekindling their relationship and bringing each of them hope. Then she remembered the way that he hugged her that time when she left as if he never wanted her to go. She knew then that God had reconciled their relationship, because deep inside, she wanted to hold on to him too. She buried her face in his quilt that sat on the wheelchair hoping to catch the fragrance of his cologne.

It was now 10:00 p.m. and she was getting almost too tired to drive herself to Bruce's home, about ten minutes away. She decided to go get some rest and come back in a few hours. She stood over her father, kissed him on his forehead and then prayed. *"Heavenly Father, please watch over my Daddy. I know that you love Him. Please comfort him and hold him close…In Jesus Name. Amen."* And then she placed her hand on the top of his head, noticing his thick black curly hair and the softness of it as she brushed her hand through it a few times. Afterward, Lizzy left.

When she drove up to Bruce's home, he had left the front door light on and the door slightly opened. She walked up the sidewalk and opened the front door quietly as there was no sound of anyone stirring. She knew they must be sleeping, so she quietly went to the right, where the guest room was, and set her suitcase down. She then got her nightgown on, went onto the bath, washed her face and brushed her teeth and got in bed. As she had just drifted off to sleep, she heard a light rap on the door.

"Lizzy?"

"Yes…?" She answered and sat up in bed.

The door opened and it was Bruce. He had tears in his eyes and came and sat on the bed next to her. "They just called me from the rehab and told me that Dad has passed."

Almost in denial, Lizzy answered, "I just left him about twenty minutes ago!" she cried.

Bruce took her in his arms, and they both held on to each other and just silently wept and told each other how much they loved each other.

"Sissy, he was in bad shape, huh?" Bruce asked tenderly.

"Yes, he was…but he was ready to go to God."

Bruce was not sure what all that meant, but he was glad to see Lizzy have some resolve. He knew she was deeply spiritual. In fact, at one time he had said, "I believe like you do Sis, but I am not as radical about my faith as you are."

Bruce then relayed, "I told them to go ahead and have his body taken to the funeral home. Oh, do you think Joe would be willing to conduct the funeral services?"

"I am sure he would… I will call him tonight… and then get some rest. See you in the morning."

"How about you singing at his funeral Sis? You sang at Mama's, so I figured you would not mind." Bruce stated.

"I would be honored." she tenderly replied as a tear found its way down her cheek. They hugged one last time, and Bruce left quietly closing the door.

The following day, Lizzy and Bruce went to the rehab center to pick up their Dad's belongings and to make sure everything was taken care of. As they walked in the room, there sat their dad's wheelchair and walker.

"I got an idea." Lizzy shared. "Let's just give this to the center and ask them to find someone who needs it who cannot afford a new chair or walker. They are very lightly used, and I am sure someone would appreciate them unless you want them, Bruce." Lizzy finished.

"I don't want them." Bruce quickly answered.

"I'll be right back then."

Then Lizzy scurried off to the therapy room in the center and asked to speak with her father's therapists. She then met Donna. After explaining who she was, Lizzy asked Donna about the wheelchair and walker, and if they would like to have them for a patient who was in need.

"You're Harold's daughter??? He was the sweetest man I had ever met!!" Donna boasted.

"My father??" Lizzy replied unbelievably.

"Oh yes…. Everybody loved him!" she agreed. "Isn't that right….?" She asked as she turned to some other therapist in the room.

"You're Harold's daughter?" another asked.

Lizzy just nodded an affirmative.

This tall man walked over with a big smile on his face. "Let me tell you Ma'am. When your dad first came here, he was really rough around the edges. He was always nice, but he had a mouth on him. I am sure that you are aware of that." he giggled. "Anyway, about three weeks ago, we all saw a big change in him. He came into therapy, and he worked harder than ever before. Also, he had this grin on his face that nothing could wash off. He stopped using those harsh words, and he started praying for us! Can you imagine that? He would ask us if he could pray for us." the man smiled. "We got to where we looked forward to seeing him."

"That's right…he was such a sweetheart. I found out that he started watching certain preachers on the Christian station and that he was reading a book one day when something happened to him. I think that book is still in his room. Anyway, it changed his life!' Donna added.

Lizzy, could not contain herself. "That book he was reading was one I had given him." she said.

She did not say that she had written it, but Donna piped up, "You're the same Lizzy that wrote that book?"

Lizzy nodded, "Yes."

"Well, he told me about that book and that it had some beautiful prayers in it. He said he was trying to learn how to pray like that." Donna grinned.

"I am so grateful that you have told me this. It does give me much hope. I knew something had happened to him, however when I arrived here last night, he was unconscious."

"We are so sorry he passed, but all of us will see him again someday. We are sure of it!" the other therapist insisted.

"Yes we will!" Lizzy agreed. "I was wondering, could you all use Dad's wheelchair and the walker?" she asked

"Oh, Yes Ma'am. We know who could use them right away!" Then two of the therapists looked at each other and grinned. "You want to come with us to give them to him?" they asked.

Lizzy thought about it… "I guess so."

Lizzy and Donna took the wheelchair and Steve followed with the walker. "This is a new resident who lost everything that he had in a house fire. He will surely appreciate the gift as the medical insurance company is bickering about getting him a new chair again. Then they arrived at the room of Dan Boyer.

"Dan, this young lady has something for you!" Donna burst into the room.

Dan was seated in a chair and watching Christian television. This is Harold's daughter Lizzy." she introduced.

"Lizzy? Well, I have heard so much about you. Harold told me that he was reading a book that you wrote. Anyway, he came here every day, and we read a chapter of that book together. He finished the whole book too!"

Lizzy who was surprised asked, "He did? I was not sure because the book marker was on a specific chapter."

"Oh yes… I gave your Dad that marker for the book. He wanted to keep it there because that is when he asked Jesus to be the Lord of His life. I was there when he did that, and he meant it! I had never seen anyone change overnight like that guy did. He and I started praying together and also for others in

269

here too. He was so desperate to tell everyone about Jesus."

"My prayers were answered, and God used you, Mr. Boyer to help my Daddy! I do not know how I will ever be able to thank you… but if you would like his chair and walker, it is yours. I hear you are having problems with your insurance company and I just know Daddy would want you to have them."

"We knew you and Harold were friends, but we did not know how his life had gotten turned around." Donna giggled. "I too know Harold would love for you to have these things." she added.

"I am so grateful! Thank you so much! I will need them when I go home next week. Oh, Lizzy, can I purchase a copy of that book from you?" Dan inquired.

She got that funny smile on her face and then asked, "Would you like Daddy's copy?"

"Wow! Sure! That would mean so much to me. He was so brave about his love for Jesus these last three weeks. It made me want to tell others too!"

"It's all yours sir. I will have them bring it to you."

Lizzy then hugged Dan, Donna, and Steve and thanked them for taking such good care of her Daddy.

Steve piped up, "Yes…we will all certainly miss him…that is except for one person." And then they all laughed.

Lizzy responded inquisitively, "Who would that be?"

Donna giggled, then answered, "That would be the night nurse. You probably know that Harold was what we call a *night owl.* Well, he would roll his chair up there at the nurse's station at night for a few hours, and he would be sharing Jesus with her, and reading from that book and sometimes just start praying for her…even if she did not want him too. She saw the change in him too, but she wanted nothing to do with Jesus, and he was a constant reminder of Jesus, so she got to the point where she could not stand him. She is a hard nut to crack."

That explained the uncaring comment that the woman had made the previous night as she walked by Harold's room. "Well, I will be praying for her, and you all keep praying. That is what Daddy would want for sure." Lizzy stated as she left the room.

Lizzy's heart was light. She was so comforted by talking to the people who knew her father and witnessed the change in him before their own eyes.

As she got back to her Daddy's room, it was all cleaned out. Bruce had loaded up everything else. "Hey bro, where is that book Daddy had on his side table?"

"I got it," Bruce affirmed.

"Well, I promised his friend Dan that he could have that book. Can I get it from you?" Lizzy asked.

Bruce seemed a bit upset about it, but went out and retrieved it. Afterward, one of the aides was standing there, and she asked her kindly to take the book to Mr. Boyd, as Bruce was anxious to leave. The aide promised she would go right away. Bruce just could not handle being there anymore.

As they got in the truck, Lizzy added, "Dan was a very good friend of Daddy's, and he needed that chair and walker too. I am glad that Daddy's best friend got them."

Bruce paused a moment to let her statement sink in, then replied, "That's nice." Tears then filled Bruce's eyes. "I am just not good at this death thing Sis. You seem so peaceful."

"Well, everyone experiences grief in different ways Bruce. It's okay." She then reached over and held his hand for a short stint as they traveled to the funeral home to make the final arrangements. Joe would be there in a few hours too, and she looked forward to sharing with him about her Daddy's Christian life.

13

Lizzy Meets Leanne and Laney

*The pain of parting is nothing to
the joy of meeting again –Charles Dickens*

A few months later, Joe and Lizzy were settled back into their usual routines and at home in Colorado. Certain circumstances that happened led them to look at the west region of Texas as a place to live. They actually had a burden for the area, though they had never even traveled there before. A pastor had contacted Lizzy to see if she would come minister in their church that fall. She insisted, *"Let me pray about it and I will get back to you."* This was something that Lizzy learned to do before accepting an engagement of any kind.

She had recently been traveling and doing more conferences. In fact, Lizzy had traveled to Guatemala as the keynote speaker at a meeting right before they left for Africa. During that conference, though she wasn't speaking on healing, ladies in the congregation were receiving miraculous physical healings and testifying in every meeting about how God had healed them while Lizzy was delivering her message. Lizzy recalled one special woman who came running up to her.

"Sister Lizzy! Sister Lizzy! God used you so mightily!" the Indian woman shouted as she ran up to Lizzy in the conference center.

As the woman approached Lizzy realized her hand-made beaded dress and was admiring her craft. The woman ran towards her with arms open wide to embrace Lizzy. Lizzy responded with open arms to receive her token of appreciation.

"What are you talking about sweet one?" Lizzy asked as the woman embraced her tightly. The Indian woman was slightly under five feet tall and when she smiled her eyes wrinkled up and her excitement filled the entire room.

The woman, whose name was Victoria, continued. "Last night when you were preaching I felt something happen to me. I have a tremendous amount of pain in my heart most of the daytime and throughout the night. The doctor has said that he cannot help me. When you were preaching I felt a warmness cover me, something I have never experienced ever before. After I left, I was telling some of the other women that I came with about it and they said God had touched me. I noticed since then, I have had no heart pain. God healed me!!!!" Then Victoria started jumping up and down with excitement and turned around declaring to everyone who was entering the next conference, "*God healed me last night!*"

Lizzy rejoiced with the woman and thanked God for His faithfulness. Lizzy had never experienced anything as supernatural as that in her sessions, but it happened, and she gave God the glory.

Joe and Lizzy were going to be visiting Aaron and his new bride in Abilene, TX that fall for Thanksgiving. Since that was going to take them to the west region of Texas, they planned on the way back to stop by Midland, Texas and try to understand better just why they had a burden for an area they had never ever seen. As they drove through, God clearly spoke to both of their spirits, and they sensed an urgency to move there. There was no reason to be looking for a move, as Joe had a good job, and they were content in Colorado.

Of course, when they discussed it, Joe said, "Maybe we are too content," he smiled.

It came to pass that God definitely moved them and paid for their home right out without a mortgage. They knew then that God definitely wanted them in Texas. While they were unpacking, Lizzy found the pictures of her twin step-sisters again. She had looked at them on and off throughout the years, and she honestly had a longing to find them. Lizzy just had no knowledge of how to do so. She had searched the internet without success, and wondered if the girls ever thought about her brothers or Lizzy throughout those years. Especially, since the twins were taken out of the home a few months after Lizzy was born. Lizzy really did not know the full story, and she suspected that what she did understand of the incident, may have been tainted. However, she wasn't sure as to what she could do about it at this late date. She still could think back and see her mother looking at these same pictures with so much longing and desperation.

As a child, Lizzy often overheard her mother say softly, *"Someday girls, I will find you, and you will know how much you are loved."*

Lizzy discussed the matter with Allen, and he said that he had a small chest with some paperwork in it that may have some helpful information. Lizzy needed information on the father of the twins.

"His full name would be a great place to start." she relayed to Allen.

Allen said he would look and get back to her, but he never did. She laid aside that gnawing in her sprit so many times that compelled her to find the girls. Every once in a while Allen would promise to look again, but he would never follow through. About a year later she called him again. "Allen, can you please stop what you are doing and go get that paperwork and look at it for me?" she pleaded.

"Lizzy...., Leanne, and Laney don't want anything to do with us! I don't know why you want to keep searching for them, but if you are insistent, I will send you the wooden box with the paperwork, and you can look through it yourself!" he blurted.

"Would you really do that?" Lizzy responded.

He softened, "Sure.... I will get it out to you tomorrow."

It did not matter to Lizzy if Allen wasn't all hyped about finding the girls, but the fact that he was sending the wooden box her way to do research thrilled her, and she anticipated its arrival the following week. As promised, Allen had sent her the box of old paperwork to go through. She carefully took it out of the packing box and placed it on the large ottoman in the living room. She was too excited to wait any longer, so she opened it up and started reading all of the papers in it. Some were tax notices to her parents, and others were some pictures. At last, she came to some critical copies of court documents that had been created on onion paper. She carefully unfolded the documents, and there before her was the name of Leanne and Laney's father. She wrote down his name and moved on. She then found a newspaper article that explained just what had happened in their household and why Samuel was granted full custody of the girls. It was shocking indeed. It all made sense now. Her mother and Harold were the ones who did the kidnapping of the twins during a visitation, and then they moved off to California without telling Samuel anything. The newspaper article had a picture of Maggie, their mother, locked up in jail for contempt of court. Everyone in the state knew about the fight that was happening over those girls. It broke Lizzy's heart to read the article. She was sure there was more to the story too, but she was not assured of what it was. She hoped that when, and if she located the girls, who were now grown women, that they would be willing to enlighten her.

Joe came home that night, and he found Lizzy at home in her office. She was searching the internet again with Samuel's full name and still not finding anything on the girls. She was frustrated but determined. Joe walked in and said hello, and gave her a kiss.

He then asked, "Honey, do you know anything? I see the papers all over the living room spread out, so I am hoping you have good news!" Joe smiled.

Lizzy paused and answered, "Yes and no. I have a name, but I still cannot find anything on the internet about their father or the twins." she calmly answered though she was frustrated inside.

"I have an idea. Why don't you join one of those online ancestry clubs or something and see if it leads you anywhere?" Joe recommended.

"That's a great idea honey! Let's see…," she answered excitedly and started querying websites for details. She found the most popular one online and joined within a matter of minutes. Better yet, after searching for Samuel's name in the registry, she got a hit. The sight opened up to a page that belonged to Samuel's son, apparently by another marriage, and that son, named Mark, had posted pictures of his sisters, Leanne and Laney.

"Honey, come here!" she called from the office.

Joe walked in and could see that Lizzy was beaming. She turned the computer monitor around for him to see, and there online were the same pictures of the girls that he had seen Lizzy hold throughout the years. It was a miracle.

Lizzy exclaimed, "Oh honey… I am so excited! I finally got a connection."

"You can write their brother and see if he responds." Joe encouraged.

Lizzy did just that. She sent off a short email explaining who she was and asked for contact information. Lizzy gave Mark, their brother, her contact information too. Then she returned to the site and saw where Mark had posted the girls married names. That indeed, was going to be helpful. She decided to look for Leanne first. The moment of truth was merely a few more keyboard entries away, or so she hoped so.

As she went back online to query Leanne with her married name, she typed it into the search engine and waited only a moment. Immediately, a website came up of a realtor in Florida whose name matched Leanne's. Then the realtor's picture scrolled into view, and Lizzy just looked at the picture for several minutes....almost in shock. Leanne looked just like Lizzy's grandmother, and she also had their mother's smile. This was undoubtedly her sister.

"Joe! Joe, come here quickly.... I found Leanne!" she cried out again.

"Praise the Lord!" she heard him ring out as he walked down the hall.

As he entered the office, she once again turned the monitor in full view. "She looks identical to my grandmother and the smile... looks just like Mamas!" she exclaimed with tears filling her eyes.

There was a phone number on the website to call for information. That is when Lizzy felt a considerable butterfly began to surface. "Maybe they really don't want anything to do with us..." she started backtracking.

"Honey? Maybe they had no idea how to find you either... did you ever think of that?" he asked.

Of course, Joe was always so logical. It still did not make the butterfly's in her tummy go away. In fact, they were stronger than ever. It was late, and she decided if she was going to call, that she would do so the next day.

Lizzy was so happy that she had located one of the girls, but her mind kept tormenting her about it. *"What if she hangs up on me when I call?"* She thought to herself. *"What if she hates us because of what happened to her when she was young,"* Lizzy thought about it again.

"I wouldn't blame her for not wanting to speak to me." Lizzy spoke out loud as she and Joe lay there in bed.

Joe was confused. "What is going on in that head of yours? It seems like you are having regrets now instead of being thankful that you found the girls....or at least, one of them. I don't understand."

"Oh honey, I don't understand it myself." She replied. "I've been looking for the girls forever...I guess I am a little overwhelmed with it, that's all." Then she turned over in bed to lay her head on his shoulder.

"Sweetheart, just rest and when it is time to call, the Lord will show you. No pressure. Just pray and then obey." he commented before kissing her forehead.

She gently patted his chest knowing that he was right, then closed her eyes and drifted off to sleep.

It took a few more days, but finally, Lizzy had drummed up enough courage to pick up the phone and call Leanne. As she dialed the number, she prayed, "Alright Lord, please go ahead of me," as Lizzy heard the phone ring on the other end. Leanne was in the bank waiting in line when her cell phone went off. Being a realtor, she answered it immediately.

"Beachfront Bay Realty, Leanne speaking." she paused.

"Um.....Hi Leanne. This might sound like a strange call to you, but I have been searching for my half-twin sisters named Leanne and Laney Milner for decades. My name is Lizzy Ryan, and our mothers' name is Maggie Milner-Ryan. I hope that you are the Leanne that I am looking for. I saw your website, and you look so much like my grandmother, and your smile is identical to my Mama's. Are you a twin, and if so, is your sister's name Laney?" Lizzy managed to get all the information out and then awaited a response.

A long moment of silence fell over the phone. For a minute there, Lizzy thought the woman had hung up on her because there was absolutely no noise whatsoever. After a very long minute, Leanne responded. "Yes, Lizzy. I am Leanne, your sister. I apologize for the long pause, but I have *chicken skin*, as I was in shock and had to leave the bank, and now I am sitting out here on the curb outside the door. I remember you because you were born shortly before we were removed from the home," Leanne cried.

That caused Lizzy to become emotional too, but she held back her emotions. As Leanne used the words *chicken skin* to describe what Lizzy called goosebumps, she knew it was her sister. Her Mama used to say *chicken skin* all the time too. "Oh Leanne, I have been looking for you girls since I was a teenager. I finally found your brother's page at one of those family ancestry sites, and he had posted pictures of you two, the same ones that I have to this day. Had it not been for Mark doing that, I would still be looking for you…I am afraid…." she informed.

"I am so happy Lizzy! I am so glad you were so persistent. Laney lives in Texas." Then she was interrupted.

"In Texas???? I do too!!!" Where?" Lizzy asked excitedly.

"Near Dallas," Leanne added. "I will give her your number if you would like and she can call you too." Leanne continued. "Oh, I remember Max and

Bruce too." She kept reminiscing. "Is Mom still alive?" she queried.

"No, Mama committed suicide in 1976, three days after Max was killed in a car accident. It was such a tragedy, but she always spoke about you girls and how she wanted to find you. I have dreamed of fulfilling her wish, and today that dream has come true!" Lizzy resounded.

"I am so sorry to hear about all of that. Listen, I want to speak with you more, but I have to get in the bank before it closes. I will call you again tonight, and I will also call Laney and tell her the good news! Love you, Lizzy." she ended.

"Love you too Leanne!" Lizzy responded then they both hung up.

"Thank you, God! Thank you, God! Thank you, Lord!" Lizzy expressed as she lowered her head on her desk. "You are so faithful God! Thank you for allowing Leanne to be receptive, and I pray that you bring the girls and me together very soon. Amen."

She jumped up and went back to the phone to call Joe and tell him the good news. He was so thrilled to hear that the call went well and he knew it would not be long before the girls all got together.

Three months later, Leanne was flying into Dallas to visit Laney, and Lizzy was flying into Dallas, TX to see her sisters for the first time. It was a beautiful day in May and only a week from Lizzy's forty-eighth birthday. The twins would be celebrating their birthdays the following week, so the girls had planned to have one big party together. Leanne flew in a few days earlier to help make plans.

As the plane landed, Laney had sent a driver to the airport to pick up Lizzy. Laney had problems driving long distances outside her own community, so she always used the same driver for longer trips. On the drive to Laney's, Lizzy was thinking about the phone conversations that she had previously with the girls. They had spoken every week since the day she first contacted Leanne.

Laney had an email address that used the name *dragonfly* in it. Lizzy thought that was very interesting, as she collected dragonflies and she wondered if Laney did too. When Lizzy asked her during one of their conversations about it, Laney assured her that she had been collecting dragonfly memorabilia and such since she was a small child. Lizzy looked down at the bag of packages she had brought. She had made each of the girls a picture album that contained pictures of them and their Mama and other pictures when they were small girls. In the collections, she was able to give them their lockets of hair that Mama had saved and hospitable birth bracelets. These were some things that Lizzy had held on to for several years in hopes of finding her sisters…and now the day had arrived.

As the chauffeur drove up into the big circle drive in front of Laney's home, there stood Leanne and Laney arm in arm and in anticipation of her arrival. It was a beautiful site. She looked at Leanne, who indeed looked just like her grandmother, and Laney, who looked very much like their mother. As she stepped out and took a few steps, the girls came running and formed a group hug together, laughing and crying and laughing some more. The girls were both a bit shorter, around their Mama's height. All of them were wearing flip-flops.

As Lizzy turned to get her luggage and pay the driver, he said, "This one is on me…I wouldn't have missed this one for the world!" he responded gleefully.

As Lizzy carried in her luggage, Laney said, "Just leave it here for now, and come on into the kitchen. Leanne and I were just fixing lunch. Are you hungry?"

"Sounds great!" Lizzy answered with joy.

By now all of the girls had kicked off their flip-flops and were sitting around the kitchen bar area. "My bunions are killing me today," Laney mentioned.

"Yours too!" Lizzy looked funnily at her. Then she got up and went to the other side of the kitchen bar where Laney was standing, and they both put out their feet in front of them for inspection. Their feet were identical. Leanne piped up, "I am glad I had surgery years ago… my feet are not so bad." She then joined them as they all put their feet side by side and looked up to heaven simultaneously and said, "Thanks Mom!"

Laney continued, "Yes…mine always hurt when…,"

But before she finish her statement, Lizzy and Laney said it together, "*It's going to storm.*" Then they all busted out laughing. They ate and then spent the day reminiscing. Lizzy met Gerald, Laney's husband, and he was cordial but left the girls alone to talk and catch up on the years they had missed together.

As Lizzy looked around Laney's kitchen, Lizzy realized that she had the same cutting board, and the same rooster décor that Laney had, along with many other things that were alike. In fact, as they visited for over a week, Laney noticed that Lizzy had the same blouse on that she had just bought from her favorite local retailer.

When Lizzy looked in Laney's closet, it was like looking in her own. Their taste in clothes and décor was identical. It made them all the more happier to know that they both had the same likes and dislikes, for the most part.

From that time on, the girls worked at getting together every year for their birthdays. Also, though Laney and Leanne were the twins, Laney and Lizzy started teasing Leanne and saying that they were the real twins, just born seven years apart. That was because Leanne did things differently. However, Lizzy and Laney could finish each other's sentences in a matter of a few hours and they were so much alike.

As time passed, Joe and Lizzy went to Dallas to meet with Laney and Gerald and had such good times with them. Joe also went with Lizzy to Florida to see Leanne and meet her husband, Richard. They enjoyed their time together so much, and many times the twins thanked Lizzy for being so persistent and never giving up on finding them.

As each year went by, the girls continued to get together regularly and always stay in touch. They started calling themselves "The Triplets." Bruce and Allen were not interested in getting to know the girls for the longest time, but eventually, Lizzy knew that someday they would come around, and the girls knew that they would never take for granted the gift that God had given them in each other.

Meanwhile, Lizzy had to get back to work. She had taken a job as a Chaplain for Hospice. Shortly after moving to Texas Lizzy had a dream. She was flying over a desolate land. Now, she was not on a plane, but Lizzy always had dreams like she was physically able to fly. So, here she was in the dream flying over a desert area where nothing could thrive. It looked like death.

Lizzy heard a voice and recognized it as the Lord's, "*Lizzy, speak My Word,*" the voice commanded. She obeyed at once.

"*But God, being rich in mercy, because of His great love with which He loved us, even when we were dead in our transgressions, made us alive together with Christ (by grace you have been saved), and raised us up with Him, and seated us with Him in the heavenly places in Christ Jesus, so that in the ages to come He might show the surpassing riches of His grace in kindness toward us in Christ Jesus.*" (Ephesians 2:4-7) NASB.

Then as soon as she finished speaking God's Word, she saw a miraculous site. There before her, trees started springing up throughout the land, and grass was growing, and flowers were blooming. The landscape had changed instantly from being barren to being alive and thriving.

As she flew on, once again she was flying over a dead and useless land. And as before, Lizzy heard God's voice, *"Speak My Word."*

Lizzy began, *"I call heaven and earth to witness against you today, that I have set before you life and death, the blessing and the curse. So choose life in order that you may live, you and your descendants,"* (Deuteronomy 30:19) NASB.

The land before her transformed from death to life. Trees and grass grew once again, then a river bubbled up from the sand and filled the valley. Birds were flying, and creatures were enjoying the goodness of the earth.

"Lizzy, I have called you here to speak life over dead situations. That is why you moved here to Texas. Remember to always Speak LIFE!" God's voice commanded.

Then Lizzy's eyes opened, and she wrote down the dream that she had encountered. Within a matter of days, she was hired by hospice to serve as their Chaplain. Lizzy would make jokes like, *"Well, you can't getter any closer to dead than that!"* She would admit to that, especially when she thought of how God wanted her to speak life into dead situations. She found her job to be very fulfilling. She was able to witness some of the most beautiful moments with her patients as they crossed over from life on earth to eternal life. Lizzy made a comment to Joe once,

"You can always tell the difference between a believer and non-believer when they die. A believer experiences such a peaceful passing, however, a non-believer wrestles with God until his or her last breath."

A few of her patients who were devout Christians claimed to see their loved ones in the room with them, beckoning them to come with them. One woman had asked Lizzy to please come to her bedside and sing her *into glory* when it was time. The lady's favorite song was "*How Great Thou Art.*"

It wasn't long before the family called her early one morning and asked, "Chaplain, can you come now? Mom is asking for you?"

"I will be right there." And then Lizzy hung up and left immediately.

When she arrived, the family ushered her over to their mother's bedside. Their mother was still cognizant at the time. Lizzy took her hand, and the dying woman nodded and smiled, and as if to cue, Lizzy began singing.

Somewhere, in the middle of that song, she passed on through the portals that led between heaven and earth. The hospice nurse was there, and tears were running down her face, but she was smiling. "You made her so happy. She loved you, Chaplain." the nurse exclaimed.

The family thanked Lizzy for coming so speedily and for being there. Lizzy took a moment to pray in that room with all the family members, and to give God thanks for a life well lived by a woman who loved Jesus and her family. The family members each hugged Lizzy before she left.

Lizzy admitted that though times like this could be stressful for others, somehow God had given her an exceptional grace and strength to always be a light of hope in times of crisis and in the midst of such moments.

Leanne and Laney both realized too that Lizzy was a powerful woman who loved the Lord, and that Lizzy was always filled with an abundance of joy, regardless of any adversity. What they did not know is that Lizzy had prayed for them all of those years. She had prayed that they would know Christ and the power of His great love. When she met them, it was apparent that they too were believers. It made their reunion all the sweeter. The twins both had benefited from her love and persistence, and they were witnessing others profit from Lizzy's years of experience, and her ability to remain calm in the midst of any storm.

Lizzy began to understand something that her Mama Maggie had written her in a letter. She had written to each of the children before she took her life. Lizzy's letter mentioned, *"Lizzy, don't let people use you for your good."* As she read that letter much later on in life, she realized that Jesus was always used for His good. In fact, people used Jesus all of the time, whether it was for comforting, healing, feeding thousands, teaching, or whatever else the Father would lead Jesus to do. Jesus was constantly used for His good. So, Lizzy resigned to the fact that God could use her in any way that He wanted, and she realized that there was nothing *good* in her except for Jesus. So, if people wanted to use her, they would never be able to do so without first hearing about the *One* who had set her free! She then realized what Peter referred to in scripture when he wrote,

"In all this you greatly rejoice, though now for a little while you may have had to suffer grief in all kinds of trials, that the trial of your faith (being much more precious than gold that perishes, though it be tested with fire) might be found unto praise and honor and glory at the appearing of Jesus Christ, (1 Peter 1: 6-7) NKJV.

Lizzy started praying daily that her suffering would bring great honor and glory to her Lord and Savior Jesus Christ. That somehow, in the midst of all the pain that she had encountered, others would find hope in knowing that Christ had been faithful to her until the end. Lizzy never looked at her hardships in life as God abandoning her. In fact, when difficult moments came along, she often could be heard speaking out loud, *"Alright Jesus, it's you and me… let's do it!"*

14

Trust and Obey

*Blessed is the one who
trusts in the Lord —Prophet Jeremiah*

Lizzy continued to travel for conferences and mission trips. She also had been to Israel and was the team worship leader as they went to all of the holy sites. It was quite an experience, and she almost did not want to leave Israel to go back home. God had shown her so much and Lizzy continued to write about her experiences and other Biblical teachings that she often referred to when she would speak at conferences. Lizzy enjoyed the written word whether it was portrayed in a book to help others, or in a song that lifted up the Name of God in splendor. In fact, one pastor called her a modern day Psalmist. None of the accolades meant much to Lizzy anymore. She had gotten to a place where she only wanted to please one Person, and that was Jesus.

After moving to Texas, Joe and Lizzy had *"Challenges and opportunities to excel,"* as Joe would put it. One of those moments came four years later when they had decided to take in a rescue dog. Lizzy had taken her dog Esther to the groomers one day and had just returned to pick her up and head home. Now Esther was a Shepherd/Alaskan Malamute and she weighed in at close to one hundred pounds. Though she was a big animal, she was very obedient and gentle and would never hurt anyone, unless they intended to harm her owner.

As Lizzy put the leash on Esther she led her out of the dog salon and outside to the car. On the way to the car something unexpected happened. Esther, being distracted by another large dog that had passed them in the parking lot rapidly turned and took off pulling the leash in Lizzy's hand abruptly. Lizzy later told the doctor, "*It felt like my head went one way and my body went another.*" Something terrible had happened, as Lizzy could not even sit up for any longer than five minutes without excruciating pain. In fact, she rode laying down in the back seat of the car all the way to doctor's office, as Joe took her there and just kept praying.

Dr. Hammond entered the room after Lizzy had some test performed. He informed her, "Lizzy, your MRI shows that a spinal nerve is caught up on a spur growth off your cervical spine and the accident has caused three of your vertebrae to become very unstable. That is why you are in so much pain and I know that this is the worst kind of pain a person can have in this predicament. I will have to do surgery, but I cannot get you in for six weeks. This is due to going out of the country for a month." he relayed compassionately.

"I cannot live like this for six weeks Dr. Hammond. What am I going to do?"

"I can have my assistant give you meds in my absence and try to keep you comfortable, until next month when I come back. If you stay on bed rest, you should be okay. It does not hurt when you lie down, correct?"

Lizzy nodded her head in agreement. She felt like she had no choice but to wait. Joe assisted her to the back of the car, where she laid down on the ride home. "I'm going to be flat on my back for a long time Joe...how are we going to get through this? And it's Christmas time too!" Lizzy added.

"Like we always have honey, with God." Joe smiled and reached back and took her hand. "Everything will work out…. you'll see."

Joe tried to make accommodations in their bedroom for Lizzy. Though he had made things as comfortable as possible, the pain was persistent and at times overwhelming for Lizzy. She knew that many people were praying for her, but she was getting desperate. She called Joe at work one day and cried out in anxiety, *"If they cannot give me anything stronger for this pain, I am going to go crazy."*

A few hours later Joe had come home early and he was smiling. As he walked into the bedroom he knew that Lizzy was at the end of her patience with the pain.

"I have a different drug for you recommended by the doctor's assistant. Now this is definitely going to help you sleep too. Let me cook you a good meal and then you can take it." he smiled.

He then rushed off into the kitchen, and prepared one of her favorite meals, and brought it to her, as he had been doing for the past month.

"Thank you so much honey…" Lizzy responded.

"You are welcome love. I just want you to relax, take this medicine and eat and then sleep. The doctor said you will be very sleepy with this, and that it is a strong medicine, equal to the sedative prior to surgery."

Joe knew that Lizzy had no real appetite the last month being in that much pain, but he hoped she would eat some of the meal that he had prepared, and she did. Then he gave her the medication and in about thirty minutes she became very sleepy. Suddenly, she had something that resembled a panic attack. Strong medication or anesthesia always made her feel that way.

"Joe, what if I fall asleep and don't wake up! I'm afraid!!" she cried.

"Honey, I am not going to leave your side... The doctor said you would feel sleepy, but the pain would be gone as long as you stay on this med every eight hours. You will be alright... I promise... trust me. Just go with it... rest."

He laid next to her in bed and placed his hand inside of hers and prayed, as she fell off into deep slumber. At last she was sleeping peacefully and Joe prayed, "Oh God, let her finally rest without pain. Let her feel better Jesus... I need her. Amen."

A few days before the surgery was scheduled, Lizzy felt herself being apathetic to everyone and life. She wished life would just end, then the pain would be gone for good and she would no longer suffer. She had to go to the hospital that day, and have some chest x-rays and bloodwork done prior to surgery. It was a big ordeal for her to take the hour trip there and back, though her church friend Anna was so willing to take on the responsibility. Anna opened up the back door to her car. It is where she had laid a foam mattress inside for Lizzy to lie on for the ride. Lizzy got in and laid down.

After they were traveling for a short while Anna asked, "Are you okay back there honey?"

"Yes, just praying though this awful pain. If there is one thing this pain has done for me it has made me a prayer warrior!" Lizzy softly giggled.

"You are an incredible woman Lizzy. Everyone at church has been praying and we know that God has this. We know that God has a purpose for allowing this to happen, and we know that you are one tough lady. I do not think that I could go through what you are going through right now and keep a sweet spirit like you have."

Lizzy thought about what Anna said and then remembered her reaction a few days ago, before her son Aaron called. Lizzy wasn't so sweet then. It seemed like every time she was ready to end it all, someone would come over or call and encourage her. On that particular day, she thought of taking all of the pain pills and just saying goodbye to the pain once and for all. It was a passing thought, nevertheless, it was there and it would pass by several times a day. She was obviously depressed. The bubbly, happy go lucky woman that everyone knew had become a beaten down, weakened desperate woman during her days of waiting. Just as she had convinced herself to take the pills the phone rang and it was Aaron. He and his wife along with the granddaughters were on the other end. Aaron had written a song... just a few moments before calling.

"Hi Mom. How are you are doing?"

"Not so well babe, but I will make it through, somehow..." she commented in an unbelievable fashion.

"Mom we were all just praying for you and God downloaded this song in me and I know it is for you and so I called to sing it to you."

Now, Aaron was a worship leader and also wrote many songs, much like Lizzy.
Immediately, Aaron started playing his guitar and then he sang the most beautiful, healing song over his mother. Lizzy lay there crying and repenting before God as he sang. That song gave her what she needed in that very moment to keep trying to hold on. When Aaron finished, Lizzy tearfully spoke, "You have no idea how timely your call was. I was laying here and I had given up Aaron. I just got to the point where nothing mattered anymore...and then you called." she cried.

"Mama, don't give up, Aaron's wife interrupted. Let's pray everyone...come in here girls. We are praying for Granny." And so they gathered around the phone and each of them said a prayer of healing and asked God to help Lizzy through this terrible time of trial. When they finished, she promised to call them the following morning.

When they hung up the verse out of John 4:4 came to here, "*Greater is He that is in me than he that is in the world."* She knew that she was in the midst of a spiritual battle and Lizzy also knew that during that time on the phone with Aaron that something in the atmosphere had broken off of her and she had greater hope than ever that God was going to bring her through, no matter how many days of pain may laid ahead.

Anna had helped Lizzy into the hospital for the chest x-ray and bloodwork, then back home. Lizzy was upbeat knowing the surgery was only a few days away. Then the phone rang.

"Hello?"

"Mrs. Dumias?"

"This is she..." Lizzy acknowledged.

'Mrs. Dumias, the hospital called us about your labs and said that you had a spot on your lung that looked suspicious. They are wanting you to come back tomorrow and have another CAT scan done to explore it in more detail. We cannot do surgery with you having a spot like that Ma'am."

"I got to have this surgery..." Lizzy begged.

"Let's hope the spot is nothing... just be there at 8:00 a.m. I have already scheduled the CAT scan for you." The clerk relayed.

"I'll be there." Then without even saying goodbye she hung up and called Joe.

Joe called the church and got them praying. Meanwhile, Lizzy called seven different pastors that she knew in the area and asked them to come to their home and to bring anointing oil and to pray a healing prayer that night. Everyone one of them said that they would be there at seven 'clock. Lizzy remembered the promise in scripture that said, "*Is anyone among you*

293

sick? Let them call the elders of the church to pray over them and anoint them with oil in the name of the Lord." (James 5:14) NIV. Lizzy had enough faith to know that God could work a miracle in her life, because He had done it many times before.

Then Lizzy remembered a time when she was pregnant with her second child, Travis, and had been diagnosed with *placenta previa.* It was a dangerous situation for the baby and a painful problem for the mother. Lizzy spent the last trimester in bed waiting for the delivery. It was difficult because she had no help with two year old Adam, as his father was gone working nights and slept all day.

Eight days before the scheduled C-section, there was a revival at the church and so she went, against doctor's orders. She was told to stay in bed, but her faith got her out of bed that night. As she walked across the street to the church the congregants were thrilled to see her but were a bit nervous, knowing her condition. Lizzy had brought a pillow and she put it down on the pew and leaned on it as the guest preacher started his message.

She was not sure it was anything that he said that made her start trusting God for a complete healing, or that she was there, and could sense the presence of God so strongly. However, something did happen to her that night when she relinquished all of her frustration and apprehension about the pregnancy to God. She gave God her problem and trusted that He would take care of her. The next day she had a doctor appointment. The standard ultrasound became part of her care during those last five months of pregnancy. So after the test had been completed, she went to the examination room and awaited to see her doctor. Her doctor was not a believer. It was difficult to trust him entirely because of that, but she knew he was supposed to be her doctor for some reason. He was obviously running a bit late so when he came in the room he apologized but he had a big smile on his face.

"Let me show you something Lizzy…follow me, if you will." He asked.

As they went into the x-ray room he placed all of her last five month ultrasounds up on the reader board and turned the light on. The last one was the result of her ultrasound that day. In the last one, the doctor explained to her that he could see that the placenta was no longer down, covering the cervix area, but it was in place and attached to the wall of the womb as it should be for normal delivery.

After he explained it all to her, he went on to say, "In all my years of practice, I have never seen anything like this! You will be able to deliver your baby naturally, after all!"

"That is an answer to prayer, doctor!" Lizzy responded

"I don't know if I would go that far…but something most unusual has happened here." he agreed.

A week later she did go into natural labor and she struggled a lot because she had what is called a dry labor. The water had broken at one time or another, and she was not aware of it. Perhaps when she was taking a shower. Anyway, there were complications after the baby was born and she was rushed to recovery. The doctor had already left before hearing that Lizzy had started to bleed uncontrollably. There were two nurses in the room at the time and they kept paging him at no avail.

"Are you in with me on this?" the one nurse Katrina asked.

"Well, if we don't do something she is going to die--- Yes!" Denise answered.

Katrina ordered, "Let's get the Pitocin on her so she will start contractions and stop the bleeding. You put the line in." she ordered.

During their conversation Lizzy was extremely weak and not in any pain at all. She was full of peace but unable to respond to anything. In fact, she knew that she was going to die, but she was okay with it. She could not explain her complete peace about the matter, though the nurses in the room were acting chaotically. She was ready to meet her Maker. She could see a bright light in the distance, though her eyes were closed.

"What have you done??" Katrina frantically asked. Lizzy's arm was all swollen up with the Pitocin. The other nurse had not put the IV-line in her arm correctly. "Let me have that!" she demanded.

Then Katrina put an IV in to Lizzy's right arm. After she was sure it was properly inserted she said, "Turn it on two, for now" Lizzy could sense the nurses massaging her stomach area, but she really could not feel it. She could feel nothing. Her eyes were still closed and she was at complete peace, regardless of their frantic efforts to save her.

"Turn it up to five!" the nurse ordered again.

After a few minutes Denise notified her, "It isn't working!"

"Turn it on full blast! We got to get this bleeding to stop."

Suddenly, Lizzy gasped as if she had not been breathing. The pain in her abdomen was very real... and very intense. It shook her to her senses.

"Lizzy, good to see you again. You had us going there for a moment Ma'am. We had to put Petocin on you because you started hemorrhaging.

Denise interrupted, "She has stopped bleeding now."

"Great news!" the nurse responded. "Lizzy, I cannot get in touch with your doctor at the time. I will let him know your update and I am sure he will see you as soon as possible. Meanwhile, I know you are in a lot of pain. This medication will keep you in a big contraction state for eight hours. I can get you some pain medication, so that you can sleep it off, but we have to leave the line on for now. Understand?"

Though Lizzy had heard the nurse, she was very weak and her husband was already gone from the hospital too, so no one back home even knew what had happened. Lizzy nodded that she understood and sensed she was being moved to her hospital room. They closed the blinds and gave her medication for the pain and she slept.

As Lizzy's mind remembered miracles that had happened in her life, she also thought of the time that God had healed her from having to have lower back surgery just five years prior. She was scheduled for surgery, but she really sensed the Lord tell her that she was not going to have surgery and that He was going to heal her. She and Joe fasted and prayed for forty days, as they felt the Lord lead them to do so. Three weeks afterward, during a worship service in her home church, God completely healed her. In fact, when the doctor took a picture of her spine he told her, *"Your spine looks like a twenty year old... completely healthy! That is a miracle!"*

Now, Lizzy was facing the demon of doubt but she had enough faith to believe that God was going to take care of this unknown spot on her lung too and so she rested in the assurance of that knowledge until the pastors showed up that evening.

As their pastor friends showed up, they were all so glad to see Lizzy. She was in a lot of pain, as she refused to take any medication until after they would leave. The men anointed her with oil and each one prayed a healing prayer over her. Her spirit was lifted and she felt an actual breaking happen....something she could not explain, but somehow she knew whatever was on her lung, was gone. Lizzy had an innate ability to sense such things and she was right. The following day the CAT scan

297

revealed everything as clear, and she got the go ahead to have surgery.

The day before surgery, Lizzy's children called to check on her. They all lived in different states, so visiting was difficult, as they each had families with young children. Lizzy understood, but Michelle and Adam had called that morning and Travis and Aaron had called her that night. Plus, many of the friends from church had come to visit her or call her and pray for her. Additionally, she had thirteen prayer warriors in her itinerate ministry who were staying in touch with her and praying. One of them drove to the hospital the day of the surgery and did nothing but pray the entire time of the procedure. At last, both Leanne and Laney called on a regular basis and sent gifts of encouragement during her injury time and afterward. Her cup was full of love and hope and she knew that the future was going to be bright once again.

After eight long hours, the surgery was completed. When she was in recovery, the doctor was standing before her calling her name as she came to. He had a huge smile on his face as she awakened. "Hi Lizzy! You did very well. How do you feel?"

"Okay, I guess. The surgery is already over?"

She never could get used to having surgeries, as they always seemed to be over with as soon as she would be given the medication to go to sleep.

"Yes, your surgery took a few extra hours. Your vertebrae were more damaged than I anticipated so you have three cadaver bones in your neck now. You did exceptionally well and I am sure Joe is anxious to see you. I will come by your room later tonight to check on you again. Just rest."

"Thank you Dr. Hammond," Lizzy spoke clearly. She was so concerned about her voice, because she made a living with it. During the surgery, the doctor told her that he would have to remove her voice box and put it back in after he corrected the spine problem. He said he had never had a patient lose their voice after this kind of surgery, but it had happened to others, and that it was a risks. Now she could tell that her voice was even clearer than usual. God had taken care of that worry for her, as well.

Joe entered and asked, "How are you beautiful?" as he kissed her forehead. They visited for a short time and then Joe allowed Lizzy to rest.

A few days out, while Lizzy was awake in her hospital bed, and older woman came in and started cleaning the room. She looked at Lizzy then continued on with her work. When she finished the woman left. However, a few minutes later, the same woman came back in and started cleaning the room all over again. At first, Lizzy thought she was hallucinating in regard to the situation, but then she decided to speak to the woman.

"Excuse me Ma'am... Weren't you just in here a few minutes ago cleaning my room? Is it that dirty?"

The woman smiled, "No Ma'am...but I can feel God in this room and so I came back in to clean again and just stay in His presence. I can tell that you are a mighty woman of God!" she finished with tears in her eyes.

A few hours later a man came in the room. He was the chaplain for the hospital. When he approached her, Lizzy sensed some sadness in his heart. He asked if he could pray for her, and she agreed only if he would allow her to pray for him too. And so, as he finished, she began praying for him and God revealed to Lizzy what was going on in this man's life, and that his wife had recently passed away. She told him that God had showed her the condition of his heart and she prayed for an overwhelming sense of peace and comfort to wash over that man. Immediately, God answered that prayer.

"I have never met anyone who has such spiritual insight like you Mrs. Dumais. Thank you for that prayer. I truly feel like something happened to me just now." the chaplain explained.

"Well….that *something* you speak of is *Someone*, and He is the Holy Spirit." Lizzy smiled.

The man shook her hand and thanked her for spending time to pray for him and then he said, "Ma'am, I came in here to be a blessing to you, and I am the one leaving with a blessing!" he then smiled and walked out the door.

In just five days, Lizzy was discharged from the hospital. Though the doctor said she would be on pain meds for a few months during the healing season, she was off her medications in just a few more days. Lizzy insisted that the healing pain that she was experiencing was nothing like the pain prior to her surgery. She really had no need for the medication. Her recovery was what the doctor called *remarkable*. Her doctor was one of the best spine surgeons in the world, and though his faith system was one of a Hindu, he allowed Joe and Lizzy to pray with him before he took her back to surgery. On her last appointment for follow up and early release, she took Dr. Hammonds hands in her open palms and said, "Doctor, God has given you healing hands. Always remember that this gift is from God. Thank you for being there for me, and I will never forget you." Lizzy smiled.

"Well, it must have been God who gave me a good patient like you. God be with you, Lizzy" he replied as she walked out of the doctor's office.

Later that day, Lizzy had an out loud thought when she was talking to Joe. "So, if the *coming of the Lord* happens and the dead in Christ rise first, will these three cadaver bones in my neck leave without me?" she laughed and continued. "Will my neck just plop over before I go to heaven too?" she laughed all the louder.

That was the Lizzy that Joe always loved and admired. She sure could laugh. Joe would tell others, *"That woman can laugh and make an entire room of people laugh with her."*

No matter how much pain and agony she had endured, Lizzy was full of joy and he loved that about her. She had learned the secret behind her pain, and that was to live her life in joy. To this day, her joy remains contagious for all to see. When people ask Lizzy why she is so different, she usually replies,

".... **the joy of the Lord is** my **strength**."
(Nehemiah 8:10) NIV.

One Last Word from the Author

I hope that you have enjoyed this novel based on a true life story… my story. All the names were changed to protect others, but you probably figured out that I am Lizzy, the one portrayed in this book.

My prayer is that no matter what you are going through, that you will remember that God loves you unconditionally, and that He will never leave you or forsake you. I know this is so true! Life affords us many opportunities to lose our peace, but do you know what I say about that? *"It's nothing to lose your SHALOM over!"*

Jesus promised us that we would have moments like that in our life. In fact, He spoke of it in the book of John:

"These things I have spoken to you, so that in Me you may have peace. In the world you have tribulation, but take courage; I have overcome the world."
(John 16:33)

Scripture goes on to say that *we too* are overcomers!

"And they overcame him because of the blood of the Lamb and because of the word of their testimony, and they did not love their life even when faced with death."
(Revelation 12:11)

I do not know where you are in your spiritual journey of life, but I hope that reading this book has encouraged you. I pray that it has allowed Jesus to take you farther than you were when you opened up the front cover. If I can ever help you in anyway, feel free to get in touch with me via my website at: www.janemorin.com

Meanwhile, always remember this great truth:

"Greater is He that is in you, than he that is in the world." (1 John 4:4) NKJV

Made in the USA
Columbia, SC
27 December 2018